"I always wanted to be a comedian..."
~ Frank L. Bellezza

THOMAS J. BELLEZZA

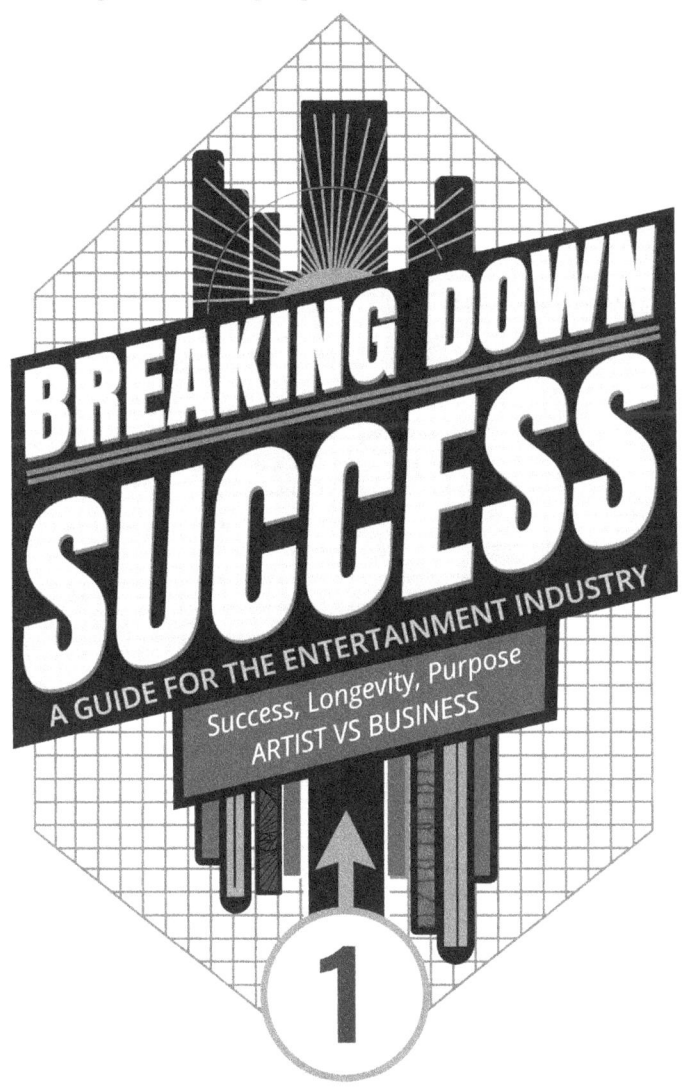

BREAKING DOWN SUCCESS

A GUIDE FOR THE ENTERTAINMENT INDUSTRY

Success, Longevity, Purpose
ARTIST VS BUSINESS

1

THE FOUNDATION FOR LONGEVITY

Copyright © 2024 by Thomas J. Bellezza. All rights reserved.

Published by BBR Productions, Inc.
All artwork by Thomas J. Bellezza.

All rights reserved. No part of this publication may be reproduced, used for AI training, stored in a retrieval system, or transmitted in any form or by any means, electronic, mechanical, photocopying, recording, scanning, or otherwise, except as permitted under Section 107 or 108 of the 1976 United States Copyright Act without the written permission of both publisher and author, except in the case of brief excerpts used in critical articles and reviews. Unauthorized reproduction of any part of this work is illegal and is punishable by law.

In other words, come on, don't steal what's not yours.

www.MakeARightLeftHere.com
www.BBRProductions.com
www.Altayon.com

"We are the results of our actions in this life, and the consequences of inaction."

ISBN 979-8-9929251-0-4 (Paperback)
ISBN 979-8-9929251-1-1 (Hardcover)
ISBN 979-8-9929251-2-8 (ePub)

"If ever there was a time to take a chance, now is that time; you owe it to yourself."

Because of the dynamic nature of the internet, any web addresses or links contained in this book may have changed since publication and may no longer be valid. The views expressed in this work are solely those of the author, but that doesn't suggest he means it, and doesn't necessarily reflect the views of the publisher, and the publisher hereby disclaims any responsibility for them.

As a quick aside, no monkeys were hurt during the making of this book. However, I did take a lot of naps, and there may or may not have been some pizza eaten.

Limit of Liability/Disclaimer of Warranty: While the author has used his best efforts in preparing this book, he makes no representations or warranties with respect to the accuracy or completeness of the contents of this book and specifically disclaim any implied warranties of merchantability or fitness for a particular purpose. No warranty may be created or extended by sales representatives or written sales materials. The advice and strategies contained herein may not be suitable for your situation. You should consult with a professional where appropriate. Neither the publisher nor author shall be liable for any loss of profit or any other commercial damages, including but not limited to special, incidental, consequential, or other damages.

Cover Design: BBR Productions, INC.

In loving memory of my pop
09.13.1945 - 06.06.2022

Contents

FOREWORD ix

INTRODUCTION

1.1 | CHANGE THE BRAIN, CHANGE THE GAME 1
    MISCONCEPTIONS ARE THE ENEMY 6
    WHAT IS SUCCESS TO MOST 9
    THE GOAL OF THIS BOOK 9
    GETTING THE MOST OUT OF THIS BOOK 10
    THE REALITY OF MY INTENTIONS WITH THIS BOOK ... 12

1.2 | WHO ARE YOU? I MEAN, WHO AM I 15
    THE RESPONSIBILITY OF KNOWLEDGE VS. UNDERSTANDING ... 19
    A QUICK REMINDER OF THE TONE 23
    AN EXAMPLE FROM MY PERSPECTIVE 24

FOUNDATION

2.1 | SUPPORTING THE WEIGHT OF YOUR MISSION	**27**
THE FUN PART IS NOT THE WORK	28
WHEN OPPORTUNITY KNOCKS	30
WHAT DOES A FINANCIAL FOUNDATION ACCOUNT DO?	32
YOU DESERVE A CAREER YOU LOVE	35
2.2 | SAYING YES TO LIFE	**37**
2.3 | CREATING OPPORTUNITIES	**41**
TIME IS A VALUABLE RESOURCE	43
2.4 | CALCULATED RISK	**45**
A LIST OF PREPARATION IDEAS	46
RISKING IT ALL ON TALENT	47
HAVING A PLAN TO TAKE CALCULATED RISKS	49
MORE THAN JUST SAVING CAPITAL	51
2.5 | BE DECISIVE	**53**
HAVE A PLAN A BUSINESS PLAN	54
YOU DON'T NEED VALIDATION	56
POSTING TO UNINTERESTED PEOPLE	57
DO YOUR JOB	59
EVERYTHING YOU DO MUST AFFECT EVERYTHING YOU DO	61
QUICK COMPARABLES TO AUDITIONS IN OTHER FIELDS	64
2.6 | STAY FOCUSED, NO EXCUSES	**65**
A DIME A DOZEN	67
IT IS NOT ALL ABOUT THE FUN STUFF	69
DOING STUFF IS NOT THE SAME AS GETTING STUFF DONE	72
WHAT DOES IT TAKE TO STAY FOCUSED	74

WHAT DOES IT ALL COME DOWN TO	75
2.7 | INCORPORATE	**77**
FAKE IT TILL YOU… STOP THAT NOW	80
2.8 | WRITE OUT A BUSINESS PLAN	**83**
ONCE ALL IS ACCOUNTED FOR WHAT NOW	86
2.9 | STARTUP CAPITAL	**89**
CAN I START MY CAREER JOURNEY NOW	91
2.10 | CALCULATE YOUR OVERHEAD	**95**
AN ACTIONABLE LIST TO FIGURE OUT YOUR OVERHEAD	96
NOW THAT YOU HAVE AN AVERAGE MONTHLY TOTAL	98
2.11 | I DON'T HAVE THE MONEY TO SAVE	**99**
WHERE DO I FIND THE MONEY IN THE FIRST PLACE	100
START NOW, WORRY LATER MENTALITY	103
HOW LONG HAS IT BEEN ALREADY?	105
2.12 | SACRIFICE	**107**
SACRIFICE WITHOUT SLEEPING IN YOUR CAR	110
WHEN SACRIFICE BECOMES A MUST, NOT A CHOICE	112
2.13 | 5 MISTAKES TO AVOID	**115**
#1—STARTING BEFORE THE MONEY IS SAVED	116
#2—NOT STICKING TO OR EVEN KNOWING YOUR MISSION	120
#3—ENJOYING YOUR FREEDOM TOO MUCH	124
#4—FORGETTING ABOUT YOUR 3 NEEDS OF PURPOSE	127
#5—NOT STICKING TO YOUR BUDGET	128
2.14 | FINAL THOUGHTS	**131**
SO WHAT NOW?	132
THINGS TO SET UP DURING THIS TIME	134

TRIANGLE OF LIFE

3.1 | HOW MANY SIDES TO A TRIANGLE — 135
3.2 | THE SIDES OF A TRIANGLE — 139
- SIDE ONE: 3 NEEDS OF SUCCESS — 140
- SIDE TWO: 3 NEEDS OF LONGEVITY — 141
- SIDE THREE: 3 NEEDS OF PURPOSE — 141
- SIDE FOUR: THE ASSETS OF LIFE — 142
- SIDE FIVE: TREAT YOUR LIFE LIKE A BUSINESS — 142

3.3 | A JOB VS A CAREER BUSINESS — 143
- THE REALITY OF THE LONG GAME — 144
- HOW IT REALLY WORKS — 145

3.4 | EVERYTHING YOU DO MUST… — 149
- IDEAS BROKEN DOWN INTO SECTIONS OF ACTION — 150

3.5 | YOU TIME — 153
3.6 | FINAL THOUGHTS — 157

NEEDS OF LONGEVITY

4.1 | THE 3 NEEDS OF LONGEVITY — 161
- WE CAN LEARN A LOT FROM THE FRESH PRINCE OF BEL-AIR — 162
- DEFINING THE 3 NEEDS OF LONGEVITY — 166
- WHAT ARE THE 3 NEEDS OF LONGEVITY? — 167

TIME MANAGEMENT

5.1 | MANAGEMENT OF TIME	**169**
5.2 | TIME AUDITING	**171**
TIME IS LIMITED	173
5.3 | BUDGET YOUR TIME	**175**
A WEEK OF WORK	177
5.4 | 40-HOUR WORK WEEK	**179**
LIFE IS A LEARNING CURVE	180
CLEAR INDICATORS OF RESULTS	181
5.5 | TIME BLOCKS	**183**
WHAT'S SO SPECIAL ABOUT TIME BLOCKS	183
THE TYPES OF TIME BLOCKS	184
BRAINSTORMING TIME BLOCKS	185
NETWORKING TIME BLOCKS	185
MARKETING TIME BLOCKS	187
PRACTICE TIME BLOCKS	187
TIME MANAGEMENT TIME BLOCKS	188
MONEY MANAGEMENT TIME BLOCKS	189
PEOPLE MANAGEMENT TIME BLOCKS	190
ENTREPRENEURIAL BRAIN TIME BLOCKS	192
TALENT TIME BLOCKS	194
REST TIME BLOCKS	195
5.6 | TIME BLOCK RULES	**197**
1. THERE IS ALWAYS TOMORROW	198
2. SAY NO TO THINGS AND YES TO LIFE	200
3. START THINGS	202

4. NO MORE THAN THE ALLOTTED TIME	203
5. WORK HOURS ARE OFFICE HOURS	204
6. ONE THING AT A TIME	206
5.7 | TO-DO LISTS	**209**
5.8 | LAST MINUTE CAN WAIT	**213**
1. TOUCH IT ONCE	214
2. DO IT NOW	215
3. A BONUS RULE: PROCRASTINATE LATER	216
5.9 | FINAL THOUGHTS	**219**
CHOOSE ONE: CAREER BUSINESS OR SURVIVAL JOB	221

MONEY MANAGEMENT

6.1 | MONEY MANAGEMENT	**225**
6.2 | WHAT IS MONEY MANAGEMENT	**229**
1. BEING CONSISTENT	230
2. TIMELY | DOING THINGS ON TIME	231
3. JUSTIFYING A PURCHASE	231
4. KEEPING DETAILED RECORDS	232
6.3 | THE PATH TO MONEY MANAGEMENT	**235**
1. CREATE A BUDGET	236
2. PAY OFF YOUR DEBT	245
3. YOUR CREDIT SCORE	247
4. USE CREDIT CARDS INSTEAD OF DEBIT CARDS (OR CASH)	248
5. EMERGENCY FUND	249
6. STARTUP CAPITAL (FINANCIAL FOUNDATION ACCOUNT)	250
7. TAKE OUT 33% FROM ALL MONEY EARNED	250

8. ORGANIZE YOUR MONEY	251
9. INVEST INTO ASSETS	252

6.4 | OVERHEAD — 255
PERSONAL OVERHEAD VS. BUSINESS OVERHEAD	257
SAFETY NETS	258
REEVALUATE WHAT LED YOU TO THIS POINT	260

6.5 | FINAL THOUGHTS — 263

PEOPLE MANAGEMENT

7.1 | PEOPLE MANAGEMENT — 267
7.2 | QUALITIES TO NOTE — 273
TRUST IN PEOPLE	274
WORK AS A TEAM	277
NO PERSON IS AN ISLAND	280
THE TAKEAWAY	283

7.3 | WHO IS RIGHT FOR YOUR BUS — 285
LIMITED SEATING	286
ADD QUALITY TO A BUS	287
SETTING THE TONE	288
WHAT DOES ALL THIS MEAN?	291

7.4 | ME PERSPECTIVE VS. WE PERSPECTIVE — 293
ME PERSPECTIVE	294
WE PERSPECTIVE	295
MANAGE YOURSELF FIRST	296
RECOGNIZE THEIR INTENTION	297
KNOWING YOUR BOUNDARIES	298

GETTING TO THE POINT	300
7.5 | CUT PEOPLE OUT OF YOUR LIFE	**301**
I AM SORRY	302
THE POWER OF RESPONSIBILITY	303
7.6 | FINAL THOUGHTS	**305**

ACKNOWLEDGEMENTS

8.1 | ACKNOWLEDGEMENTS	**309**
AUTHOR FRIENDS	**313**

FOREWORD

In April of 2017, I attended the Actor's Pro Expo in New York City. I arrived eager to gain knowledge and make valuable connections in the entertainment industry, but I never expected that a single encounter would forever change the trajectory of my life. That day, I crossed paths with Thomas J. Bellezza.

He was hosting a seminar on finding success in the entertainment industry. I sat toward the back, casually observing. The moment he took the stage, his commanding presence was undeniable. As soon as he opened his mouth, his wit and charisma had me hooked. He started the session by asking the room a seemingly simple question:

"What is the most important factor in having a successful acting career?"

The audience shouted out their answers—"Talent!" "A great agent!" "A degree from a top school!" "Luck!"

The responses were varied, yet Thomas remained unfazed. After a moment, I called out my guess:

"Your network."

Bingo.

That was the answer he was looking for. And from that moment on, I was mesmerized—not just by his words, but by the way he thought, the way he challenged conventional wisdom, and the way he reshaped the very foundation of what so many of us believed about success. His perspective was unlike anything I had encountered before. He spoke with passion and authority, not just theorizing about success but proving it through his own life. A musician, theater owner, writer, consultant—every venture he pursued, he excelled in.

Thomas has cracked the code on success—not just of the entertainment industry, but of life itself. His approach isn't based on luck or vague motivation; it's a blueprint, tested and proven, that he lives by every day.

One of the many principles he shared that day was that we are the sum of the five people we spend the most time with. That idea struck me deeply. I thought about my own circle and thought, I need to upgrade. I knew instantly that Thomas was someone I wanted to learn from, someone whose insight and wisdom could help me grow.

Over the next several years, our connection deepened. He became a mentor, a trusted friend, and one of the most influential people in my life. He didn't just teach me about success—he embodied it. Through his guidance, I built an incredible network, unlocked opportunities I once thought were out of reach, and transformed the way I approached both my career and personal growth.

I am endlessly grateful for the impact Thomas has had on my life. I know that after reading this book, you will feel the same way. If you absorb his words and apply them, I have no doubt that you, too, will experience incredible transformation.

~ Gabi Faye - Actress/Filmmaker/ALS Advocate

CHAPTER 1.1

Introduction

1.1 | CHANGE THE BRAIN, CHANGE THE GAME

The entertainment industry is filled to the brim with people who want to be successful and people who are successful. Successful people may be well-established, belong to a group with a specific goal, or have achieved their "big break," among other factors. People who want to be successful—well, they're still waiting to be called up.

And there are two kinds of brains, one that hinders individuals and one that helps them achieve their success: the **Artist Brain** and the **Business Brain**.

The Artist Brain focuses only on the end results of success and is therefore driven to succeed on the weight of their talent. "Be so good they can't ignore you," as Steve Martin once said. This by itself is not great advice. There are layers to its wisdom. However, the Artist Brain believes in their talent over process and that their talent will lead them to success.

This way of thinking feeds the misconception that the better one is (and the more people who see their awesomeness), the more it will give them a chance to prove they have value and be rewarded for it. This is the core concept that fuels the Artist Brain: "If I'm good and people see that I'm good, I'll have proven myself, and this will lead to my success."

The Business Brain focuses on The Process involved in how to reach the end results and uses that information to achieve success. This perspective takes into account the several Needs of running a business, or rather, a Career Business, before relying on the byproducts of that business. Talent is only a byproduct of a business—a result, if you will. And the Business Brain understands this.

Those who view their career as a business understand how others have developed their own careers and successfully achieved their goals in the entertainment industry. The Business Brain breaks down The Process that led to the achievements of others and then analyzes it, organizes the steps it took to succeed, and places those steps into actionable tasks.

There is a difference between getting a chance to perform because you waited in line long enough for someone to call your name and following The Process that will lead to meeting the right people to skip the line. The right people will hire you because you are their friend, not because you are an unknown talent.

In this book, I have taken apart these two brains to show you what those in the entertainment industry have and have not been doing to accomplish their dream careers, which I firmly call a Career Business.

Before I go any further, here is something to think about. When I ask people why they want to be in the entertainment industry, there is a very specific and consistent answer I get from them.

"I want to make a living doing what I love."

That's a great answer for any ambitious person with dreams. In reality, this is not a plan but the motivation that drives the Artist Brain.

This book will explain the misconceptions about the entertainment industry and clear things up. What we hear from others in our current positions can and does corrupt our paths to success. Between the *advice* of others and their own ill-informed data, the Artist Brain actually builds walls of inaction. They believe that what they are doing will lead to actionable results. In reality, this belief creates inaction.

I'm not saying what you know is wrong or right. I'm saying that it's all you know. Until we put in the work to understand what we've learned, our knowledge remains limited to what we think we know. And until you're in the industry itself, everything is hearsay. The unknown limits your understanding of that knowledge, whether it's your uncle, a random celebrity interview, or even an idea you had while lying in bed dreaming about success. As the saying goes in the entertainment industry, "A day on set is a college education."

For example, when an Artist Brain performs, they feel like they're doing something, yet all they are doing is performing. They are showing off their talent and hoping someone takes the time to pay attention to them. This is why the Business Brain also focuses on building relationships off and on the side of the stage.

As a person in the entertainment field, I'm sure you've heard this dreaded question, "What have you done lately?" This question always refers to the results of the Artist Brain's recent endeavors, whether they just started their career or not.

"You're a writer. What have you published? Anything I've read?"

"You're a musician. What have you released? Anything I've heard?"

"You're an actor. What have you been in? Anything I've seen?"

This is the downfall of any career. The number of albums, movies, books, or comedy shows someone has done doesn't equal the measured value of a person's success. Yet, this inevitable question from friends and family will secretly drive an Artist Brain to try and *do* things to show that they're indeed *doing* things.

These accomplishments translate to inaction and will keep you from taking proactive steps toward running your Career Business successfully, i.e., tricking the brain to think you'll be successful if you do things. The old, "I must be doing something creatively," illusion isn't the solution; instead, the reality of it all is that you should be doing your *job*. By the time you finish this book, you'll know what doing your *job* really is.

Ego is the sin of inaction. Ego makes it difficult to tell someone they're doing it wrong when they believe their way is the right way. Ego makes it hard for a person to listen when they believe they're right or fear being wrong, especially when their way is the reason they're not seeing results. Ego conquers any doubt about misinformation in a way that makes sense for those who follow blindly. Ego will creep in and lead the mind with that "I can't be wrong" mentality.

This way of thinking is dangerous for any career in any industry, as it places a person in the position of A) believing what they know and B) only knowing what they believe.

Worse still, if you believe that performing will help you succeed and someone in the same position as you says, "You should be performing as much as possible," it only serves to reinforce the misconception you're already invested in. And why wouldn't it? This is a trusted friend doing what it is you wish you were doing: performing (or doing whatever artform you want to do).

But, Thomas, they *are* performing, so I should listen to them.

Let's say they *are* performing. And let's say performing is your goal. Their performance on stage isn't what got them on the stage. Someone had to say, "yes, you can play on that stage." Let me explain.

Success is not about performing. Success comes from so much more than getting on stage or acting in front of a camera. You have to think of performing as the *result* of doing your *job*. And true success comes from the opportunities that allow a person to perform. Performance didn't open the doors. Something else opened the door for the opportunity to earn the result of playing on a stage or going to auditions, etc. Someone, somewhere, had to like that person and say yes to them to give them the chance to perform on stage.

I assure you, there will always be someone, somewhere, at every level of this industry, who has to say yes for an opportunity to happen.

But, Thomas, none of this makes sense. If I want to be an actor, shouldn't getting a chance to act be my goal? I can't be a successful actor if I'm not acting. So shouldn't I be doing everything I can to audition so I can get on stage or in front of a camera?

My point is that you should be doing your *job*, and in doing so, you'll be given opportunities to perform without having to ask.

For example, if a person were a teacher, the act of teaching would not make them a successful teacher in their field of interest, nor would teaching get them an opportunity to teach. In fact, they couldn't even get the opportunity to teach until someone said to them, "Yes, you can teach in this school."

It's highly unlikely that they were randomly teaching in some school or home, and someone came into a room and told them that they could continue doing what they're doing and, oh, yeah, here's some money. What would probably happen is the cops would get called because they were trespassing.

There is a process. Sure, working in your field of interest might be the definition of success for some, but for this book, it is not. There is more to success than performing. To clarify, *performing* would be equivalent to *teaching* a class. Teaching is what a teacher does, but it's not their *job*, just as performing is what a comedian does, but it is not their *job*.

But, Thomas, if you teach, you're a teacher. If I tell jokes, then I'm a comic.

Correct. But performing, or doing the thing you do passionately, is not the same as being successful within that field of interest. If a person writes, they are, without a doubt, a writer. A person is a comedian if they write, perform, and tell jokes. A person is an actor if they memorize lines and perform them emotionally. And yes, a person is indeed a musician if they play an instrument, write music, or take the plunge and play covers.

Doing something is not the same as being successful at it, nor is it doing the *job*. And being good at something is also not what I'm talking about in this book when I talk about being successful. Success is something we all define for ourselves, and later on in this book, I will define success, longevity, and fueling one's purpose.

This is one mantra I'll repeat a lot in this book: What you *do* is not your job. Your *job* rewards you financially to do the thing you do passionately.

Now let's break that down.

What you *do* is your passion, your craft. This is the thing you'd do for free. Actors act, writers write, etc. This is the artist's part of your life. This is where the Artist Brain feels free.

Your *job* is everything you do to create opportunities to do what you *do* and get paid for it. The *job* is taking on the responsibilities of your Triangle of Life. Networking is your *job*. Marketing is your *job*. Managing your time, money, and the people around you is your *job*. Every side of the Triangle of Life is going to end up being your *job*.

Now that we have that explained, the point I'm trying to make is that solely doing anything that is considered your passion does not reward you financially or with opportunities.

You might believe, or have heard, that performing and being seen is what will lead to your discovery or success. This is a misconception. It's the idea that if I do A, then B will happen. "A" usually refers to performing a talent or selling products, and "B" is usually the result in the form of money or achieving success.

How many times have you done the *things* you love, like acting, music, etc., and not gotten paid for them? Doing *things* is not your *job*. Your *job* is not about mastering your craft, performing, or selling products. With that said, this is where the book's version of success comes into the equation.

I'm going to get us all on the same page. To do that, we need to define what success means in this book: *Success* is making a *living* within your field of interest. A *living* is not a *lifestyle*. A *living* is affording an average monthly overhead.

Now why did I define what success means in this book? We should define things so we can understand them as we learn about them.

There's a word that'll come up a lot: understanding. Understanding is also going to be a consistent theme in the book. This is because knowing something is not the same as understanding it.

With that said, having a definition gives us a chance to see a word in a new light. Now that success is defined, it gives us a chance to analyze it in a way that makes more sense for this book. So any time the word success is present in this book, you'll know that it means the following:

Success is making a living within your field of interest. A living is not a lifestyle. A living is affording an average monthly overhead.

MISCONCEPTIONS ARE THE ENEMY

Misconceptions are the enemy that spreads like a sickness through people, both inside and outside the industry. Friends, family, and associates all think they know what is best for us. They all have some form of information that will be the missing link to our success.

In the end, all this information is priceless and should be heard. However, one of our job responsibilities is to take that information (whether we agree with it or not) and do some research, research, research. Never take new information at face value, but also never ignore it, as there is always something to learn while doing the work to understand it.

Listen to what is said when people speak so it can be analyzed later. We should always *hear* what people have to say, even if we don't want to hear it. *Ego* can lead to our own ignorance if we do not pay attention to our choices.

We, as people, do not know it all. We can't know it all at the beginning stage of a career. Even people who are examples of success might not know how they got there in the first place. Some successful people will believe it only took dedication and talent. That answer does not mean they didn't do what was required of them. It means they have not connected the dots themselves, even though they are doing what they should be doing instinctively.

Misconceptions stem from the belief that we know what we know and that there are no other explanations so therefore, my information is correct.

Let's assume you're an unknown comic who wants to have a successful career. You end up speaking with a fellow comedian who just got off stage at a comedy club in Long Island, New York. And now you walk over to them and ask, "How do I become a successful comedian?" There is a high chance they'll respond with, "Write as much as possible and get on stage often."

And you know what? That's what they know to be right. They know nothing else. They do not know the value of running a business. They only know that when they write, they get better, and being better makes them look good on stage. Stage time gives them a chance to improve and find their voice. This, in their minds, leads to opportunities.

My follow-up to them would be, "How long have you been performing comedy for?" I then would ask what their day job is (a survival job), regardless of their response. If they have a survival job and have been doing comedy for more than three years, they are a failed business.

According to the latest data from the U.S. Bureau of Labor Statistics (BLS), nearly 1 in 5 U.S. businesses fail within the first year. What's insane is that almost 37.9% of businesses fail within their third year. Most small businesses fail because of a complex and multifaceted nuance of reasons, some being that they don't have enough capital, have an ineffective management team, have a bad business model, try to market themselves but fail, etc.

But, Thomas, I'm not a business; I'm an entertainer in the industry.

Entertainers—comedians, actors, musicians, writers, etc.—are businesses. It's called the entertainment industry, and anyone in that industry is a business, even if that business is a sole proprietorship. This is why it's important to realize where one is in their Career Business when trying to analyze if they're successful or not.

If one is not making a living within the industry of their choice within three years, they are, by definition, a failed business. Is this the end of the line for them? No. It means they have to regroup and start over. What is interesting about the idea of a performer being a business and failing is usually the same reason why most businesses fail within their first three years.

1. Lack of capital or funding
2. An ineffective management team
3. A bad infrastructure or business model
4. An unsuccessful marketing initiative

These four points, and there are many more, will all come into play later in this book and the Breaking Down Success series of books. For now, I want to get back to the conversation with the person who thinks they're a successful comedian from Long Island, and yes, I said that in the New York accent I was born with.

Since we had an answer from the comedian, I want to turn it around and give you the same question. This will create a baseline for where you're at, as this book educates you to help change your brain to change the game.

The question was, "How do I become a successful comedian?"

What does success mean to you in that question?

But, Thomas, I'm not a comedian

Oh, my bad. In that case, what makes a successful add your talent and dream job or passion here—comedian, writer, actor, musician, director, etc. successful?

What is success to you?

In this book, I defined success as making a living within your field of interest. A living is not a lifestyle. A living is affording an average monthly overhead. For now, why don't you write down what you feel success is for you? Then write what you feel success is for a comedian, or, any entertainer and creative type.

Then move on to the next section: What is Success to Most?

WHAT IS SUCCESS TO MOST

Most people believe that success is obtained through the validation of their skills or the craft and talent that they are honing. A musician might feel successful if they succeed on the merits of their songs, how crowds cheer for them at shows, or how well their products sell. Comedians may measure their success by the laughter of an audience or the approval of their peers. This can go on indefinitely with actors, writers, producers, etc.

The truth is "How do I become a successful XYZ?" is not a complete question. When asking someone how to be successful, it needs to be defined, which leads me to the answer for a comedian.

That comedian from Long Island is not wrong when they said a person should write and get on stage as much as possible. This will indeed make a person a successful comedian over time. The reason is because they'll be good at writing and performing. What they're not successful at is their Career Business, since they cannot afford their average monthly overhead with writing, performing comedy, or working within their field of interest.

That's the thing about definitions and success. If the definition of success is being awesome, amazing, and unique, then their plan of attack will be based on talent and not growing their business. To be awesome, you must practice until you reach a certain level of skill, then practice some more. But for a business?

THE GOAL OF THIS BOOK

The goal of this book is to give you the power to make choices, protect yourself, and learn how to get the most out of what you do. And the truth is, everything you *do* must affect everything you *do*. This is why I want to bring light to the misconceptions of the entertainment industry. Hopefully, the tools I show you in this book will help you find solutions by thinking outside the box in a proactive way.

Part of that learning process will give you insight on how to take the knowledge in this book and understand it in a way that allows you to utilize it in a proactive way. Anything you learn in this book, don't take at face value. Remember, like with all knowledge, you need to research, research, research to help you better understand it. This is because knowledge is one thing; understanding that knowledge is another.

As this book breaks down the information so you can understand the knowledge within it, you'll develop the skills to keep others from taking advantage of you. If you're starting out in a career that is either brand new, five, or even ten years old, then let this book be an opportunity to give you a different perspective.

I'm not saying your way is wrong. I'm saying if you haven't seen real results in comparison to where you thought you'd be at this point, then let this book be a chance to reevaluate what you thought you knew. There's nothing wrong with looking at new information with the intention of at least analyzing it through research, research, research.

> *A good rule of thumb* is to use this book as a guide, a tool to change your brain, so you can work to change the game. Take what you learn here as another option on the path to success. Whatever you learn in this book, I implore you to research, research, research until you begin to understand what you have learned.

GETTING THE MOST OUT OF THIS BOOK

Over the course of each chapter, take notes, ask questions, and push back without saying no or this is wrong. I am not challenging what you know; I'm introducing you to new information, options, skills, and Value Sets to help you succeed in the entertainment industry.

People who will probably feel the most hurt are those who've been doing what they've been doing for over ten years with little to no results. At this point in their career, it's only a matter of time before they become jaded by the experience of their industry.

And you know what? I'm not even going to say the insanity quote that people often say in this situation right now. Oh no. There is no need to say that "insanity is doing..." I almost said it. Let us save that for another chapter.

The greatest gift you can give yourself is new information to explore. When you were younger, you had beliefs that were based on your youthful and limited powers of perception. This perception guided your deductive reasoning of situations until you had a position or belief about it. Deductive reasoning is a way of using logic to move from broad ideas to specific conclusions. And with each new year you're alive, you gain wisdom and new perspectives that help influence your perception of things. Which means your power of deduction has new information and tools at its disposal.

Deductive reasoning is often contrasted with inductive reasoning. *Inductive reasoning* is the process where one starts with specific observations and forms general conclusions.

You may also have heard the terms top-down reasoning or deductive logic. Inductive reasoning is the Artist Brain's favorite way to win, whereas the Business Brain uses deductive reasoning to plan.

Most people use inductive reasoning. They think of an idea, or the results, and work out general conclusions about that idea. "If I get on stage, then someone will discover me."

Deductive reasoning examines The Process that had led to the successful person being discovered. Yes, The Process is a powerful term I use all throughout this book. Studying The Process is when a person looks for conclusions and works out the steps of The Process to get end results.

- If person "A" was discovered on stage, then how?
- What led them to that moment?
- What was it about them being on stage that got them discovered?
- Was it being on stage that got them discovered?
- Marketing perhaps?
- Did developing relationships help in any way?
- Did they follow up quickly or wait a long time?
- Was it their stage performance that was interesting?
- Or was it the way the audience spoke about the performance?
- Did they hear about the show beforehand?
- Did they know someone who brought them to the show?
- Did someone randomly see them performing to be discovered?

These are only a few questions you should ask yourself. All of these questions will lead to deductive reasoning as you work out The Process of how they were discovered. And once you see The Process, you can now take action on the steps (The Process) of how they got there.

Luckily, I've written a book that looks deeper into The Process of breaking down success. That is why this book is The Process broken down into simplified explanations that are condensed into terms, mantras, skills, Value Sets, and tasks for any individual or group of people to utilize.

THE REALITY OF MY INTENTIONS WITH THIS BOOK

You should keep in mind that my intentions are not to give you the impression that this book is the only way. There are many ways to make it in the entertainment industry. This book, in particular, will be one way where I show you The Process broken down on how to be proactive in your Career Business. It'll break down elements needed for success, longevity, and fueling your purpose.

These elements are Needs that have to be worked on, but the variables in how you work on them are all up to you. I will give examples, ideas, Value Sets you should develop, and even skills you can use to do what is needed to find that successful longevity in a career fueling your purpose.

For example, in this book series, you will learn that networking is a skill you need to do. Relationships are vital in a way that has loosely influenced the misconception that the one in a million chance of making it comes down to "who you know." But who you know is only one-third of the reality of a successful Career Business.

The three realities of The Process are "who you know," "who knows you," and "how well you know yourself." This book series will go over each of these Needs for all three versions of the valuable relationships you should be developing. For now, think about the people you know, who know you, and how well you know yourself.

As an example of what you'll learn and how there are variables to what you "have to do," here is a quick look at the dreaded concept of networking.

Networking is a Need that you'll have to work on developing as a skill. Why is networking a Need? Networking is all about "building" and "cultivating" relationships as you establish a strong Circle of Influence. And even though networking is a Need, you do not have to do it in a specific way. Relationships are vital, nonetheless, but how you build and cultivate them is not.

You have to be comfortable with what you do and how you do it. So in this series, I'll go over ways you can network to build and cultivate relationships, but they're not the only way, nor even the *correct* way for everyone.

The correct thing is that you do Need to network. That's the point of this series, to learn how to utilize the Needs of Success, Longevity, and Purpose. Once you understand these Needs, you'll be able to see through the misconceptions of the entertainment industry so you can take proactive action and achieve your dreams.

CHAPTER 1.2
Introduction

1.2 | WHO ARE YOU? I MEAN, WHO AM I

This is the part where I am supposed to assert my credibility—the "look at what I have accomplished in life, so listen to me" part. If anyone ever tells you, "Do you know who I am?" Ignore them. I mean, be nice, but ignore them. They don't even know who they are. You know how I know? I used to be that person back in the day, when I was younger, but now I'm older.

This book is not about who I am or what my qualifications are; it's about you and what you are capable of. Knowledge is power, and understanding that knowledge puts possibility at your fingertips.

The short and sweet of it all is that I'm a successful individual who works in the industry, has worked in the industry, and continues to work in the industry since the 1990s.

Milestones?

In 2011, I owned a playhouse theater for several years; I currently have a nonprofit called Team Rise Together, and my notable successes were my touring metal band, my days as a comedian, being a writer (I probably will always be one), being a union actor, and so much more. Truth be told, what I have accomplished isn't the point of the book. I've studied success my whole life and learned a few things. One of which is that all careers in any field of interest succeed, have longevity, and fuel their purposes the same way as a business.

With that said, my qualifications are that I don't think anyone is qualified to give advice. Even experts have contradictory information. If you look hard enough, you'll always find people giving advice, saying this and that or they heard from so-and-so, and from the people around you in your everyday life.

Most influential mentor advice will come from celebrities, who are either giving a motivational speech, telling someone in an interview about their big break, or you're watching their career happen and making assumptions about how it all came together.

The big takeaway is this: What they tell you is all lies until you do your research, research, research to understand it. Advice is moot if you don't do the work to break it apart.

If someone tells you that performing will get you discovered, what does that mean? You need an album to build fans. Oh yeah, how does that work? Actors without headshots or reels won't make it in this industry. Okay, that's interesting; why is that?

Advice is useless without understanding The Process of both why and how it works. You need to ask yourself why is this advice useful, and how does this advice lead me to XYZ? Until you can follow the breadcrumbs to the results, the results mean nothing. PS: Results are going to be the end reward of your effort. This is why performing is a result and not The Process.

I love hearing advice like above for entertainers, but also when people say, "Save money and do it this way." Oh yeah? You're telling me to save 30% of my paycheck each week and I'll have X amount of money by Y date? I mean, that's true, but saving 30% of my check that needs to pay my bills is crazy.

Even that advice is without laying out The Process. Yes, you do need to save money. That is true. Unfortunately, this is not advice. Yes, you do need to organize your finances. Yes, you need to regain control of your spending habits. But no, this is not complete knowledge for just anyone to take action and try to do it. It is simply knowledge without understanding it. Experts often give us tidbits of what we should be doing, yet they rarely go into The Process of how to do it.

But, Thomas, they did tell you how to do it. They said to save 30% of your paycheck to save up money.

Right. They tell you the results and then say some obvious things to make it sound like you should have been doing it all along. If you want to be a millionaire, save X amount of money each month, and you will be a millionaire in X years!

Now what?

Do you go home and save that money?

What about the other parts of The Process?

Where do I place that money?

What about getting other aspects of your life in order first?

Should I earn the right to save money before blindly saving?

No one, including me, has the right answers. We only have ideas, and sometimes they are not the right ideas for you. The one thing I can say for sure is that I see through that advice and know I have to do my due diligence to understand it, which led me to break down The Process for myself.

> *A fun side note* is that if you really want to be a millionaire by saving X amount of dollars a month, you have to first do this: Create a budget based on what your overhead expenses are (there are many ways to do that, one of which is in this book), live by that budget, and afford your overhead before saving any money. What's the next step? I go over that in this book too.

All I can say is that you should always research, research, research what people tell you. Even Oprah can give bad advice, despite how successful she is. Her advice comes with danger. If Oprah gives advice like "take a leap into a career or you'll never know if you had a chance," that's absolutely horrible advice.

I'll explain why that's horrible advice in a moment.

Or, you may have heard Steve Harvey give random chunks of advice on his shows (and I love both Steve and Oprah). There is that one video of his I see often, the one where he gives a lot of general advice on how to take action. The advice I am talking about is his advice on success and how one should "jump and let God open your parachute," which to me is less advice and more motivational.

What about Oprah's advice to prioritize self-care? This is the quote: "If you put yourself last and burn out, you won't have anything left for others, let alone the goals you're striving to achieve."

That's how, according to Oprah Winfrey, you too will find fulfillment—which is how she defines success. I do like that she defined success in her advice. This is great advice, but not for the person trying to succeed in a career.

People who hear or read that specific advice from Oprah will begin to prioritize self-care over taking action or making sacrifices for their career. I've seen it firsthand where people who can't afford their overhead decide they have earned a spa day instead of doing background work on a film that day.

That whole mindset of "after all, it's only background work and not a speaking part, so, I need my beauty rest" is why I do not think general advice is good advice because it does not come with real direction, or rather, a detailed breakdown of The Process.

What you will notice in this book is that I first give advice, then direction to that advice, followed by suggesting that you research, research, research. In reality, it's not about me; it's about you and what you do with what I write in this book or what you hear from others in and out of the industry of your choice. No matter how much of an expert I am in my field of knowledge—and I have many fields of expertise—you still need to understand what it is I am presenting to you.

But, Thomas, what is your area of expertise?

My areas of expertise are the following: the study of success, the longevity of that success, and ways to fuel the purpose of that success. I achieved my expertise through research. I did a lot of research into individuals in all fields, businesses, and creative minds to simplify The Process of turning a passion into a career.

Even when I was willing to start multiple businesses and fail at some of those businesses myself, I still used those experiences to learn to improve my next venture. My Business Brain has always guided me, even as I ventured into a career within the entertainment industry. A Career Business that I've had since 1997 as a writer, musician, actor, director, producer, and comedian. That was a lot to write on a business card, I tell you.

And within these industries, I've had the privilege and honor of mentoring people who have gone on to earn a living doing what they love. And for myself, I was privileged enough to see several lifelong dreams come true before I reached my forties.

None of this is validation for why you should take my advice. I could write stuff in this section like, "I once traveled around the world in fifty days." Unless you do a little deep diving, you might believe or disbelieve that statement at face value. My advice to you would be to research, research, research anything and everything you hear, read, or see. Never take anything at face value just because it aligns with what you believe you know or because it feels like the information is accurate.

The fun part of my life is that I am a nobody to random strangers, but I'm somebody to those who know me. My value among those I have a relationship with was built over a great length of time. One thing that is true is that when I meet new people, I maintain the cordial kindness that all deserve; this is my "be nice to everyone; you never know who someone is or knows." mantra. This is why you should not give value to celebrities or famous people and their random, tossed-out advice simply on the merits of their success in life.

THE RESPONSIBILITY OF KNOWLEDGE VS. UNDERSTANDING

When you learn things in this book, from others, or simply realize that what you know is all you know, allow yourself the freedom to recognize that you may not know everything. This is why you need to research, research, research when you learn new things. Blindly letting information become your dogmatic truth will lead you to fail and to believe that Jupiter does not orbit around the sun because its orbiting barycenter is just outside the sun, even though Jupiter still rotates around the sun's orbit as the fifth planet of eight planets in our solar system (look up Kepler's Laws of Orbital Motion).

A fun side note is that you'll deny yourself opportunities to succeed when you accept what you've learned in one viewing. Taking a stance on knowledge you don't yet understand will stop your growth. If you believe you understand it without doing the research, research, research, you'll fall into the "I can't be wrong" camp. This'll isolate you from potential Circles of Influence. For more on this, research the Dunning-Kruger effect.

I want to look at the orbit argument as a way to get you used to the benefits of deductive reasoning. For those wondering, an orbit is a regular, repeating path that one object takes around another object or its center of gravity (notice that there is an "or" in that definition).

The following are the argument positions:

Position 1: Jupiter is so large that it rotates around a barycenter between the sun and the massive gas planet itself.

Position 2: Jupiter orbits both the barycenter between the sun and the gas planet itself and the sun itself, as Jupiter is the fifth planet in a cluster of eight planets.

Merriam-Webster states…

Orbit (noun)
    A. : a path described by one body in its revolution around another (as by the earth around the sun or by an electron around an atomic nucleus) also : one complete revolution of a body describing such a path
    B. : a circular path
    C. : a range or sphere of activity or influence
Orbit (verb)
    D. : to revolve in an orbit around : CIRCLE
    E. : to send up and make revolve in an orbit

Deductive reasoning would suggest that The Process of elimination means that position 2 is right, while position 1 ignores the fact that both realities are true because two things can be right at the same time.
    If you find yourself believing something so deeply after directly reading it once, then turn to your friend and tell them what you discovered is fact as your friend pushes back using logic; don't take the stance that it is absolute truth because you read it once.
    Unless you are an expert in the topic being debated, you are merely training your brain to ignore The Process of what to do when you learn new information.

We cannot debate, argue, or take a stance on things we do not understand. What does this all mean? It means that anything you learn, whether in a first reading or not, requires due diligence and research, research, research to understand. Once you understand it, take a stance on the subject with the willingness to be malleable in adjusting that stance.

> *A good rule of thumb* is that even if you understand something, it is okay to listen and absorb new information from the debate and allow The Process of research, research, research to help you grow and understand it. The point of it all is that successful people listen to learn, not to be right.

My point is, whether it's knowledge from celebrities, strangers, friends, or your own research, all knowledge seems valuable if you don't know any better.

When it comes to celebrities, their knowledge comes with the value of their accomplishments and something else: your emotional connection to their brand.

Emotional connections increase the value of their knowledge; who and where they are is the result that fans or admirers want to be. If I do "A," then "B" will happen. Oprah hosted her own show; therefore, if I do "A" (host my own show), then "B" will happen (lead me to success).

There are so many factors involved in taking information from anyone, including celebrities. Without knowing the full extent of what it took them to accomplish "A" in the first place, the knowledge one discovers is only data without direction. Accepting data with "blind certainty" is dangerous on many levels. When that data is accepted as an objective truth on the grounds that they discovered new information, it is even worse.

No person should ever take what they have learned on the internet as gospel. Moreover, they shouldn't accept an article by an unknown author as reliable validation for new data. This kind of response to new information from those you admire, know in person, or have found after a few hours of research leads to fueling the misconceptions of our industries.

Data, relevant or not, should not be spread because you now know it. Knowing and understanding are not the same, and understanding something you think you know leads to the perpetuation of misinformation that turns into misconceptions.

Overall, this is what happens when we ask others for advice in the industry. When they are at the same level as you, or slightly higher but not really "doing" anything, their advice is fueling misconceptions. Well, unless you do something very important after receiving said advice. That's right, take what you heard from them and go to your... Well, you should know by now, but, just in case, here's a reminder to make it stick: Research, research, research!

I promise I won't repeat that phrase too often in this book after the introduction... maybe.

No person should blindly absorb or share information. Just because they know it, read it, or heard it does not mean they understand it enough to A) explain it to another person or B) even rationalize it as an absolution in life. Never let your ego get in the way of your ability to listen, learn, and grow. You are better than that kind of behavior. This is the behavior that will destroy relationships, opportunities, and your reputation. All this comes to the point that you should always research, research, research any information you read, hear, or conjure up in your head due to the guidance of people you know and do not know.

If anything should come from your perception of me and the knowledge I lay out in this book, it should be to not accept what I say or what anyone else says. Words are only going to be words. And without putting the time and effort into dissecting those words, you will simply know the information but not understand it. It's good to hear other perspectives and consume knowledge wherever you can, but don't just take action based on what you learned.

However, there is a risk in blindly taking information from anyone, anything, or even yourself. People only know their perspectives on the information they discover. Ultimately, their advice needs to be researched.

Things are what we perceive in our observations. Letting your eyes be the final factor in accepting new data is foolish. Always look deeper into information with as many senses as you can to give your brain enough data to make sense of it all. And as for yourself being the source of your knowledge, we are sometimes the worst villains in our lives when it comes to misconceptions or misguided directions. This is how ego-driven inductive reasoning leads to ignorance. You only know what you know. And what do you really know?

If you do come up with a plan or an idea that makes sense to you, just do the research to figure out its value. When bands combine their lack of knowledge and believe the path to success is based on recording an album, just stop what you are doing. It is okay to want to record an album and even actually record an album. But do your research. After doing that research, you will quickly realize that albums do not make money. Marketing a brand and advertising help sell albums, not the album itself.

But, Thomas, does that mean if I focus on marketing, I'll make money?

See, right there, the mind is focused on the end results. Marketing is an important part of The Process, but it's not the key to reaching your end goal. You have to work out The Process by doing research. Enjoy your ideas, but never let the blind lead the blind, no matter how smart you are.

> *A good rule of thumb* is to focus on The Process of achieving the end result and not the end result itself, especially if the end result is money. Money comes when you do your job and earn the reward of a financially secure Career Business.

A QUICK REMINDER OF THE TONE

I need to disclose something important: If you haven't noticed yet, I'm going to approach these chapters, at times, with straightforward and blunt energy. What seems harsh is a realistic look at what I've learned as I've grown in the entertainment business.

This book is a collection of things I've learned through experiencing my own Artist Brain moments, from the people who taught me, and from working with clients as I learned to make sense of the knowledge I've gained over the past twenty-plus years. My examples will be based on actual conversations, responses, and ideas that were supposed to be world-changing for my career, friends, and others I've known in this industry of entertainment!

Raw verbiage allows me to not hold back. Whatever comes off as rude, arrogant, or even placing me in the "know it all" category, I want you to understand this very point: I am not doing it to be rude so that I feel I am above anyone in this world. I'm doing it because I wish that people had been straight with me when I first started. It took me years before I met some of my mentors, and even more years of my life to get out of my own way and listen to them.

And let me tell you, they laughed in my face often. They made fun of my ideas, my ambitions, and every single one of my selfishly motivated plans that involved the path of least resistance. And when push came to shove, they were always right.

AN EXAMPLE FROM MY PERSPECTIVE

Here, as an example, is a moment of agony from the mind of one of my mentors. There I was, sitting in a chair across the table from a person who knew the music industry inside and out. Imagine being a young me, a musician who knows it all, and being told that music is not what makes you money in the music industry.

But, Mentor, what are you saying? How does music not make you money in the music industry? It's literally the music industry. Music is in the term.

What they were telling me and my ego was that my music, the music I poured my soul into, was not an important factor in my success. And at the time, my Artist Brain believed that if my music wasn't good enough, then I wasn't good enough. And my success had to come from my music because I was awesome, amazing, and unique.

And to be fair and clear, yes, music does have some value in the music industry. Music contributes to a musician's career longevity. But one will never see longevity if they can't first create success to have a presence within the industry itself.

Any example or explanation I give in this book is me telling you how something is, was, or could be, and, to be honest, a lot of my examples are things I have said, experienced with others, and even fought against because me and my fellow friends could not accept a lot of the information people gave us—people who were literally record label presidents. And somehow, me and my friends knew better than they did. "Young and dumb" is a saying for a reason.

Knowledge is not wisdom. Oh, and I know, as you should know by now, that we do not take anyone at their word simply because they have value. But I might have taken it to another level when I ignored the president of a record label giving me their *free* time.

The thing is, we, me, okay, it was I, as in all me. At the time, I was not taking their word, as they freely gave it to me with the purpose of clearly hearing what they had to say. It took years. I mean, it took lots and lots of years to get out of my own way and try a different process that could work and did work. And that process began with listening to what they had been telling me all along.

Before that happened though, I had to fail and fail a lot to finally stop myself from being right all the time when I clearly didn't know the industry as a musician. My Artist Brain knew this and this alone: write music, perform on shows, sell merchandise, get on tours, I need a manager, I need to get signed to a record label, and once all that happens, I can focus on only the fun part while others handle the business stuff.

I was wrong.

So I say to you: with this book in hand, go on, get to reading, please take notes, and get out of your own way. At the end of the day, when you finally finish this book, don't take it as gospel, but allow it to guide you in doing your research, research, research so you can take the knowledge you have learned and work to understand it!

CHAPTER 2.1
Foundation

2.1 | SUPPORTING THE WEIGHT OF YOUR MISSION

A career lives or dies on its foundation. No standing structure maintains stability if its foundation is frail or weak. The Knap of Howar in Scotland is a testament to how valuable any foundation is for long-lasting results.

This is especially true for a career in the entertainment industry. If your Career Business should be treated like a business, then that business should have a foundation of resources to build on. This means one must have patience while developing their foundation.

A foundation is the first step in taking control of your life, which will allow you freedom in the form of time. Time is a limited resource, but when used well, it can help build a structure with stability, strength, and purpose. These aspects of your time will evolve and mature into opportunities.

The power of time, due to its foundation, grants you the ability to say *yes* or *no* when and where opportunities arise. If a foundation is neglected during its creation or maintenance, it'll collapse. Even the tallest structures will collapse on themselves if the foundation is weakened and neglected.

> ***A good rule of thumb*** is to have a Financial Foundation Account (FFA) in place before taking a leap of faith into a dream career. An FFA should be filled with the essential startup capital needed to run a business. If one's Career Business is considered a business, allocate startup capital to cover overhead for a minimum of eighteen months. This startup capital is the basis for an FFA that makes everything come together.

THE FUN PART IS NOT THE WORK

There has never been a shortage of people in the entertainment industry who are living off the fumes of their misguided passions to be successful in their field. Who can blame those who have a dream? Dreams keep us motivated. They drive us to pick ourselves up when we fall. That passion in us takes on the negativity of those who keep telling us to have a plan B, and yet, we still push forward. Nothing is going to keep a dreamer from waking up until they achieve their goal!

This is one of the main reasons I often find myself hearing the repetitive banter of clients who seek the same results in the end: "to make a living doing what they love to do." I.e., making a living playing their music, doing comedy, acting, writing, etc. This rhetoric is so similar in conversation that I can tell you what they will recite to me verbatim. Again, I get it. An entertainer with a dream focuses on the results of what they love instead of The Process. After all, the results *are* the fun parts, so I get it.

Acting is fun when you jump inside a character's motivations; therefore, an actor will do what they can to get as many chances to act. Telling jokes and hearing an audience laugh is amazing. This is why comedians will try to perform as much as possible, and they want to "practice" their sets. Headbanging while you blast through a metal song on stage is pure awesomeness when performing, so why wouldn't a musician work hard to get booked on more shows?

These examples are the same things that influence the divine power of being an author when it comes to creating absolutely anything their imagination conjures, which is an adrenaline rush that never ends.

Art and being creative are absolutely the fun parts to do. So why would anyone want to do the boring business stuff? And I completely understand this;

I, too, am an artist who wishes to play my guitar indefinitely, write novels and scripts, tell jokes on stage, act, direct, etc.

And the insane part is that I took action for years without real direction, without any foundation to stand on. I basically hoped for the best outcome, which led to that old saying, "If something happens, that's great, but until then..." And I just kept doing whatever I was doing to feel the joy of the fun part.

Something in me made me believe that the *work* was getting booked to perform. It took me a while to realize I was putting more effort into the results than I was into my job requirements for my Career Business.

And each sentiment varies between individuals depending on how long they have been doing what they have been doing. You get individuals who believe they deserve a chance because of how awesome, amazing, and unique they are. But for these individuals, there's no doubt in their minds that greatness will be achieved simply due to these elements of being awesome, amazing, and unique. They have an awesome stage presence, they're amazing at their craft, and they bring a *unique* element to the experience. All that's needed is to get in front of the right people.

But who are the right people? A lot of the time, it's believed that the right people are audiences, managers, shakers and makers, and the movers who make things happen.

Then you have those subtle, hopeful Artist Brains who believe in themselves but downplay their inevitable failure. It becomes that old way of thinking, "I'm having fun doing what I do, and if something happens, then great, but when it does happen, I'll put all of my attention exclusively into creating my art while others handle the boring stuff, like marketing."

These mindsets, and the variations of them, heavily rely on what they do creatively or artistically to succeed, but not necessarily what their jobs are. They have little to no direction or foundation to grow off of.

A fun side note is that the Artist Brain is dedicated to succeeding on the power of their creative energy, while the Business Brain takes proactive steps to secure their paths of opportunity.

A good rule of thumb is that what you do is not your job. Your job rewards you financially to do the thing you do passionately.

WHEN OPPORTUNITY KNOCKS

These two mindsets produce an all-too-common outcome, which is typical of people whose Artist Brains are in charge. These are the people who work a survival job that has *nothing* to do with their field of interest while they wait for their dream career to take off.

This creates a difficult situation. One where they have no way of paying for their overhead without that job or jobs in general. And by having a survival job, they limit the opportunities that are available to them to take those random leaps that could elevate a career. The issue with working a survival job is that now the person can only take these leaps when the random opportunity has an extreme value or benefit behind it. Otherwise, to the Artist Brain, it's not worth it.

The smallest opportunities that present themselves to a person could lead to greater results over the course of a career, one that will take time to build. Waiting for the big opportunities stunts growth within the industry. How can you only say yes to big opportunities if the little ones are what help you develop relationships, leave your brand's impression on people, and establish Value Sets at the tables you join?

Mental behavior like this is a game of gymnastics that keeps people isolated in their dreams while potential careers pass them by.

But, Thomas, I need to pay my bills.

That makes sense. Bills need to get paid, and a survival job does just that, and I get that one hundred percent.

Why would anyone leave a job that pays consistently each week? When it comes to the security of a survival job over the small percentage chance of success in the entertainment industry, it all makes sense. But honestly, that fear is why people think this way. Doing so is the first step in creating walls and not solutions.

And I completely understand that fear and those worries. Besides, how else can the bills get paid if a person is not making money until they are making money doing what they love? This is where it's time to change the brain; to change the game to get you thinking outside the box in a proactive way.

It's not about making money doing what you love.

But, Thomas, that's the only reason I'm reading this book: to make money doing what I love.

It's not about making money doing what you love; it's about making a *living* in your field of interest. The longevity you create will give you the power to combine your success with the power to do what you love because you want to, not because you have to pay all your bills.

But, Thomas, how do I make it so I can make choices because I want to and not because I have to pay for my fifteen streaming accounts?

In these Foundation chapters, I'll show you how to establish a powerful and reliable Financial Foundation Account to break the chains of a survival job.

First, we need to cover a few things. A person who needs to work a survival job to pay their bills turns their Career Business into a hobby; hobbies cost money to maintain. In this situation, the survival job has the benefits that a Career Business fails to have at the start. Some of the benefits of a survival job are that you most likely will get a raise, more hours, promotions are possible, paid vacation days, and you develop relationships in that particular industry you have no desire of staying in, which, by the way, is not the industry you're interested in.

This survival job plan leads to extremely annoying stereotypes: an actor working as a waiter till they get their big break, a musician having a job as a mechanic, or a writer working as a janitor. I know, without a shadow of a doubt, that for these people, it wasn't a conscious choice to make their Career Business a hobby.

But, Thomas, why is it a hobby?

If it costs you money to sustain the effort of doing this "thing you love to do" without a return on your investment, then it's a hobby. People who love building model airplanes spend money to buy the materials but make zero dollars in return for that investment. That makes it a hobby.

The other side of the argument is that one cannot build a Career Business if they're working all the time to pay their bills with a survival job.

Here's what I'm saying. Imagine, for a moment, that your Career Business (dream career) was your hobby. Now, imagine, if you loved doing that hobby but you just didn't have time to do it. You know why? Because you work at a job that has nothing to do with it. You can't build model airplanes and you can't build a career if you're working down the street at the local supermarket.

One more example: being an actor is easy. Anyone can act if they recite memorized lines with some emotion behind them. A person can act in a local community theater, set up their own performances in the living room, etc. Acting is the easy part, even if it's bad acting. Now, getting paid to act in things that you emotionally connect with—well, not everyone loves being a tree in the local play. Also, are you really choosing to do the herpes commercial or did it just pay really well? See my point?

You have to put time into an acting career by being seen and being present in the industry. This allows you to meet people, market yourself, and get involved so you can lead, follow, and advise at the tables you're invited to. And this is why if you have a 9–5 job five days a week just to cover your bills, it becomes difficult to turn that hobby into an acting career.

But, Thomas, I still don't get it.

Let me put it another way. How can you build your dream business of opening a donut shop if you also have to work at a gas station two towns over just to pay your bills?

You cannot put any real time into your donut shop if you have to be at another job. You either have to choose to grow a career or not. If you want to grow your Career Business, you need to be able to afford the overhead for both your life and the business. In this example, owning a donut shop is the Career Business.

This is where a Financial Foundation Account comes into play. Having startup capital in your Financial Foundation Account allows you the time to focus on building said donut shop or, since you want to be an entertainer, replace a tasty donut shop with your career as an entertainer when you have a solid Financial Foundation Account.

WHAT DOES A FINANCIAL FOUNDATION ACCOUNT DO?

A Career Business develops when a person can put time into their job responsibilities for that specific venture. A Financial Foundation Account allows a person the freedom to put time into those job responsibilities to develop that venture. Which, in this situation, would be your Career Business.

But, Thomas, what's the difference between putting time into my job responsibilities and a hobby during one's spare time until something happens?

That's a great question. Let's create two individuals to answer that question. We're going to call these people Person A and Person B. Now let's generate lives for these people.

Person A wanted to be a novelist. Instead, they work at an architectural firm. This job was their backup plan, their Plan B if writing a novel didn't pan out. Since they still haven't sold one of their ten novels to a publisher, they need to continue to work at the architectural firm to pay their bills. Of course Person A would rather be paying their bills with a writing career, specifically writing their novels. Unfortunately, they still need to pay their bills with their survival job at the firm that comes with benefits, vacation time, etc.

Person B also works at the same firm and loves their job. Why? Because there is a big difference between Person A and Person B. Person B wants a career as an architect. This was their Plan A, their dream career, and the hobby they turned into a Career Business. However, they also love building model airplanes on the side as personal relaxation time.

Being an architect does pay well. So this allows Person A to pay their bills. But how does Person A get their writing career off the ground? Their plan is simple: work at the firm during the day to pay their bills by clocking in on time each morning, and then writing their book on their hour break, and then again after clocking out at the end of the day. This leads to them running home to eat dinner, relax, and then write their book a bit more at night.

Person B, on the other hand, wants to make being an architect their Career Business, so they show up early for work, eat with the other employees, especially makers and shakers, stay late when needed, and go out to dinner with the partners and fellow architects after work.

Now, here's the interesting part about all of this: Person A is actually the better architect on paper. They went to college, graduated at the top of their class, and were hired for more money when they began at the firm. Person B was only able to attend a local college and graduated with passing grades. They were hired at the same firm as Person A, but their salary was the base starting rate of that firm. Additionally, Person A has been at the firm for two years, while Person B just hit their six-month anniversary.

Who do you think is going to get the promotion?

If you said Person B, then you are correct.

Now let's take a look at Person A a bit closer. For them, both their writing and architectural careers are going nowhere.

Why do you think that is?

Logistically, Person A is putting some time into writing at the expense of their architectural career. Doing this affects both career paths negatively.

Now I want to examine what it would look like if Person A decided to work hard to save up a Financial Foundation Account so they could dedicate their efforts toward building a Career Business as a writer.

First, they would have to focus on saving money to build up enough startup capital for their Financial Foundation Account. This is where a survival job, or several, makes sense. Instead of focusing on the Career Business at the start of their plan, they begin by saving up enough capital to invest in that Career Business.

Second, once they have their eighteen months of startup capital in their Financial Foundation Account to take the leap, they do so and take the leap. This leads them to step three: get involved in their field of interest.

See, the Financial Foundation Account gives a person the freedom to pay for at least 18 months' worth of overhead costs. This freedom gives a person a chance to volunteer their time or work at a job within their field of interest for less money than is reasonable.

But, Thomas, why would anyone want to do that? All I want to do is the thing I love doing. Who would ever want to play music for someone else's band or help another author with their book?

Someone who understands that success has three parts: one being relationships with other people. And this is what having startup capital does for a person. It gives them a chance to get involved in and around their industry. This allows them a chance to build and cultivate relationships with other people within that industry. While they are in the field of their interest, they're leaving an impression on others and learning the industry through practical application as they do things in their field of interest.

The big difference between having a Financial Foundation Account and working a survival job "until something happens" is the ability to give time to the career a person wants to nurture. When a person can only devote some time to a career as it becomes available, it will lead to a long road of chance that is less proactive and more passive.

Attacking a Career Business aggressively with the ability to make choices, take opportunities as they come, and get involved in the industry itself places the career in the hands of the person. A hobby is something we give our free time to, and a career is something a person puts real time into so they can build it up.

> *A good rule of thumb* is that if you want a specific career, you give it the time it deserves by treating it like a real business. It might look different for everyone; however, the real-time commitment toward anything worth developing is over forty hours in a seven-day work week. In the beginning of any business, the owner needs to sacrifice their *wants* so they can put time into the *needs* of their business; in this situation, that would be a person's Career Business.

YOU DESERVE A CAREER YOU LOVE

I don't care what anyone says to you; you deserve the career you want in this life of yours. And honestly, you deserve it because you're valued. You're a human being and deserve to have a career that you're passionate about. Your dreams are no less important than the dreams of the next person.

What will get you there is how you choose to take action. We're the captains of our own lives, molding this world with action and sinking in our inaction. A real proactive effort to take action is going to take time to execute, and most of that time is spent getting the foundation of your plan ready.

So, the first step in getting ready is to put time and effort into your Financial Foundation Account. If you have a strong Financial Foundation Account, you can start working hard on your Career Business the moment you open up your proverbial shop.

One of the most powerful benefits of a Financial Foundation Account is that it gives you the ability to take a chance. And you know what? It's not just any kind of chance; it's a calculated chance. Jumping off a cliff into the wild blue sky, hoping your parachute opens through divine intervention, is insanity. Not the having faith part, the believing it's not in your hands once you take a leap part.

Jumping without the tools to take action is what taking a *chance* looks like. However, taking a calculated chance is when a person has the capital to cover their startup costs, makes a plan to execute said goals, and takes the knowledge they've consumed and puts time into understanding it.

That's what this book is going to teach you. It will show you how to pack your parachute yourself, trust when to jump, and, with the right effort, float down safely. Maybe even with those smoke books that make the colorful trails behind you.

CHAPTER 2.2

Foundation

2.2 | SAYING YES TO LIFE

You have the right to say *yes* to your life and to the things you want to accomplish. We all do. And truthfully, life is beautiful when we can contribute to it with our endless creative passions. Creative outlets give our imagination a chance to explore the human condition and make real the emotional truth of what art can be for all of us. That passion can come from construction workers, designers, teachers, chefs, and more. These are all forms of passion where people want to have a career making a living doing what they love.

Like traditional creative outlets, each of these forms of expression is designed to add value to this world and elevate our perspectives. The way we approach our passions in order for them to touch others is part of the beauty of the life we choose. And you deserve to be a part of that magical assimilation of hope—a hope that makes us aspire to greatness in a way that potentially inspires others.

You're filled with pure joy because of a dream that burns inside of you with an unwavering, unchanging passion. You've held steady even in times when people might have tried to discourage you; you ignored their disrespectful advice and kept your head up and focused forward. And through your efforts to make a living doing what you love, hours turned into days, weeks into months, and years into decades as you worked hard to learn and master what it is that you love doing. Even when it seems like there's nothing you can do or the career you want has slipped away, you can still add your voice to the endless stream of art. That's the foundation of the passion all of us Artist Brains have, and it is beautiful.

Then it happens. Somewhere in your life you find yourself fighting more uphill battles with little to no results. Every bill that exists seems to surface, costing you a fortune. Instead of collecting outcomes, you're collecting debt—a debt that now officially fuels your purpose in life. What is that purpose? The purpose is to make money and pay those damn things off. Yet all you wish you could do is what you love to do. And, yes, life wants you to succeed, but you must work for it.

At some point, maybe not today, tomorrow, or even the long gone yesterday, you'll find yourself making excuses to do what you hate while watching your passion fade away into "if onlys." These excuses are the villains that motivate you to work a dead-end job, give value to that self-doubt, and find yourself further away from your dream. And where you once said yes to life, you find a way to compromise your purpose as if you have no choice.

It happens. A person ends up working hard at what they don't want to do so they can justify being able to do what they love doing occasionally when work or time allows it. Next thing you know, you're the manager of some seafood department at a local supermarket, and ten, maybe even fifteen, years have flown by. This is what happens when you cannot say yes to life because your preparation failed to help you stand your ground and develop your financial foundation to take action.

The truth is, we all deserve a chance to fight back against the negative no's and walls built to hinder our potential for success. No one, not even ourselves, should be the reason we accept no for an answer. I deeply believe that anyone can make things happen when they take control of The Process. By not letting our passion direct us, we can take a more strategic approach to our Career Business by setting up a Financial Foundation Account, a plan with tasks and goals, and establishing everyday job responsibilities that all lead us in the right direction.

But, Thomas, what is that direction you speak of?

I'm speaking about a person who is specifically proactive in every aspect of their responsibilities to build a successful Career Business. That proactive path isn't an easy journey, nor will it have instant results, no matter how much time is put into it. Whatever those tasks are, I can say this much: they have nothing to do with the craft of being a creative individual.

Every element that needs attention will be focused on the Business Brain. There's a major difference between succeeding through a creative endeavor and being proactive in making things happen. Making things happen is always going to come from the job responsibilities one must fulfill and never from the things we do passionately.

With that said, this book has a lot of pushback when it comes to one's craft. My lessons are less about becoming an awesome, amazing, and unique craftsperson and more about running a career like a business. Think of it as the backend aspect of a career: all the things people should be doing to run their business, yet no one ever sees the work that goes into it. That work will be laid out in sections while building on the foundation of what a person should be doing to get the most out of their effort.

The way I look at it is that you don't need my help with the art of it all. You've lived with that passion long enough where no one needs to explain it to you. My job is to show you behind the curtain of The Process, which most people don't get a chance to see in their lifetime. Once I show it to you, then I'll explain The Process to you.

When the work begins to turn into habits, the results start showing up. This is true with anything; nothing can happen if we don't choose to take action, even a little at a time (a little is better than zero). A foundation helps you find the yes you deserve, and that'll make sense and be possible once the insight in this book goes from being knowledge learned to being knowledge understood.

What you'll find in this book is The Process laid out for those who want a career within the entertainment industry. Each step will give you the tools to best guide you to success, longevity, and fueling your purpose.

A fun side note is that the *work* is networking, marketing, and practicing; managing your time, money, and people; finding solutions and using your talents to lead, follow, or advise; organizing capital to protect, grow, and reward yourself; and treating your life like a business.

CHAPTER 2.3
Foundation

2.3 | CREATING OPPORTUNITIES

A strong Financial Foundation Account gives you the option to say yes to your life by creating the freedom to make choices. When you have the freedom to make these choices, it potentially opens doors to opportunities. Or, rather, it affords you the freedom to take action toward opportunities when doors are opened for you. More importantly, a proactive lifestyle leads to more productive outcomes.

But, Thomas, what does that mean for me?

It means that you can take advantage of opportunities when they are presented to you or have the availability to create opportunities yourself. And this is only possible when you have the freedom to say yes. Without that freedom to say yes, you can't make things happen because you don't have the time.

As I often say, "don't work too hard, but be productive." I've seen it all too often where people do a lot of things but not a lot is getting done. Being productive is more important than working hard at nothing. That mantra is all about us becoming the creators of our own destiny by being proactive in creating opportunities and being available to say yes.

Of course, being able to say yes to things doesn't mean you should say yes to everything. You might have certain desired outcomes that are important to you, but when you achieve them, no matter what, they should ultimately influence your big picture. That big picture is allowing everything you do to affect everything you do. So when you do say yes to things, they are based on choices that best suit your brand and needs of the Triangle of Life.

The direction of your brand allows you to make choices that influence consistency in the overall impression you leave on others. That consistency left on others pulls you into a community of like-minded individuals who share similar missions, morals, and purposes with you. These perspectives lead you to have things in common with others who add to your Circle of Influence. And when we share perspectives in an emotional connection to something bigger than ourselves, it increases our chances of being asked to join tables and to be suggested to other tables.

All I'm saying is that with a solid Financial Foundation Account it frees you from the constraints of time, money, and our own fears. When you want something to happen, *you* have to make proactive choices to achieve your goals. You're less likely to make active decisions over passive ones when time constraints, financial obligations, and personal fears control you.

Passive decisions are based on making choices for opportunities only when you have the availability to take that action. The advantage of an active decision is having both the freedom and the ability to be proactive in making choices, even if the outcome ends in failure. The more active decisions you can make, the higher your return will be on your investment of time.

Success will not come to you without the ability to make choices, attempt things, and take action. The more you're able to take that action, the more you'll learn, grow, and can change to fit your situations. The more you learn to fail and rise again, the stronger you'll be in your next attempt. These attempts are only possible because of a strong Financial Foundation Account that gives you the ability to fail, and fail often, then get back up.

I love that a strong Financial Foundation Account helps sustain that initial venture into the entertainment industry. It gives you a real sense of security because the startup capital you've saved up gives you more options to try to make things happen.

If it isn't clear yet, a Financial Foundation Account gives you the power of choice. That power of choice is what allows you the option to say yes to your life. To your dreams. Your freedom is directly proportional to the value of your Financial Foundation Account. So remember that when you're saving up money, organizing your overhead, and getting ready to start your journey into a Career Business.

> *A good rule of thumb* is to make things happen by making things happen. This is the mentality of a proactive Business Brain who finds solutions by thinking outside the box in a proactive way—take action to create reaction.

TIME IS A VALUABLE RESOURCE

Time is a valuable resource that you, and most other people, are happy to trade for money. The formula feels like it works: work a few hours, get paid. Done. But you must also be willing to trade time for opportunities even when there is no direct or instant financial reward.

But, Thomas, I need the cash to pay my bills.

If you focus on earning money over wealth, it leads down a path to debt. More debt means more outside forces creating stressful limitations on your freedom to take action. Being able to say no to things and yes to life is a freedom that gives you control. That control in life enables you to create opportunities yourself. These opportunities are the residuals of having the choice to say yes to life and make things happen by making things happen often.

But, Thomas, how many opportunities do I really need? I'd rather have cash. Which I hear is almost as good as money.

All of them. That's the simple answer. You need opportunities to develop to the point where you're not asking anymore; they're coming your way. And the more opportunities that come your way, the more likely a better opportunity will present itself. But you have to say yes to a lot of crappy opportunities that you probably don't think are worth it at first. I assure you, they absolutely add up in a positive return.

This is why it is better to have money to cover overhead than to be working to afford your overhead. If you have to work to pay your bills, then it's less likely that you are frequently able to get involved in your field of interest.

See, getting involved in your field of interest allows you to build relationships and brand awareness. Getting involved is how opportunities present themselves. The smallest yes with the least amount of return can, in time, result in greater returns on the investment of your resources. The entire point of having a solid Financial Foundation Account is to allow you the freedom to focus on your Career Business rather than trying to pay the next bill.

But, Thomas, what does this have to do with creating opportunities?

You can't create opportunities if you don't get involved. And opportunities will quickly dry up if you can only say yes when you're available. The Financial Foundation Account covers your overhead so you're not working a day job or a survival job to pay your bills. Instead, you have every day available to meet new people, interact with them, follow up, and say yes to helping them when they need it. If you get involved in the entertainment industry and people see how competent you are, they will ask you back.

But, Thomas, that sounds too easy and too good to be true.

Let me ask you something. Would you rather work with your friend and people you actually like, have stuff in common with, and know you can rely on them or would you rather randomly approach a stranger on the sidewalk somewhere and ask them to help you do something?

The rule is simple: make friends by getting involved, which then allows them to see that you're not only capable but are friendly; go out of your way to help the mission of the tables you joined; and then they will come back to you for more opportunities. That's the way of life. Friends like hanging out with friends. And you know what? Friends like working with friends too.

One of the better ways to create opportunities is by having a Financial Foundation Account cover your overhead. This gives you the freedom to get involved within your industry of choice. And the more freedom you have, the more you can get involved with others so they can witness your Value Sets when joining tables to lead, follow, or advise the best you can.

A career doesn't just happen because you're awesome, amazing, and unique. No matter how awesome you are, if an opportunity presents itself and you cannot take off work to say yes, this makes you the *no* person. Having to say no is a negative thing for anyone's brand. And if you give people enough no responses, you will be written off.

CHAPTER 2.4
Foundation

2.4 | CALCULATED RISK

Every new venture must necessitate a significant amount of planning. This doesn't mean a person should take months or years to plan out their course of action. The beauty of building a Financial Foundation Account is that it helps take the strain off of getting all the necessities together at once. While saving up your initial startup capital, you can utilize this time to work on each side of your Triangle of Life—among other aspects of The Process before taking a leap. The more prep you put into the Triangle of Life, the better off your starting position will be once you step into your field of interest.

But, Thomas, can't I just save money and then take action?

You could, but I'm sure you've heard, "Success occurs when opportunity meets preparation." You can thank author and salesman Zig Ziglar for that gem.

So yes, you could just take this time to save up money. But success comes when you place effort into The Process, and preparation is part of that process.

With that said, here are a few ideas for preparation to keep you busy during this time. Know that these ideas will be continually explored in greater depth within the Breaking Down Success series.

A LIST OF PREPARATION IDEAS

- **Network**: People are your first line of offense and defense. So put time into growing your Circle of Influence. Whether you have time or not to hang out with people, you always have time to interact on social media, send friends their way, or show your support when and where you can.

- **Market**: You need to market who you are and what you're capable of. You might not have time to get involved, but you could use this time to discover who and what you are. Who are you in terms of your missions, morals, and purposes? Can you lead, follow, and advise?

- **Practice**: You're going to spend a lot of time on your talent, but in reality, you need to be practicing your industry. Knowing and understanding how your industry works gives you the insight to make better, stronger, and more educated decisions. Learn how and why things work.

- **Manage your time**: Know how to control your time to give yourself a step up on others. Time management is knowing yourself. How long does it take you to do something? Are you a late sleeper? Train yourself to work with schedules, where to adjust, and how to live on no sleep.

- **Manage your money**: Capital leads to longevity and success, and how you spend money is really the whole experience. We spend money to be born, live, and, oddly enough, die. Work on improving your spending and budgeting skills. Don't earn money to pay bills, earn to invest.

- **Manage the people around you**: The right people will take you time to find, and while you work to find them, learn about the people around you. Who's celebrating only themselves, helping others, and do you trust them? Are they team players with similar beliefs and end goals?

The truth is, when it comes to your Career Business, you should be setting your proactive tasks around networking, marketing, and practicing, as well as managing your time, money, and the people around you. None of these Needs are more important than the others; however, keep in mind that people make the world go around and around.

All of this simply means that in an industry where people run things, you need to know people, those people need to know who you are, and you need to know yourself. People. A simple word with big results. People are the secret to networking, growing a career, and making choices for the people they believe in.

When I say you should manage the people around you, what I mean is that you should organize them and the time you put into certain people. This will help you with a plan of attack when you begin networking with others. You can do this by organizing those you know, or don't know, into a Circle of Influence. This list of people will give you a better idea of who is already in your network, who you want to bring into your network, and who knows who within that network of people.

Now this is the crazy part: none of this matters if there is no Financial Foundation Account giving you the freedom to make choices and take action. There is a reason I'm placing a great deal of emphasis on having a strong Financial Foundation Account; it's essential for taking action and will give you a significant advantage in your industry when you take calculated risks.

Notice I said calculated risks, not risks. There is a major difference between taking calculated risks and taking risks in general. Calculated risks are planned and prepared for. Far too many people jump without a real plan and hope God opens the parachute for them on the way down. To me, that's a risk not worth taking.

RISKING IT ALL ON TALENT

Stop me if you've heard this before. Craft and talent are usually the be-all-end-all of every plan the average person with a dream believes in. These are people who want to be successful within the entertainment industry. To the point where they're going to take risks—not calculated risks, but risks that risk it all on their talent.

That approach usually begins with, "Be so good they can't ignore me," all the way to, "My talent will get me to the top," and of course, "Once something comes from it, I'll be able to afford to put all my attention into my career."

The idea that your greatness will get you discovered or that your talent is the answer to your dreams will only fuel your hope with logical fallacies. Now, I understand that there's a nuance to all the in-between stuff, but let's be honest with ourselves: talent alone is not the secret to success. And when you rely on talent, you're cutting off your legs of potential on the risk that you're so talented that all these strangers in the entertainment industry are going to drop everything once they see that talent in action and think, "Who's Brad Pitt? Sign that background actor next to him right now. They're the next big thing!"

Hell, even Brad Pitt almost didn't get cast in Thelma & Louise until Geena Davis pushed for him. And this is after he worked his butt off doing background and extra roles in film.

Then there's the notion that once you're in the industry, signed, or whatever the victory pole is, you'll stay and advance your career because you're great at what you do (rather, you're talented). But that's not how it works. You can't wait until you're there and then do the work. And you can't wait until you're there and then rely on your talent alone.

People need to like and trust you way more than them thinking your talent is enough. If they can't stand you, no one will want to work with you. Don't believe me? Lindsay Lohan had faced issues with reliability and professionalism on set, leading to clauses in her contract. Same with Brando. That's not enough? How about Axl Rose or R. Kelly?

But, Thomas, isn't R. Kelly a criminal?

Okay, yeah, that's true. My point still stands. Those people were talented and because of their reputations (brand value) and their relationships being hurt, they lost the level of success they once had. You know what? For fun, look up Marlon Brando and his career's history.

Talent is the killer of careers when relied upon. The more weight you place on talent being the pathway to your success, the greater your chance for failure becomes in securing your Career Business.

Another example of dangerous mentalities are actors who say, "Get me in the audition room and I'll get the part." Another person might say, "Hire me and I'll prove myself." Yeah? How about proving yourself first?

HAVING A PLAN TO TAKE CALCULATED RISKS

Where was I? Oh yes, taking calculated risks. Talent shouldn't be ignored, as it's one side of your Triangle of Life, but that's not why you should feel confident taking calculated risks. To take calculated risks, develop a plan that gets some of your ducks lined up in a row before taking a leap into your Career Business.

But, Thomas, having all my ducks in a row is being extra prepared.

Yes, you could put the time into having all your ducks in a row, but, in reality, it's about having enough preparation to get through the first few years. I say this because there are certain things a person cannot prepare for until they are involved in the industry itself.

Your plan is only going to be able to help you with what you do know. From there, a lot will change once you get involved in your field of interest. You'll naturally learn how things work inside the machine once you're able to look behind the scenes. Which means you should focus on what you can anticipate in advance without worrying about what you will know once you're inside.

This might seem like you're leaving a lot on the table when it comes to your preparation, but I assure you, it isn't. As long as you focus on the Needs of each side of your Triangle of Life, you'll be more than ready.

> *A good rule of thumb* is to also use this time to map out what you will do with your first six months after taking the leap. Use this preparation time to write out where you want to go, need to go, and could go. Knowing these elements helps gauge your progress as you begin doing things.

One thing you can do to set up calculated risks is to work out a plan that has milestones in place. You should have reasonable milestones that guide your effort after you begin your Career Business. I say this because your Financial Foundation Account should be covering eighteen months of your overhead. That means you need to accomplish certain things within a certain time.

I did say reasonable, which means don't overextend beyond what you're capable of at first. Yes, you should be meeting people, but scheduling ten meetings in a row for thirty minutes would be impossible. It's not about doing one thing a lot; it's about doing a lot of little things over time. However, you should be doing things that help you get the most out of it, even if it'll only pay off in a few weeks, months, or a year and a half.

But, Thomas, what kind of milestones should I create?

That's a great question. For example, here are a few milestones from a much larger list of hundreds of things you could be doing. Take this list as a way to brainstorm your own list. Everyone is different, but a lot of these items are generalized realities filled with variables that anyone would benefit from. Basically, you need to meet people, but how you meet them is up to you.

- Schedule five lunches a month with very specific people.
- Find three ways to get involved with tables that fit my brand.
- Find ways to volunteer once a month with the union of my industry.
- Go through five people a week to see what they are doing and if I personally can help them or know someone who could help them.

But, Thomas, how are these risks, calculated or otherwise?

What makes these risks is that they don't have instant rewards or a high capital return on your investment in the beginning. What makes them calculated risks is that you have the capital in your Financial Foundation Account affording you the right to put real time into these actions.

You're ultimately putting time into relationships that you will be growing over X amount of time, volunteering for things that probably won't pay off right away, and introducing people to others when it doesn't directly benefit you at first.

The value of calculated risks, as opposed to general risks, is having the strength to say yes to an opportunity without worrying about your efforts failing or not. Having that Financial Foundation Account gives you the choice to take action, and it gives you the power to make that choice because you want to. More importantly, you can say no to things that don't have something in common with your missions, morals, and purposes.

Plus, there is a refreshing peace in being able to do things because you want to, not because you have to just so your bills are paid. This is something to really understand. You never want to make choices for the sole reason to recoup capital. Situations like that will lead to quick, emotional reactions. Quick, emotional reactions take away the control you might have had over guiding your career through the pits of opportunity.

The whole point of a Financial Foundation Account, plan of action, and taking calculated risks is to control the outcome of your choices. Having limitations on them will create negative consequences. To be honest, and to get real with you, you can't afford the consequences of your choices when you A) don't have the capital or B) are working with that limited eighteen months of capital.

But, Thomas, didn't you say that my eighteen months are protecting me?

Yes. Yes, I did. And it is. The issue is, you have capital covering your first eighteen months. This means everything you do in that time needs to affect everything you do more so than later on in your Career Business. You can't just say yes to anything, especially if it's to pay your bills. You should have been doing the work to figure out where and why you should be involved with someone, their table, and other opportunities. All of which should be a reason that fits your missions, morals, and purposes.

All I'm saying is that when you have a Financial Foundation Account, you can put thought into your choices: Is this the right choice for me? Should I say yes to this thing that seems a little outside my character as a person, a brand, or my reputation?

When the fear and stress of having to pay a bill come into play, taking the big money seems like the right choice over making the right choices for the right reasons. It's not always about saying yes when having the ability to say no builds your character as you develop your Career Business and reputation with others.

A fun side note is that when you take matters into your own hands, calculated risks are meant to help you find the best possible solution. Knowing what you can afford to lose, both in time and money, gives you an immense amount of confidence in each calculated risk you take.

MORE THAN JUST SAVING CAPITAL

It's going to take time to save enough capital to put into your Financial Foundation Account. In fact, it might take a lot of time. Does this mean you're wasting time? No. There is still plenty to do before you have the capital to take a leap into attempting each and every calculated risk out there.

The time it takes you to build that capital up should be used to set up a plan of attack so your risks are calculated. That's right, saving up for this account gives you some time to plan out those future calculated risks. And I assure you, it's going to take time to save up that capital.

Which means you're being given a gift of time. Take that time and organize your circle of influence; brand yourself by figuring out who and what you are; write out SMART goals; and figure out what calculated risks you're going to take once you're out there in the field.

Additionally, you should write out your marketing and business plans during this time. Those two plans should clearly define what your one, three, five, seven, and ten-year goals are going to be during the proactive effort you put into your Career Business. Once you start, you need that plan to help guide you, realign you, and keep you on point.

A fun side note about what a SMART goal is. It's an acronym: specific, measurable, actionable, realistic, and timely.

A good rule of thumb is that it's better to make moves knowing you can say no rather than having to say yes. Ultimately, not all great opportunities are great for you; it is this freedom that helps you make choices based on the best possible yes or no, instead of having no choice at all or just saying yes to everything.

CHAPTER 2.5
Foundation

2.5 | BE DECISIVE

At the end of the day, you have to trust your gut and be decisive. This is your life; you're going to be responsible for making the majority of the decisions that lead to success. When it comes down to it, all the advice you get is worthless if you are not making the choice to take action. More importantly, what good is advice if you do not have the freedom to afford to make a choice or take calculated risks when opportunities present themselves?

To take action, you have to be proactive in doing "research, research, research" on any information you receive or discover. Variable perspectives can influence your collection of what you've heard and know about certain topics.

This is why there is no harm in understanding multiple sides of an equation. Be aware that when it comes to understanding information, it will take time, effort, and dedication to dissect new or, more often than not, unfamiliar data. You have to take what you hear, see, and discover as the variable perspectives meant to fuel The Process of making stronger, more educated choices—choices that will help you assess any calculated risk that stands before you.

For example, you need to network. But how you go about networking is up to you. There are many tricks to building and cultivating relationships, but it's up to you to find the one that works best for your specific needs. When you find it, hone it and work with it. After a while, if the desired results are not being seen, change things up.

Networking is the answer to one-third of success, and the variables in the equation that you have to solve are how you get there.

But, Thomas, what are the variables?

These variables are what dozens of people tell you, things you learn, and what this book will show you to better help you network so you can build and cultivate relationships. My ideas are not always the right ones for everyone. Just as with most successful celebrities, their ideas on how people should take action are not always going to be right for everyone.

This is why all information is valuable, but it is worthless if you do not do your research to understand if it is right for you. Again, networking is something you have to do. But how you network is up to you, and research will show you if the method is truly right for you.

> *A good rule of thumb* is the rule of three. A minimum of three options is a great way to decide which option will be the best for you. You can find more than three, but three is a great starting point. Three options will give you insight into the pros and cons of each option. Break the habit of choosing your first choice just because you thought of it, heard of it, or discovered it.

HAVE A PLAN A BUSINESS PLAN

One of the best ways to be decisive is to have a plan, specifically a business plan. Knowing where you are coming from and where you would like to get to is a wonderful guideline. The goals within this plan will help you climb your own ladder to success.

A business plan will have both your *needs* and *wants* written out for your pathway to a successful and long Career Business. This plan allows you to establish ground rules for how you attack certain things and accomplish them in a timely manner. Some of the helpful items within your business plan will be SMART goals.

There are big picture SMART goals and micro SMART goals. The big picture SMART goals are focused on the very specific results of long-term goals. Micro-SMART goals focus on all the steps that lead to those long-term goals.

One long-term SMART goal might be to increase the number of valued people within your Circle of Influence to thirty individuals by the end of your third year.

The micro-SMART goals for that long-term goal might be the following: setting up one meeting a week for the first year, then two meetings a week for the second year, and so on. Additionally, you'll organize any follow-up schedules for those meetings and do research on the ones you're meeting. They might need certain things, things you can help with by either offering your services for free (at first to build the relationships) or referring someone who'll be a great fit for them.

But, Thomas, why do I need to break up the long-term SMART goals into micro-SMART goals?

Reaching three hundred new relationships in three years will feel visually overwhelming. It will also be an insane goal to try and achieve. This is why we divide the task into smaller micro-SMART goals to help ease your visual mind. As time goes on, you can reasonably adjust your task goals to better fit your needs. If you're not getting the results you want or need, it is time to change things up.

Having a business plan adds a great value to your journey. The plan has specific SMART goals (long and micro) that give you a chance to stop when you feel overwhelmed, lost, or you're going in a circle with nothing coming out of it. All you have to do to get back on track is stop, breathe, and look through your business plan.

A detailed business plan provides you with a great opportunity that your mind cannot achieve on its own. It gives you a chance to examine the big picture laid out in smaller increments. Being aware of the bigger picture reminds you of your direction. Seeing how you will get there gives you a plan for action.

Having a destination lets you make choices on how you'll get there. And when you find yourself straying from that path you set up, you will realize how possible it is to waste time on unactionable tasks and goals.

But, Thomas, how will I know if I'm wasting my time?

When the outcomes are minimal or nonexistent, it's a clear sign that what you're doing is not worth your effort. Seriously, that's the best indicator that what you're doing is not worth the effort. Before you ask, the best way to know if nothing is happening is to look at your business plan. If you're not hitting your realistic SMART goals for your first, third, and fifth years, you have to change course and reevaluate your process against your business plan.

Your success is based on taking proactive measures. Actions need to have results that match your business plan and realistic goals. Sure, it feels great to finally record and release that song after all these years, just so you can post it for validation. It's important to remember that your job responsibilities hold greater importance than any thing you make or do creatively. Recording two songs a month will not help elevate your Career Business and open any doors to potential opportunities. To elevate your Career Business you need to network, market, and practice to learn and understand the business of your industry.

> *A good rule of thumb* is to keep track of your social media engagement. This'll help you figure out if people are emotionally connecting with your brand. The proof that no one wants your creative things will be when your posts get no responses, interest, or return on your effort.

> *A fun side note* is that your numbers don't count if your engagement numbers only grow after you've posted it over and over again, repurposed it, and then shared the link with all your friends and family until it became blindly annoying. Don't believe me? Stop doing that immediately and see if the responses are still almost nonexistent after two weeks.

YOU DON'T NEED VALIDATION

Why am I telling you this? You should not be posting anything for validation. Validation is for you, not your audience, and it does not affect everything you do. Needing validation from others is not part of your brand, so why do something if it's not part of the plan?

But, Thomas, I didn't post for validation.

Yeah? You didn't post it for validation? Did you post it to make money? Perhaps you posted it because you felt it would help you achieve success. Did you post a song, book, or stand-up video to inspire people with your message? I know why you posted what you did—you did it to build your audience. Once they hear, see, or experience your creative talent, they'll become your fans!

And logically, I get it. But that's not how a person builds fans.

> *A fun side note* is that posting "byproducts" is not the way to grow a fanbase, just as performing is not the best course of action to build a reputation. Do you realize how many amazing byproducts or performances you need to produce to justify your efforts? Unless your next song, book, film, or painting is going to be the same every single time, posting a "byproduct" will not help to create a reaction unless you have audiences connecting to your brand first.

> *A good rule of thumb* is that scarcity is the secret to rewarding your audience and creating a demand for more of what you offer. Avoid frequent posts about performing dates or buying my product. Audiences want those things; however, if you don't have an audience, then posting about those things is called pushing. Pushing does two things: pushes people away and pushes an agenda. If you're going to push anything, let it be your brand.

POSTING TO UNINTERESTED PEOPLE

As you will learn in this book, you don't make money from byproducts.

But, Thomas, selling byproducts makes me money.

No. You're not selling byproducts. You're pushing and trying to convince people to buy your byproducts. That's what earns you money: convincing people to buy your stuff. But you can't ask strangers to buy your stuff just because you believe you're awesome, amazing, and unique. I'll explain that later in this series. For now, let's just focus on "posting to uninterested people."

Success does not come from the things you create. Your art does not inspire people because you posted one byproduct that is going to be different from the other byproducts next week when you post something new. Hell, if you post daily, weekly, or monthly, it won't have a major effect on your audience unless you already have the demand from an established audience.

Audiences want *things* from you, and they really do. But first, you have to build that audience. To do this, you must first establish a brand. Then you need to establish a strong emotional connection between your brand and that audience. This is how you create a relationship between them and you (and what you have to offer). Until you do that, they won't want anything from you without that emotional connection to your brand.

But, Thomas, a brand doesn't give them anything like selling a book does.

Not true. A brand has your missions, morals, and purposes associated with it. When people align with some, most, or all of these aspects, they're more inclined to support the brand because they feel connected to it. Once they feel connected to that brand, they'll spend money to support it and want to feel even closer to it.

However, if you don't have an audience that demands something from you, posting the same thing every day, week, month, or year is going to have a negative effect on your audience's growth. Sure, straggling impulse buys may lead to some people purchasing your products, but it won't build an audience.

Audiences do not attach themselves to byproducts. Byproducts are just a thing. It has no real value beyond what it does. There's a reason people buy Coke or Pepsi. Their connection to Pepsi is based on both the value of its brand and how the audience is emotionally connected to that brand. Brands aren't byproducts.

When it comes to marketing, byproducts do have brands, such as the packaging and associated messages, that align with their intended uses. However, the companies that represent those products also have brands. That's why Walmart is blue and yellow.

Here's the biggest lesson to take away from all of this. Posting a song, poem, book, or video of you doing comedy is not going to yield real results. These are things that you're trying to sell to an audience that: A) doesn't know who you are and B) has very little interest in clicking on them. It's not like you posted "Taylor Swift concert this weekend!" In fact, you could post that on the day of the show, and people would likely click on it to check the availability of seats. Of course, we both know that the event has already sold out.

A good rule of thumb is that everything you do must affect everything you do. If you are posting a song, book, etc., it will not affect the bigger picture. If your goal is simply to post things for an already established audience, then post as much as you want. However, the moment you want to make money doing the thing you love, that's when you have to change the brain to change the game.

DO YOUR JOB

This concept may seem overwhelming at first. I assure you that it's not as complicated as overthinking every action to make sure it affects everything. A strong, thorough business plan is going to be your first line of defense to guide you. Your plan outlines your one, three, five, seven, and ten-year goals, for a reason. This is what helps you make decisive decisions towards all your primary goals.

But, Thomas, how do I affect everything I do?

In this book, you'll notice I talk about doing your job over what you do. Because what you do is not your job. Your job rewards you financially to do the thing you do passionately.

When you do your job, opportunities and doors open up for you to act. Essentially, an actor secures a job not because of their acting abilities but rather because of their job responsibilities, which create opportunities and open doors. These opportunities allowed the actor to perform and receive cash money for it.

For an actor to succeed in the entertainment industry, they must do their job, which, oddly enough, is not acting. Acting is a byproduct of doing their job. If they only focus on acting, they're not doing their job. Technically, when an actor is acting, they're not actually working. The act of acting is the reward for doing their job responsibilities correctly while establishing a Career Business in their field of interest.

But, Thomas, how is acting not considered working? It takes work to act.

It does take hard work to act. It's a hard craft to hone. I've been an actor for a while, and it takes years and years of practice to get really good. However, anyone can act for free in their home, a theater production, independent film, etc. So to answer your question, acting is not considered work; rather, it's a job you were hired for. It's the reward for doing your actual job.

The real question, however, lies in examining the actor in question and their results. Is the actor receiving money for their acting, or is their acting a consequence of the opportunities they create through their job responsibilities?

But, Thomas, if I'm getting paid to act and can cover my average monthly overhead from acting, therefore, logically, I'm successful according to your book.

1. How did you get paid for acting?
2. Did you meet people?
3. Did you leave the house and let others know that you're an actor?
4. Are you hanging out with other actors?
5. Do you work within the field of your desire?
6. Did someone magically discover you at your house?

But, Thomas, obviously I have to meet people to get work.

Yes. Yes, indeed, you do need to meet people to get work. Logically, this means you're not getting paid for acting; you're getting paid for doing your job responsibilities. One of those responsibilities was networking to meet people. Another responsibility was leaving your impression on them, which is marketing. Did they ask you to work on another project? If yes, this means that they saw your Value Sets in real time, helping to elevate the table to best lead, follow, and advise. This is considered practicing and utilizing your talent.

Doing your job is what creates opportunities to do the *thing* you love doing. That's why, if you're writing, you're not networking. If you're acting, you're not marketing. If you're playing music, you're not learning your industry.

We all have different work hours for the careers we invest in, which means we all have different personal hours to do the things we enjoy. Just like when we go to a 9-5, we're expected to work, work, work during the scheduled business hours. Once we're home, we get to play all we want, doing what we want. This is why you can't act at a job. You can't play the guitar at a job. You have to do the job to keep that job and create new opportunities for promotions, etc. And that's the same with your Career Business.

What does this all mean? It means that if this is a career you desire, then you have to give yourself Career Business hours. Real business hours are not the few hours here and there that are dedicated to a career in between the fun stuff you love doing. It's the stuff you need to do to grow your business.

Think about it. Does any of the following sound like networking, marketing, or practicing to learn your industry: recording your music, writing a book, or telling jokes at a club?

EVERYTHING YOU DO MUST AFFECT EVERYTHING YOU DO

One thing I hear my actor clients often say is, "I need more auditions." To which I respond, "Why do you need more auditions?" The average answer is usually "so I can get more work."

Actors believe that they have to focus on getting auditions to get cast in a project. Projects that sometimes don't pay, but hopefully a few of them do. They put their time into this because, to them, acting is the work.

In reality, the first step is placing time into trying to get auditions. The second step is hoping they'll get a chance to actually audition. A third step is going in to do the audition. And finally, the fourth step is getting selected for the part.

The issue with this is that the actor is putting a lot of time into one thing with the hopes that after four potential steps they'll get rewarded with a chance to act. This is where being decisive comes into the equation. You can't just put time into things that don't influence other aspects of your Career Business. You need to be decisive with your choices in a way that allows everything you do to affect everything you do. With that said, it's time for some deductive reasoning; let's focus on "getting auditions."

If I do A, then B will happen. "A" is "getting auditions," and "B" leads to "being cast in a project," therefore "I'll get paid for acting if I do auditions." Argo, more auditions equals greater opportunity for being cast, and bam, cash in the hand in the form of money!

Ask yourself, does getting auditions really equal getting cast in projects?

But, Thomas, I'm awesome, amazing, and unique. You get me in that room and I'll wow those casting directors!

Unfortunately, auditions don't get you work. Auditions are simply opportunities to be seen as a potential option for a specific role where dozens of other actors have already been seen. Through this deductive reasoning, we can eliminate the *need* to focus on getting auditions and suggest that we should focus our efforts elsewhere.

But, Thomas, I still want to get cast in projects so I can act.

Great! I wonder what The Process of getting auditions really is. Is asking "How do I get auditions" really the right question to be asking? Sure, on the surface, that's an interesting question, but is it the right question?

Here's an example of how a Business Brain works out the solutions by thinking outside the box in a proactive way. First, they study The Process more than the results. By being decisive, they search for the path less traveled and work on The Process of how to achieve results toward their long-term goals. That long-term goal is to make a living within their field of interest.

Let's use our Business Brain to simplify your desired results, which in this scenario is really that you want "to get cast in projects so you can act."

But, Thomas, how does one get cast?

The quick answer is: network to build and cultivate relationships; market your brand by getting involved with others; and practice learning your industry so you can increase your Value Sets to give you a chance to prove your worth at the tables you join. These elements are the 3 Needs of Success and they give your desires a chance to come true.

But, Thomas, that doesn't answer the question of how to get cast.

Oh, you want the longer answer? Or do you want the most direct answer that'll lead to an instantaneous result? The answer that says, "If I do A, then B will happen"? Maybe you should do a little "research, research, research" into who casts projects. Oh, wait, you already know who casts projects, right? Well, who casts projects?

Did you say casting directors? If you did, then you're incorrect.

But, Thomas, how is that wrong?

I'll tell you, but first, who has the final say on the role?

The answer is: producers, directors, and writers. Usually, it's in that order of importance. A producer has the most power because they're the ones with the money and have the final say in decisions. The director comes next because they make the creative decisions. The writer, unfortunately, comes last but still has a say because they created the characters. Though a writer may have created a blueprint for the narrative, it's the director's vision and the producer's risk.

Right there, you have to say to yourself, "Why am I not trying to build and cultivate relationships with writers, directors, and producers?"

Here is the real kicker: You were probably thinking about reaching out to established people in the industry. But how about those to your left and right? You're growing up in a time where the next big writers, directors, and producers are developing their Career Business right alongside you as you develop yours.

Your generation's Patty Jenkins and Quentin Tarantino are standing right next to you, and you do not even realize it.

So, how do you get more acting gigs? Make friends with those who will ask you to be a part of their journey.

What I'm saying is that going to auditions is just the first step toward the next step, which is getting cast. An audition will never provide an absolute answer as to whether you'll be cast in a project, as auditions do not produce *results* for your bigger picture goals.

This is my point: You must make sure that everything you do affects everything you do. Auditions do not affect everything you do. They affect nothing but a small, almost unapproachable probability of the impossible. Relationships give you a chance to prove your brand value while getting opportunities to showcase your Value Sets to best lead, follow, and advise.

But, Thomas, why do they affect nothing? That doesn't make any sense. If I get an audition and I'm cast in something, that feels like it affects something. Won't that influence my career?

Auditions specifically don't affect anything because you have no real control over the outcome. The outcome that an Artist Brain believes is that if they are given the opportunity to audition, they'll indeed be cast in the project. Therefore, they need auditions to have a career. And being cast for an Artist Brain, means working, and working means they are successful.

Focusing on auditions to get cast so you can work more is not focused on getting hired to work, or rather, and more importantly, being focused on getting involved in your industry of interest. Focusing on auditions is not the same as focusing on the longevity of a Career Business. An audition is only focused on getting a small chance to be seen.

Auditions are not for getting cast. Auditions are simply for a person to get in the room or do a self-tape to try out for a role as an option for the part being cast. You're a choice, not the option.

Additionally, being cast is just another result you have to work for, not The Process of success. This is why breaking The Process down into smaller steps helps you make better decisions that lead to success. Focus your efforts toward actions that will help *what* you do affect *everything* you do.

This is why I'm telling you to do your research, research, research and break down The Process of how things work by looking at each step of that process. It's all about what it'll take to achieve the desired long-term results. If you're affecting one thing by doing one thing, then you're doing the wrong thing. Auditions lead to casting is a logical fallacy only because auditions don't always lead to casting. They *could* lead to casting, but the chance is minimal.

That is common logic for a Business Brain. They know that auditions give them a chance to be rarely seen, but even if they are seen, it doesn't affect everything else they do. Which, in turn, is wasting time. Focus on opportunities to "be seen, be present" by getting involved with others to grow relationships.

> *A fun side note* is that relationships, marketing your brand, and getting involved leads to the longevity of a successful career. Instead of putting time into one result, as in the above example of getting an audition, focus on a result that affects everything you do. A relationship now with a person starting out as you are affects everything you do. Strong relationships now lead them to refer you to others, hire you, be the person who helps you, and pull you up as they rise.

QUICK COMPARABLES TO AUDITIONS IN OTHER FIELDS

1. When musicians record albums to make money or build a fanbase
2. Comedians who perform to get discovered or build a fanbase
3. Writers who do spec scripts, author a book, etc., to get hired
4. Directors who submit projects to a festival to get their big break

These examples are basically one-and-done actions; they're not worth the time you put into them. If you want a bigger return on your investment, look at your choices and place the idea into the "if I do A, then B will happen" equation.

If the results come in the form of one thing happening, then think twice about doing it; everything you do must affect everything you do.

When you think about how what you do will affect everything you do, the results should affect multiple aspects of your journey.

Building and cultivating relationships opens doors for opportunities, just as marketing your brand leaves an impression on people when they think about who they want to work with, and getting involved gives you real-time practical experience in the field. This means you should be putting effort into your Triangle of Life.

CHAPTER 2.6

Foundation

2.6 | STAY FOCUSED, NO EXCUSES

This chapter is all about staying focused without making excuses. Excuses are the killer of careers. You need to be focused on taking action to make things happen by making things happen. So, what did you accomplish this week to take steps for your Career Business?

But, Thomas, I had no time this week because things came up.

I completely hear you and understand the conundrum you're having. As far as excuses go, this is one of my favorites from an Artist Brain. When I hear any excuse, I usually follow up with one of these:

1. Did you go to your survival job this week?
2. How many episodes did you watch of Gilmore Girls this week?
3. What kind of music, art, acting, etc. did you do for fun this week?
4. What about the time you put into going out with friends at the bar?

Trust me, I have plenty more of those questions to easily call out the excuses people make for not doing their job. And I get it; the fun stuff is getting to work on your craft, hang with friends, or watch Lucifer.

Artist Brains fail at becoming successful when they put time into the things they want to do and not the things they need to do. Being creative is not an excuse to do none of your job responsibilities. I know you want to be a successful XYZ in the entertainment industry, but that will only happen if you put time into the Career Business side of things.

But, Thomas, being creative is the part that motivates me.

I get it. I'd rather be writing than networking, doing stand-up comedy instead of investing, or anything creative really over doing the work. You need to separate yourself from the mentality of Artist Brains who inspire the bad habits of focusing on the wrong things. You can't put little to no time into your job responsibilities and expect to have a career in your field of interest.

A Business Brain develops strong, proactive habits to run their Career Business like an actual business. When you're doing your job, you will earn the right to do the things you love to do. Those things might not be fun, and I get that. In reality, you have to sacrifice now so you can benefit later.

You don't want to fail because the Artist Brain is controlling you. You can't be the person who finds time in the weirdest places to be creative at the expense of your potential success. A Career Business is going to take a lot of work to get going before you're earning the free time to write, do comedy, act, etc.

All I'm saying is that you have to make better choices instead of writing a book for four hours a day, performing at local open mics in dead bars, getting cast in a local unpaid community theater show, or going to your survival job.

My favorite Artist Brain choice—I mean, excuse—is to relax in front of the television and binge watch their favorite shows. When a show is 30-60 minutes long and they've watched five episodes... that's between two and a half hours and five hours in a day. This is time they could be giving to their Career Business. After all, they did say, "Things came up."

A good rule of thumb is that when it comes to talent, it won't lead you to success as defined in this book series, though it does help maintain longevity in a person's Career Business on the backend. To reach that point where longevity is a factor, one must first find success in their field of interest.

A DIME A DOZEN

There are a lot of talented people out there who never find true success. They struggle, work a survival job, and all the while hope that one day they'll get their big break in the industry. A break that comes out of the magical shadows where a person miraculously appears and recognizes how awesome, amazing, and unique they are.

The issue with this kind of thinking is that your success will never be solely dependent on your talent. It takes networking, marketing, and practice to find success. Remember, talent is always going to be worthless at the beginning; however, it does help later on. And yes, talent could get you noticed; it could get you called to the table; hell, it might even get people to notice and pay attention to you. That kind of discovered talent gets you one thing: fifteen minutes of fame.

But, Thomas, don't they love me for my talent?

No. This is the entertainment business. That means people are out to make money first and foremost. You and your talent are just another opportunity for them to take advantage of you. And they know when a person wants success and what they are willing to do to make that happen. This means that people will use the naivete of people focusing only on their talent and doing what they can to suck them dry.

To be fair, this does not happen to everyone. Sometimes a talented person might meet the right connection. Like Dr. Dre and Eminem. Though honestly, cases like that are rare and often still fade away after their fifteen minutes of fame. Only the few that get those opportunities can maintain the level at which they were discovered. Because once that million in one chance happens, you must still create longevity.

Again, look at Eminem and the businesses he created, the artists he developed, and the life he had to get back on track because of drugs. He almost did not make it. The lifestyle almost took it all away from him. When he began taking his Career Business seriously, he opened avenues beyond only rapping and touring. He's made appearances, but look up how many major tours he went on since 2014. He has the freedom to not have to rely on touring to make money. More on that later in the book series.

Talent is not the secret to success. I'd almost argue that you don't need talent to find success, at least not in the beginning. You do need talent to create longevity. That's why I've said it a few times before; that talent comes into play later in the game. If you don't believe me, then ask yourself this question: How many times have you watched a movie, listened to a song, or heard a comedian perform and said:

1. These people suck?
2. How the hell did they get there?
3. I'm better than this crap?

But, Thomas, who's *these people*?

That's a great question. *These people* are the ones who have a career in the entertainment industry. The people who are not only still successful but way more successful in their careers than you are. These are people who have the ability to make things happen by making things happen in the industry. The people I'm referring to are those who have direct access to industry's movers and shakers. They can get the funding, pop on a tour, elevate others with a quick word, or have the freedom to say no to projects if they want to.

If you've ever heard someone say the above lines that "these people suck" or something similar, it's clear that talent isn't the issue. When I hear people say, "These people suck; how did they get cast, on the radio, thrown on the show, or whatever, and I didn't?" I shake my head. Not because I used to be that person, and I was, but because I know that this person believes that they're more talented and deserving of the opportunity than those other people.

Just because you're amazing, awesome, and unique doesn't mean you deserve a shot. It takes more than talent to earn that spot and opportunity. Anyone with the right connections (or, in some cases, the right amount of money) can get their shot. Even people who don't know anyone or have very little money can get their "shot."

It's not unheard of for a band to buy tickets to play on a music bill. It's not uncommon for actors to pay to be seen by agents. It's not rare for performers to be scammed into paying for casting opportunities.

If you *need* to get these spots to feel successful, you're going to be waiting a very long time. You can want success all day long. Dream all day about acting, singing, and writing by getting your big opportunity. The problem is, you won't succeed that way. I mean, you could succeed that way; maybe. Anything is possible. There's always going to be that one in a million chance that a singer is heard at a random gas station (Toni Braxton) or a kid is discovered at a school play (Topher Grace).

No, really, I'm serious, at a school play. Even casting directors, producers, and showrunners could have children, because they're people. And if they're at the performance to see their child perform and manage to catch the next Topher Grace, well, then, success!

But you and everyone around you should never rely on this mathematical possibility. You have to do something different to get to the next level. I say this because there are only 2% of actors and writers who make a living in their field of interest. Musicians? Now we're talking about the 0.04% who make a living in their field of interest.

But, Thomas, what could I do differently?

First, it shouldn't be about how you could showcase your talent that you believe is way better than the others in your field of interest. What it should be is about breaking the bad habits of the Artist Brain. Second, get involved in your industry after you have saved up your startup capital and placed it into your Financial Foundation Account.

IT IS NOT ALL ABOUT THE FUN STUFF

An Artist Brain is not always willing to do what they hate doing to get to where they love being. Who really wants to do the crappy parts of building a career? No one wants to meet random strangers, market themselves, or spend hours learning the ins and outs of their industry.

What an Artist Brain does want is the reward part—the fun part. I do, too. As much as anyone wants the fun part, they really should focus on the business side of their Career Business until they've earned the right to do the fun part. This is the part that sucks for a lot of people. I personally have grown to love running my life like a business to grow my Career Business. It has led me to have the freedom to shut my Business Brain off and enjoy getting to do what I love to do.

That's right, when I do any and all of my creative ventures, I turn off my Business Brain. When it comes to running my business, I shut off my Artist Brain. The two of those brains are never meant to play together. You don't want your creative endeavors to be tarnished with business ideas as much as you don't want to approach the business of your industry like an artist.

This is why I've always found it odd that people find reasons not to do what they hate in order to succeed at doing something they love. Yet, these same people will work a 9-to-5 job they hate just to make a buck.

But, Thomas, the 9-to-5 job pays me every single week.

Sure, but why do people put in all the right effort for that job they hate and not put that same mentality into a career they love?

But, Thomas, if I put in the work at the job, they'll reward me over time. With my dream of making a living within my field of interest, I need to make money quickly or I won't be able to afford my bills.

Whether it's a survival job or a Career Business in the entertainment industry, it's all the same thing. You don't enter the world of acting as a lead in a big, major studio role. Just as no one starts out as a store manager (without experience) when they get their first job as a cashier.

You will have to do the grunt work in both situations just to advance in your chosen career. The part you want to do will come with effort, but not if you only focus on trying to do the fun part.

Imagine needing a regular job. You go in, ask for an application and tell them you want to be the store manager. They say no, you've never worked in a supermarket before. So you go to another supermarket down the road and they say no. So then you go to another one and they say no. Now, to cover your bills, you get a job at a local gas station and continue to only apply to store manager positions.

It makes no sense. You have to work within your field of interest in some capacity until you've developed relationships, established your brand value, and shown your Value Sets in how you lead, follow, and advise. Only then will the right people elevate you with a promotion. Keep in mind that these people are the ones who have eventually become your friends.

This is the same for people in the entertainment industry.

We love doing what we love doing, and when it comes down to getting dirty, we find reasons to divert from our responsibilities. We love what we do so much that we want to find ways to just do the *thing* we love and hope something comes of it. Most people are willing to work a job they hate outside their field of interest until they get their big break into the industry.

Personally, there's no way I can blame anyone for wanting to do what they love. I love doing what I do, and it means the world to me that I can pay my bills doing it. Well, I don't get paid to do what I love to do. I get paid because I do all the stuff a Career Business needs me to do, so people see me, like me, and hire me to do what I love to do.

I don't get hired to write books because I wrote a book. I got hired because someone knew I wrote and referred me to someone who needed me to develop their novel or write the book itself. And you know how many times they've asked to see my work before paying me? None. The weight of the relationship held the value of my referral.

And it's common for people to become easily distracted in life by their favorite activities. Who really wants to work on their Circle of Influence by going out or getting involved to network? Between that and, say, getting to go out on an audition for that part you know you'd be perfect for, it's clear what an Artist Brain would pick. For the Artist Brain, this is an easy choice. Go out and audition.

I have seen people give up opportunities to go out and get involved in an event for networking purposes because they'd rather act in a play for free at the local library.

But, Thomas, I'd choose acting over networking. I want to act.

Acting sure is a lot of fun. So of course you'd choose acting over doing the crappy work needed to succeed. That's why you became an actor—to act. This is why "I'd act for free" has become the motto of the Artist Brain. In fact, they'd probably do it for free often if the opportunities continued to reach out to them.

Stand-up comics, bands, and spoken word artists—all performers, really—will be happy to attend an open mic over doing something they despise. Who wants to be home organizing their schedule with potential meetings, let alone setting up those damn meetings?

I probably could count on two fingers the number of people who would choose budgeting their money over getting on stage on a Tuesday night at some local dive bar just to work on their material. Of course performing is going to beat out sitting at home and figuring out what other people are working on. Why would anyone want to spend time trying to figure out how to help others when it's their own career they're worried about?

I don't know about you, but performing sounds like a lot more fun than working on whatever boring job responsibility I have to do. So, I get it. If my brain still thought that way, I'd choose to perform or create every single time.

In reality, you need to change your brain to change the game. Think about what is important to you and your end goal. Once you know what the end goal looks like, you have to figure out all the crap involved in getting you there. Saying that you want to be a successful comedian does not mean that you should go up and only perform when and where you can. There is a lot more involved.

Look, I get it. And trust me, I say this knowing that there is no harm in being a weekend warrior who does gigs on their time off from work. This is considered a hobby or a side gig, and that's okay.

But maybe there's a writer who wants a career as a writer. And to do this, they get their work done for their Career Business first and then write at night for as long as they can.

Believe it or not, both of these choices are absolutely fine. But one path is a hobby, and the other is a career.

But, Thomas, how are they different?

The writer does their work first: build and cultivate relationships, establish a brand by getting involved with others, and learn the business so they can develop Value Sets for when they're called to the table. The art is what they do second. Do your job first, then enjoy the art of it all.

DOING STUFF IS NOT THE SAME AS GETTING STUFF DONE

I believe it comes down to a few factors. Artist Brain people love to feel like they're accomplishing things that are tangible. When a person goes to rehearsal for a future performance, it gives them instant gratification that they're doing the very thing they love to do. Rehearsals make an Artist Brain feel like they're doing something. And they are, but is what they're doing to stimulate their brain worth the reward of immediate results?

Think about it. If they rehearse, they're actually doing something, and it's something they love doing. But are they actually getting stuff done? I might make the argument that there's a difference between *doing stuff* and *getting stuff done*. They're not the same. You can do things all day, but if you're not getting stuff done, then what are you actually doing?

Acting is doing stuff, but what is getting done? You know your lines, you understand your blocking, and acting might even make you feel amazing afterward. I mean, you killed that line delivery! But what is getting done?

At the start of your Career Business, anything that has to do with the creative or performance of your passion is a one-and-done action. It's passive at best, and the things you do after rehearsal can be the beneficial and proactive aspect of it all. The *afterward* is where you can get things done. Or, more importantly, this is where you get to do your job.

If you go to rehearsal and leave afterward, you did nothing. The part you should be most concerned about is the meeting with people afterward; spending time with the other actors, directors, writers, or producers is the real job and the part that makes it all possible. Yes, you might be tired afterward and want to go home, but you just spent X amount of time at rehearsal doing nothing. By putting in the time to cultivate relationships, you're doing something that will affect everything you do, including what happens in the future of your Career Business.

And when you act, the "return on your investment" is that you had a chance to perform. However, when you network, the "return on your investment" is that you're developing relationships for the future that will ultimately lead to more opportunities.

But, Thomas, what's the difference whether I get to know them during rehearsal or if I get to know them by hanging out afterward when I'm tired?

Ah, that, my friend, is a great question. They are absolutely both opportunities for networking. The big difference is that during rehearsal it's going to require that you focus on learning your lines, blocking, and listening to the director. Yes, you might have fun, laugh a little, and hopefully, you're easy to get along with. The big difference is that you can compound that energy by putting in the time that is specifically dedicated to the relationship part afterward. It's hard to get to know someone when they're reading back lines someone else wrote.

And you might think that you can build and cultivate relationships while doing the art part of it, but try speaking to a comedian who leaves after their set or an actor in the corner learning their lines. Even when I was in a band, we hung out after rehearsal so we could be human with each other and not focus on the art of it all.

Ultimately, stay away from the "A = B" mentality. It should be A leads to B, which creates C, which, over time, awards you Z.

WHAT DOES IT TAKE TO STAY FOCUSED

But, Thomas, if I have to stay focused on developing my Career Business, how would I go about doing that?

You must first create a powerful counter to potential fears of change, inconsistencies in habits, and a willingness to try something different when real results are not being realized. Next, you want to start doing what needs to get done: your job.

This is why we have a business plan with our SMART goals written out in great detail. It shows you what actions you should be taking. When you feel lost, it's always best to revert back to your business plan.

To get the most out of your plans, and stay focused, make sure you write out specific goals to follow along your journey in the entertainment industry. When it comes to SMART goals, set up daily, weekly, monthly, quarterly, and yearly to-do lists for a better system of accountability and guidance.

Your to-do list is an amazing tool that should never run out. If you run out of to-do items, then what are you really doing? It's not about finishing a to-do list. Plus, a to-do list is there as a reminder for when you feel lost and/or are without direction. When you feel this way, jump on your to-do list and take action. It's literally listing out what you need to do.

The to-do list should follow the Needs of your Triangle of Life, which should keep you focused on doing your job. And ultimately, a to-do list is more about starting things and less about getting things done. This means that you should create time blocks that will have general tasks to keep you moving forward.

A *general task* might be in your networking block. This is a block where you spend X amount of time doing anything and everything that has to do with networking. Specifically, you should be working on your networking long-term SMART goals that are broken down into micro-SMART goals. These micro-SMART goals would become the items on your to-do list.

I'm going to go into time blocks later in this book, but, as an example, in your first year after taking action in your Career Business, you should work at least nine hours per day.

Each hour should be, or could be, a time block.

When you reach a general time block, work the full block—no more, no less. When the time runs out, move on to the next time block.

If you're working on a networking to-do list filled with ten tasks, it's not about finishing the ten tasks you have written down. In fact, the next day, you might add several more task items to that networking to-do list.

Time blocks and your to-do lists are all about working on tasks until the block's time expires; it's not about completing tasks. Over time, the tasks will get completed.

One of those general time blocks in your nine-hour workday schedule should be dedicated to networking. If that's the general block of action to take, a specific micro-SMART goal for networking might be:

- Clean up my contact notes in my phone
- Text three people I know a message of admiration
- Schedule three meetings with people to have lunches
- Research what three friends are doing so I can support them

> *A good rule of thumb* is that you should use your to-do list as a device for direction, not a list of things that need to get done. It's a to-do list, not a to-get-done list. A to-do list is about starting things, not finishing them.

WHAT DOES IT ALL COME DOWN TO

I keep saying that what you do is not your job. Your job rewards you financially to do the thing you do passionately. And in this section, my goal was to add that you need to stay focused on your job responsibilities and maintain accountability for your actions or inactions.

Your job responsibilities are what you need to do to get your Career Business started and keep that business going as you move through your first eighteen months. As you take action in that timeframe, maintain accountability and change things up if and when they get stale. You don't have a boss; you're the boss, and it's your responsibility to hold yourself to certain standards.

During this time, you have to follow and adjust both your business and marketing plans. You'll have to organize and adjust your SMART goals into daily, weekly, monthly, and yearly to-do tasks as more comes into view. You have to look at these new responsibilities for what they are: your new job. And the more you get involved within your field of interest, the more new goals will appear. These new goals will be both things you were expecting and the unexpected.

This new job comes with a collection of tasks that'll be filtered through the Needs of your Triangle of Life, which is the blueprint for your Career Business. This blueprint shows you what you "need" to do to find success, ensure the longevity of that success, and fuel your finances back into the system.

As I've been saying throughout the book, acting, writing, music, etc. are all things I'd consider the fun stuff, the play time. They are not going to get you where you want to go. They might allow you to dip your feet into the water, but you can't go swimming into the deep end and expect a boat of opportunity to be there and help you up if you begin to drown.

What you *need* to do is your *job*. And this is what your job is:

- Network, market, and practice.
- Manage your time, money, and the people around you.
- Find solutions by thinking outside the box in a proactive way.
- Add to the tables you join by developing your Value Sets.
- Know when to lead, follow, or advise at the tables you join.
- Organize your money to protect, invest, and reward yourself.
- Invest in assets to develop passive income.
- Maintain a Financial Foundation Account to say *yes* to things.
- Always treat your life like a business.

This is the introduction to the reality of your job responsibilities. Doing your job will reward you financially to do the thing you do passionately.

CHAPTER 2.7
Foundation

2.7 | INCORPORATE

When I first began my adventure in the entertainment industry, I ran my Career Business like an Artist Brain. I made a lot of Artist Brain choices that produced tons of "results" where lots was happening, but nothing was happening. Those results were a combination of the band doing shows, writing a gaggle of songs, and practicing often, so often that the experience became dull.

So while lots of stuff was happening, nothing was actually happening and I was trapped working a survival job that I hated. At the same time, my free time was dedicated to getting my music career off the ground. This is why I stand by my statement: Treat your life like a business.

What changed for me was my mindset, from an Artist Brain to a Business Brain. When I performed, practiced, or did anything creative, I let my Artist Brain run wild. When it came to my Career Business, I turned on my Business Brain.

My Business Brain had me analyzing my choices. When I felt stuck or like nothing was happening, I'd think back on my statement for direction: Treat your life like a business. Then I would ask myself specific questions: am I treating my life like a business? Is what I'm about to do what a business would do? Then it hit me. My original business, the band, was failing.

I had been working on this music career for over three years, heading into my fifth at the time, and realized my business had failed completely. I had two choices: to keep pouring money into my dream with the hope something would change, or change things up by starting over.

This is what led me to think like a Business Brain running a business. And all businesses need a strong Financial Foundation Account that holds their initial startup capital.

Startup capital is more than money in the bank or cash to open your doors. It's meant to sustain your business for eighteen months or more, giving you time to create some momentum. And by having that Financial Foundation Account, I could take all the calculated risks I wanted as long as I was doing what my business needed me to be doing first.

But, Thomas, what makes a business a real business?

You have to open up a legal LLC or S corporation. This is where you turn your dream into a reality. I knew I had to take the next step and this led me to incorporate my dream into a company. Which meant that my band (Career Business) would now be pushed into the next level.

But, Thomas, an artist is not a business.

Odd? If an artist is not a business, then why do you sell creative byproducts or have services people hire you to do? If you have creative byproducts, you're selling something creative. If you're a performer, then your performance is a service. Such as with an actor acting or a musician going on tour, maybe you're a hired gun for another band, etc., this all makes you a business that provides a service.

But, Thomas, I can't start a business now. I have to wait until I'm making money with my career, or rather, my business, as you call it, before I can turn it into a legal business.

Wrong. You're a business the moment you want to make a living doing what it is you love to do. This is where a Financial Foundation Account is more than the capital that supports your mission. Think of a Financial Foundation Account as a tool for you to create a strong underbelly for a building you'll be adding layers to over the years. And if the Financial Foundation Account is the concrete below your building, then your LLC or S corporation certificate is going to be the metal bars inside that concrete, adding stability.

If you wait until you have something going on or money coming in, it takes away from the invested time of getting your Career Business ready. By having a business legalized at the beginning, you're now adding equity and value to your company's name. In a sense, you're establishing wealth of both time and worth in your business.

> ***A good rule of thumb*** is that there is no better time than now to start your legal business. By establishing your wealth now, for both time and worth, it helps your business grow on paper for banks, investment opportunities, potential partnerships, etc. You need this equity of time for future efforts, opportunities, or general attempts when you are trying to expand your business ventures that influence the larger part of your Career Business.

If you do your research, research, research, you'll find that there are other options to create a legal company. Two of those examples are a limited liability company (LLC) or a sole proprietorship. These are both good choices for certain needs. One is the "you have to pay for it" venture, the LLC, and the other is how you're classified on your taxes when you get paid for a service without a legal certificate.

I was told that an S corporation is the best way to start a business, which I agree with. There are a lot of tax benefits and available options for those who create S corporations. However, no matter which route you go, I recommend always doing your research, research, research and speaking with a professional accountant or lawyer to allow yourself the best options for making a decision.

I'll say it often, and you need to keep hearing it: knowledge is always going to equal power, but only if you truly understand it by gathering enough intel to solidify an informed decision. My advice to you is to set up a business entity, either with an LLC or an S Corp, and not go the sole proprietorship route.

Setting up a legal business can have a *power of value* return to it. What was once just a person who wanted to be an entertainer is now a Career Business ready to join the entertainment industry. An LLC or an S corporation is going to be that extra level of encouragement that will push you to take your Career Business seriously.

You're a real business now: Entertainer, Inc. Even if you don't make money after incorporating, you're accumulating time equity the moment you sign the paperwork for an LLC or S corporation. Being a real business is going to feel different than being only an entertainer in the industry.

FAKE IT TILL YOU... STOP THAT NOW

I'm not a major fan of this quote, "Fake it till you make it." This is manipulative, both for the people you meet and for yourself. It's a lie that doesn't solve the issue. Instead of faking it until you make it, start The Process to make it a reality by turning your dream into an actual business.

This is what taking proactive steps to work in the industry of your interest looks like. This will begin your journey toward truthfully making it while actually doing the work. Not only are you literally working in the field of your industry, but you're also developing a reputation within said industry as you develop your Career Business.

You don't have to specifically be an actor acting in the entertainment industry to have made it. It's about being in the industry itself and earning a living. This is because what you do is not your job. Your job rewards you financially to do the thing you do passionately. It doesn't matter if you're working as a PA or an assistant. What matters is that you're working in the field of your interest, and that's the truth.

This goes with any form of entertainment. A musician should be getting involved in their industry doing anything that gets you closer to people to build relationships and show your Value Sets. This goes for comedians, writers (screen or author), directors, producers, etc.

Incorporating yourself makes you a real business with real goals. And even more so, taking this step is you taking a step in a serious direction on a path less traveled by others in your industry.

But, Thomas, if I'm a business, what kind of business am I?

Being an entertainer is what makes you a business. You specialize in all the things that you do and the services that you provide. Before I break down what those services are, think about it yourself. What do you do? No, really, think about what you do and break it down. More on that later.

All I'm saying is that you need to take your career seriously, and it will reward you with an amazing return on your investment in the form of opportunities. Those opportunities will reward you with more opportunities, capital to fuel your system (business), time, and the Career Business you're growing.

These rewards will give you the freedom to enjoy your life, have the ability to make choices because you want to (not because you have to pay bills), and live the life you wanted from the beginning—the one where you can focus on doing the thing you love.

Okay, stepping backwards for a moment. Let's talk about services.

I asked you what you *do*. Then I asked you to break it down. I'm sure you said that you can offer your craft, whatever that might be. Maybe you're an actor, musician who plays the cowbell, etc. So yes, in the entertainment industry, you can offer your craft (or any special skill you have—playing the guiro).

We'll focus on these two things: your craft and a special skill. Your craft could be the thing you do, which is acting, singing, playing a guitar; maybe you're a comedian, writer, etc. And your special skill might be time management, networking, maybe you have a knack for social media marketing.

In either case, you as a business provide these two services. People could hire you and potentially pay you to get involved with them, especially if you do your job competently. More importantly, are you adding value to the tables that you were invited to? If so, then that's a bonus!

But, Thomas, what do you mean?

How about we break down what it is you actually *do*? I'm going to start with the *thing* you love and break it down into smaller subskills. For anyone following along, the *thing* you love to do is your craft; to be more specific, writers write, actors act, musicians... musician?

When people like you as the person that you are, they'll hire you to do the *thing* you do because you're their friend. However, can you do more than the thing you do, or are you only able to get involved with others if they let you do that thing?

Believe it or not, you don't have to get involved working with them only to do the thing you do. You can also teach the thing you do. In fact, you can break down what you do and teach those things too. Actors act, but they also understand how to break down scripts, film self-tapes, memorize lines, understand how to take direction, etc.

But, Thomas, what does that even mean?

It means that people will pay you to A) teach them how to do what it is that you do and B) hire you to get involved to make sure their people can do the thing you do too and that they are doing it correctly.

When it comes to your special skills, people will want you around because you have specific skills to help elevate their table by leading, following, and advising. These are the skills you provide naturally: your knowledge of things; maybe you understand marketing, problem solving, brainstorming, leadership attributes, etc.

For example, I do it all in the industry: music, comedy, writing, acting, etc. I've been a performer in multiple areas since before I could remember—I'm old. But for this example, my focus will be on my skill as a writer.

As a writer, I can write scripts, novels, books, jokes, lyrics, a few speeches if you need me to, and pretty much anything where words need to be written down. This is what I do as a writer: I write. This means I can be hired to write those things. I can also be hired to advise on those things as a script doctor, developmental editor, or story consultant. Additionally, I teach outlining, brainstorming, character development, and joke construction.

But, Thomas, what else can you do?

What else can I do? Oh, let me tell you. I can speak on these things at events, in communities of my industry, at local comedy clubs, and even in bookstores. The world opens up when you look past what it is you just do creatively through your craft.

Every aspect of everything you do and can provide will help you get invited to join the tables, giving you an opportunity to best lead, follow, and advise others. So instead of trying to get involved only to do the thing you *do*, you can instead provide other aspects and qualities to the tables out there. And more importantly, these opportunities could potentially be paid opportunities that benefit from you being incorporated or having an LLC.

To be a business, you have to be a business, no matter if you believe you're one or not. It begins with changing the brain to change the game as you start treating your life like a business the moment you incorporate.

CHAPTER 2.8
Foundation

2.8 | WRITE OUT A BUSINESS PLAN

A business plan is going to be the ultimate tool to help turn your dream into reality. A business plan is more than just a plan of attack; it's a reminder, a guideline, and a resource to help align future goals with present actions. It's designed to provide you with a comprehensive understanding of your potential challenges and opportunities, outlining strategies to achieve your goals.

During your journey, a business plan has thresholds, milestones, and SMART goals to show you your needs for the beginning, middle, and end stages of your Career Business. Not only does it show you the way, it also shows you how to handle things when you seem lost or out of place. The business plan is there to refocus the direction of your Career Business on where, when, and what your efforts should be allocated toward.

But, Thomas, I already know what to do. Why have a business plan?

It's easier to look at a business plan that specifically maps out the entire first ten years of tasks and objectives than it is to throw spaghetti at the wall and hope it sticks. Even loosely mapping out your journey sets the stage for a proactive initiative. You never want to begin your Career Business by rambling on with uninformed concepts equated to: if I do "A," then hopefully "B" will happen.

If everything you do must affect everything you do, you want your actions to have a worthwhile return on your investment of effort. The objectives that need to be accomplished will highlight the reality of success's horizon in the form of detailed numbers, statistics, and the researched results that should come out of any effort.

All companies need a business plan, and this includes entertainers who want to have a successful career in the entertainment industry. Every business has objectives that will need to be given actionable tasks to see good results. These objectives range in size from seemingly insignificant daily tasks to elaborate month- or year-long objectives that can take up fifty or more pages of strategy in your business plan.

The detail that goes into a business plan is more than just data you write out. This is information you have been doing research, research, research on to figure out the best course of action for your desired results. A great business plan is not just information for you to write down and leave in the drawer. During The Process, you should be learning how and what it takes to run your business. As you do so, you're figuring out what works and doesn't work for you in the business plan before taking action. This helps you learn what makes the most sense for you and your journey.

I understand that it appears that a business plan is the be-all and end-all of a Career Business. But I assure you, a business plan does not need to be perfect, nor is it written in stone. You're allowed to adjust the business plan as things happen, courses change, or whatever variable makes you have to realign The Process. Remember, you're going to learn the industry better as you get more involved in it. This means that you and your business plan must be malleable to The Process of adapting in order to take action.

A business plan is not law. A business plan is a guideline to help you stay on track when you get off track. It's there to guide you when you feel lost. The point of a business plan is to get you started on your journey, while it also sets the tone for what you should be working on. And depending on what you want to achieve in your Career Business, your business plan will be tailored for your needs.

Additionally, sometimes a person feels so lost that they start making up new ideas to compensate for that anxiety-driven worry. A business plan is right there, waiting for you to read it and remind yourself of the original plan before it's too late and you're just doing anything and everything until something works. Ultimately, when it all feels lost and nothing is happening, step back and ask yourself, "Am I doing what's in the business plan?" If the answer is no, then you know why things are probably not working out based on how you thought they would work out.

But, Thomas, I'm not a physical business, what goes in a business plan?

You might not be a mom-and-pop brick-and-mortar shop, but you are still a business. This means that traditional business information should still be in your business plan. To make your plan a highly practical business plan, it would be filled with marketing strategies, income and expense opportunities, and SMART goals, detailing objectives for the day, week, month, and year-end goal lines.

Other elements within a business plan will have their brand missions, morals, and purposes written out for the business to uphold, honor, and become active in proving through action the truth in what they believe. Knowing what a company wants and how to get there is a powerful tool for maximizing impact.

A good rule of thumb is that a business plan is a blueprint for your success. The more time you put into doing the research, research, research, the more your business plan will benefit. Allow The Process of how you write your business plan to also be a direct reflection of how you will take action.

Before a building is built, its blueprint must be finalized and given the green light. This blueprint shows important details about every part of the building, from the foundation to the materials that will be used. Elements of the building show the size, shape, and design of each floor, room, and doorway, which are all important parts of a highly useful blueprint.

Like a building, a career needs a foundation, walls, and ceilings to understand the limitations of what is possible for that particular project. Once a blueprint is finalized, the owner of those designs can now take the time to start construction. In this situation, it means taking action for your Career Business.

And as with all things, this proverbial construction will take time and effort to get started and completed. For you, as a business, that *construction* will be how you take action to network, market, and practice, and how you manage your time, money, and the people around you.

A quick reminder: time is the most expensive resource you have. This is why it'll be laid out and managed over the course of one, three, five, seven, and ten years. Every moment is important, so a schedule as small as each day, week, month, and quarter must be organized for a more specific allocation of time as a resource.

To get the most out of that time, money will be budgeted to ensure the materials are affordable, and, in the rare case of issues, these mishaps will be dealt with. The budget shows what will be needed to get the project running, finish it, and address any contingencies that might occur.

No matter how much you account for the time spent or the budget organized, none of these things matter if the people around you are not there to help with construction, maintenance, and keeping The Process in motion. This is where networking, marketing, and practicing come in.

Networking is who you know; marketing is who knows you; and practicing is how well you know yourself. This means that you will be building a strong Circle of Influence while showing your Value Sets to best lead, follow, and advise those around you at the tables you join. Since you'll be practicing by getting involved with your industry, you will bring yourself to the people by being proactive and not reactive.

ONCE ALL IS ACCOUNTED FOR WHAT NOW

You have your business plan finished and organized, and now you're ready to get started. First, you need to make sure you have the correct amount of startup capital to cover your overhead for at least eight months (more is good too and encouraged). This amount should be firmly secured in your Financial Foundation Account ready to afford your overhead.

This startup capital gives a business (you) a chance to get started, maintain a presence, and attack its goals without having to worry about bringing in cash money right at the start of its (your) journey. All business owners know that they need this startup capital to open the front doors, keep it running, and have that extra money to support their budgeted overhead.

But, Thomas, why do they have to support their overhead?

A Business Brain knows that nothing is as it seems. As the saying goes, "hope for the best, prepare for the worst." When it comes to running a business, you have to be able to secure the presence of that business in case no one walks through those doors while building that presence up. In this situation, "no one walking through the door" is the same as you having no return on your investment of time, money, and the people around you. That, and when you're networking, marketing, and practicing within your field of interest, nothing is panning out. And you know what? It shouldn't pan out. Not at first. Eventually it will. I'd say about, oh, I don't know, twelve to eighteen months from the day you start.

A solid Financial Foundation Account is there to give your Career Business the stability it needs so you can take the calculated risk outlined in a clear business plan. This is because even after all your ducks are lined up and ready for you to take your shot, it still might take a good six to twelve months for you to establish yourself within your field of interest. And the secret to success is all about how deeply you can get involved within that field of interest—where people are calling you and you're not the one calling them for opportunity.

> *A good rule of thumb* is that you don't have to wait until you start your Career Business and get involved in your industry before you take action and create potential opportunities. Remember, while you're saving up that startup capital, you can network, market, and practice. No one is stopping you from building and cultivating relationships, establishing your brand on social media (while building a platform), and learning your industry before you step outside and into your Career Business path.

CHAPTER 2.9
Foundation

2.9 | STARTUP CAPITAL

Startup capital is one step toward being a well-versed Business Brain who thinks like a business. That startup capital is one part of The Process for a Business Brain. They approach opportunities with preparation, protection, and potential. And as a person in the entertainment industry, a Business Brain should approach their Career Business the same way a smart business owner would when opening their donut shop. They do this with a business plan and a solid Financial Foundation Account filled with startup capital.

To get the most out of your Financial Foundation Account, you need to start a business with a solid stash of startup capital. This capital will cover your overhead for at least 18 months. This startup capital, also known as seed money, refers to the funds required not only to open a business but also to handle all of the pre- and post-startup responsibilities that come with a new business venture. This includes the money to sustain said business while they gain traction.

Remember that overhead includes a marketing budget, day-to-day costs, and the financial burden of running a business when money isn't coming in right away. That's the thing: money, at least real money, will not come in the moment you begin your Career Business journey. You might have a few paying opportunities here and there, but until you're fully involved in your industry, small money is not consistent money. Keep in mind that most of the time, your best opportunities are going to be you volunteering your time for free.

The smart move is to have this startup capital finance you through the first eighteen months of your Career Business. This money is there so you can spend the majority of your time trying to get involved by being able to say yes to things. When you're not worrying about your overhead, you can focus on doing your daily, weekly, monthly, and yearly tasks to increase your odds of being called to the tables.

As was already said, investing only a few hours a month in a hobby rarely rewards a serious Career Business. This startup capital already places you and your Career Business in the correct lane to reach your potential. Think like a business, grow like a business, and you'll develop your Career Business.

And as a reminder, it is indeed called the entertainment business, which is an industry that will chew you up and spit you out if you don't prepare. You need the ability to control your calculated risks by protecting yourself from having to say yes to "things" that won't help your Career Business in the long run.

> ***A fun side note*** is that if you focus on getting working *doing* what you love to *do*, then that's not considered getting involved. What you're doing is dedicating time to your hobby at the expense of your potential for success and longevity. Don't ignore your Career Business just so you can play—put time into it.

> ***A good rule of thumb*** is that when opportunities present themselves to you to play, then say yes. There is a difference between asking to play and being asked. Being asked means you're doing your job, and it's paying off. Additionally, when they ask you, now you're officially getting involved because they want you there. Don't put time into asking people to play. People will ask you to play when you put time into your Triangle of Life to generate opportunities.

I probably can't say this enough about your Financial Foundation Account, but it holds your startup capital and gives you the freedom to focus on your job responsibilities full-time. A major pro of this capital is that it'll reduce any fear that makes you feel like you need a survival job. The reason you won't need a survival job is because your survival job is the capital you have saved. At least in the beginning.

The whole point of your startup capital is that instead of working while attempting to make something happen on the side, with this capital, you now get to devote more time toward working in your field of interest. If you have the capital in your account, you can proactively take action without having to work a job to pay your bills.

> *A good rule of thumb* is to sacrifice your *wants* now so you can afford your *needs* while establishing your financial strength. Your financial strength gives you the freedom to make choices because you want to, not because you have to pay the bills. It's better to sacrifice now while you're building a Career Business than it is to spend your financial strength on *things* that won't help that mission.

And you need to understand that you've accomplished a great task the moment your startup capital is in your Financial Foundation Account. This sacrifice of yours has given you the greatest gift ever: time. This capital is your future because it gives you the freedom of your present, a present that allows you to finally jump out of that plane with a working parachute filled with calculated risks.

You've opened the door to the next step in your Career Business by having this startup capital. At this point, if you have that capital, you've successfully sacrificed your *wants* to save up this money. Take a moment to realize what kind of accomplishment that is. This is the hardest part because of how long it takes. Nothing feels like it's getting done when you're only working to save money. But now you have earned the "time" to get it done: your Career Business is ready for you to take full-time action!

CAN I START MY CAREER JOURNEY NOW

But, Thomas, can I start before I have eighteen months of startup capital?

Sure, why not? Anyone has the ability to do whatever they choose. These concepts within this book are ideas for people to try. There are millions, if not tens of thousands, of different ways to achieve the desired results in your Career Business. My method is one of those ideas. This method is designed to protect people first and take away the need to wait for an opportunity to come to them. Everything I suggest you do in this series affects everything I suggest you do in this series. Each step helps the other steps. That's the difference between this method and the other methods out there.

To get the kind of protection I'm talking about, you need startup capital in your Financial Foundation Account, which is there to provide you with stability. With this stability, you can dedicate time toward elevating your power and status within your industry of choice because of the freedom you'll have to get involved in that industry. Or more importantly, you can say *yes* to things. Things that have similar missions, the way you approach life with your same morals, and the purposes you have dedicated your life to.

The secret is to be able to get involved because you want to, not because you have to pay your bills. Therefore, your choices are directional instead of being reactionary to the stress of having to pay your bills. And also having to hope that the number's game works out for you while working a survival job. Or worse, living off just enough money to survive for a few months, hoping a big break comes.

My way will take you time—a lot of time—before you're set up in a position that allows you to take action toward your Career Business. Yes, there will always be that one-in-a-million chance where you get discovered, but that's passive effort. I believe in proactive effort. The more you are prepared to take action in your Career Business, the greater your ability to say yes to the opportunities that come your way.

I don't believe waiting for opportunities where you get discovered solely based on how amazing, awesome, and unique you are is proactive either. Can you do it your way and begin your career before your startup capital is established? Yes, you can. Do I recommend that? No, I do not.

In fact, to be proactive, you need that startup capital, which allows you to take action and get involved before opportunities present themselves naturally. Besides, how can you say yes to things when you've already used up all your sick time at work?

The thing I know to be true is that no matter what you do or how you do it, your success will always come down to three things: networking, marketing, and practicing. No matter what you do—music, comedy, one book after another—it'll all amount to nothing because, inevitably, the thing that will lead you to the promised land is your 3 Needs of Success. And if you have that startup capital helping you take action, it'll become something you're in control of. It becomes about the effort you choose to put into your Career Business.

You'll see. One day it'll happen as it always does: you meet someone (networking), they see your Value Sets in action and love the impression you left on them (marketing), and they bring you in on their projects because they like you, which allows you to be seen doing what you're capable of doing in real time (practicing). From there, you'll elevate yourself in a group through consistent involvement because you are on time (management), think outside the box to find solutions in a proactive way (entrepreneurial brain), and find ways to lead, follow, or advise others at the table (talent).

CHAPTER 2.10
Foundation

2.10 | CALCULATE YOUR OVERHEAD

To finalize the total amount needed for your initial startup capital, you'll need to do a little research and math. Once you know that number, it'll give you a targeted total amount needed to build a solid Financial Foundation Account (FFA) that'll support you for your first eighteen months. This amount is designed to cover your overhead so you can take calculated risks. As stated in early chapters, those eighteen months will give you the freedom to focus a full year on getting involved in the entertainment industry and making a name for yourself. The remaining six months of capital are there as your contingency reserve—your "oh crap" money in case something crazy happens. And trust me, something crazy can always happen.

To get this total amount, you'll need to figure out every expense that you're comfortable with. Keep in mind that these expenses should include everything necessary for the lifestyle you want to live and the cost of running your Career Business. Knowing these costs will help you determine the total overhead you'll need for those first eighteen months.

Personally, I'd limit my expenses to what I *need* rather than what I *want*. This doesn't mean you won't eventually afford those *wants*; it just means your main focus should be on what you *need* to survive. Remember, every dollar counts in the beginning, so saving where you can at the start of your Career Business, the better. As you build the financial system that is your 3 Needs of Purpose, you'll be able to afford your *wants* without compromising your mission. This happens as you hit certain financial milestones, allowing you to increase your overhead as needed.

But, Thomas, how do I figure out how much I need for my Financial Foundation Account?

Set up a budget that will afford and cover your *needs* and any *wants* you absolutely feel you can't live without. These *needs* should include personal expenses, business expenses that'll help you maintain and grow your Career Business, and any other expenses that could come up.

Those "can't live without" wants should be included too. *Wants* are things you don't *need* but personally enjoy. For example, if you like buying a specific brand of sneakers that cost $400 a pair or if you want to buy the latest game consoles for $500 every time they come out, these are *wants* that aren't necessary for running your Career Business or affording your life.

When it comes to your "wants" that you can't live without, you have to add them to your budget. Alternatively, over time, you can earn the right to these wants through your Dream Need Account, or as your budget increases, you can allocate more to the leisure column.

AN ACTIONABLE LIST TO FIGURE OUT YOUR OVERHEAD

1. Go through your 12-month bank and credit card statements.
2. Organize shown expenses into specific grouped categories.
3. Add each category total up.
4. Divide that total number by twelve months.
5. Now you should have the average for each individual category.
6. Add all those category averages together.

This total is known as your starting *average monthly overhead*, specifically for your personal expenses. Your personal expenses are the easy part to figure out. But right now, you're halfway there. I know, I just started singing the Bon Jovi song too, but we must stay focused.

Now it's time to figure out your business overhead expenses. To do this, it's going to take some work on your part to research, research, research and learn what specific categories your industry of interest would have. These will be expenses that might, or a majority of the time, come up within your industry when working within it.

As an example, how much traveling would you have to do to get around in your industry—gas, train, MTA, etc.? Some careers generate headshots, websites like IMDb, Actors Access, DistroKid, URLs, and hosting costs.

Each field of interest will be different within the entertainment industry. Do the work to figure out what your Career Business costs are and what the potential costs would be for your Career Business. When you do figure out these costs, add an additional 20–40% to the total to give yourself some wiggle room. This is a fair and quick contingency increase that all budgets could benefit from.

At this stage of The Process, by adding your *business expenses* to the total, it might be clear that your total monthly average overhead is higher than expected and it should be. The first budget that is calculated is based on the last twelve months of a particular lifestyle, and the second budget is based on the projected first twelve months of your Career Business *needs*.

Having a large total is not that bad. It gives you a chance to really think about what you truly *need* in your budget. This is why the next step in The Process is to go through and cut, cap, and even cancel any personal expenses that lean more towards *wants* and less than a *need*.

When you stop spending extra money on things like daily coffee or pizza (okay, pizza can stay—that's food for the soul), you'll be surprised at how quickly that first total amount drops.

I wouldn't fear taking action to reduce your costs and expenses. These caps, cuts, and cancellations on your spending will help you take back control over your budget and give you the power to take action. More importantly, it'll give you the power to afford to take action.

A practical approach to The Process is to cut costs for eating out and switch to buying groceries. As a first cut, that's quick and easy. When you realize how much you spent over the last twelve months on entertainment, hobbies, all those subscriptions for streaming, etc., you might be shocked.

Being shocked is good. And seeing your numbers play out on the page and watching those totals grow or shrink will put your spending into perspective.

And hopefully, this book helps you realize that making those cuts, caps, and cancellations is a way for you to actually take back control. And remember that control will give you the freedom to take a chance on yourself by sacrificing your luxuries (for now) so you can afford to spend time on your passions.

As your budget grows and your FFA gets stronger, you'll be able to add any *wants* back into your overhead. The Process of increasing and strengthening your finances will be discussed in later chapters; for now, think of this part of The Process as training your brain to change the game.

NOW THAT YOU HAVE AN AVERAGE MONTHLY TOTAL

It's time to figure out what your total startup capital will need to be to have a strong FFA. For this example, I'm going to make up an arbitrary number. This total is based on me doing all the work to organize my budget by using my bank and credit card statements for the last twelve months. After it's all completed, my average monthly overhead total is $2,500 a month.

- Multiply the average monthly overhead by eighteen months.
- $2,500 x 18 = $45,000

This makes my startup capital goal $45,000. I can now begin my Career Business journey once I have that $45,000 saved into my FFA. I cannot take a step into turning my dream into a career until I have that total protecting me and giving me the freedom to take action.

For me, I'd consider incorporating or creating an LLC and opening up a business checking account once I had $3,000-$6,000 saved for my startup capital. Mostly because you need the corporate or LLC filings to open a business account, and depending on the bank, you'll need $3,000 or more to not get penalties for having less than.

Once I have that business savings account, which will be considered my FFA, I can continue to place money in there until I have the total amount needed. This $45,000 in my FFA will cover my overhead and protect me for my first eighteen months. This means I can officially take action.

Now, your turn!

CHAPTER 2.11
Foundation

2.11 | I DON'T HAVE THE MONEY TO SAVE

But, Thomas, how can anyone save up $45,000 if they have other bills to pay, like rent, a car, food? All I'm saying is that I don't have the money to save $1,000; how am I going to save $45,000?

That's a great question. And anyone can save up that kind of money if they take the right course of action for themselves. There is no timeline on how long it'll take to save it. You "need" that startup capital if you "want" to have a successful Career Business. So it's less about the total amount and more about setting up a plan of action to accumulate that amount.

I know that the $45,000 is based on a monthly budget of $2,500, but, for argument's sake, let's consider some factors before learning how to save up that total amount. We should consider where you live, what you want to accomplish once you get your Career Business going, and the variables that each specific field of interest entails. If you need that extra lifestyle cost budgeted into your overhead, it will increase your average monthly overhead total. More than likely, it'll be way more than $2,500 per month.

For example, I worked with a client who needed $3,500 a month to cover their average monthly overhead. This included college loans, car payments, a desire to live in New York City, etc. Sure, a person can always room with others, get rid of their car living in a city, cut out entertainment, and so on, but the truth is, it's different for each person. At the end of the day, the amount is going to be what it is unless a person cuts their *wants* down or completely out of their budget.

But, Thomas, where would I find the money in the first place?

WHERE DO I FIND THE MONEY IN THE FIRST PLACE

Do you have a rich uncle or aunt? No? Alright, well, in that case, you're going to have to do it the hard way. This means you'll have to pull up your sleeves and start taking action by sacrificing your comfort zone for a chance to live the dream! Here are some ideas to get your brain thinking outside the box in a proactive way.

The first thing to do is get a second job.

But, Thomas, I don't want to work two jobs.

Great. This means you need to find a job that pays better than your current one, unless you're okay taking however long it will take you to save up your startup capital. Saving up that capital is part of The Process. And to do that, you need to bring in more money than it costs you to cover your overhead. If you don't want a second job or your job doesn't pay enough, you'll have to think outside the box.

P.S. Please don't do anything illegal or anything that feels like a quick fix, it will probably cost you in the long run. It's really not worth it. Additionally, if you're working a part-time job, you'll need to find another job that allows you to work those other open hours. You need to be working 40+ hours a week, or bringing in enough to earn over that overhead of yours.

But, Thomas, I won't get anything done if I'm working that much?

Think of this time as your "save as much money as possible" phase of your life. You're not sacrificing potential but accumulating that startup capital for your FFA. Think of your startup capital as a way to help you better your odds by giving you the freedom to take action. You need capital to "run your business," and in this situation, your career is your business.

You could work one job, but I recommend doing whatever you have to do (legally) to save up that money. Personally, I once worked three jobs and rarely slept while saving up as much money as I could until I was able to quit all three jobs and focus on my original Career Business path, music. This took me about a year, give or take.

There's always a solution if you search for it. That's what sacrificing looks like. The good news is that whatever job or jobs you take on will be jobs you can leave once you have your eighteen months of startup capital saved. Allow these jobs to be what they are—a means to save up capital, not a future career path.

One, two, or even three jobs is a fantastic way to take action so you can save the money needed to explore your freedom. Again, that freedom is what'll allow you to fully commit to the Career Business of your dreams.

This next option is a bit more aggressive. You're a business venture getting ready to open its doors, which means you could potentially approach it the same way a business owner would: investors.

Try the following *think outside the box in a proactive way* ideas:

1. Crowdfunding
2. Bank loans (especially business bank loans)
3. SBA loans
4. Family members
5. Investors

Let me touch on *investors* for a moment. If you're searching for investors who believe in you and want to invest in your future, then this option is extremely risky. I repeat, this option is extremely risky. The reason being, besides having to pay them back (if that's part of the deal), you also have to give them equity in your business as part of the bargain.

Investors might say you can pay it back when you have the money, within six years after a grace period, etc. However, no matter how long they give you to pay them back, they often want a percentage of the company and a return on their investment above their initial contribution.

Even though some investors will give you a grace period or work with you to pay them back, some options, like bank loans, will require you to start paying them back the next month after you've accepted the loan. If you go through SBA for a business loan, they might allow you a certain amount of time to pass before payments are due.

I'm not going to go into all the ideas. But I do recommend you research, research, research, which option would best accommodate your needs and resources. And sure, these five options are available to you, but my personal suggestion is always the same: get multiple jobs, work hard, and save money on your own. Rushing to get to the Olympics before you're ready is never worth the failure of preparation. Be prepared to take that first step into your new venture with zero money owed.

But, Thomas, can I start my Career Business before I save up that insane amount of money? I really want to start sooner rather than later.

This is a great example of what Artist Brain thinking looks like—or, rather, I should say, what panicking or worrying looks like. This is when the brain tries to find reasons not to save up money. Questions like, "How can anyone save up that kind of money?" arise. The answer is simple: work and save. Work long hours and save as much as you can.

I'm assuming you have a job right now. Maybe you have a part-time job or you're lucky enough to be full-time. And sure, you're making some money but not enough to jump into your Career Business tomorrow. In fact, at this rate, it might take ten years to save up your startup capital. I know, ten years sounds overwhelming. Time is so important. Or is it?

But, Thomas, I don't want to age out.

Trust me, age is not an issue. When you begin is also not an issue. The worries we have are often in our minds. If you do some research, you'll find that many successful careers began later in life. The thing you should focus on now is building that Financial Foundation Account.

> ***A fun side note*** is that I had a full career in the music industry for ten years, then another career as a standup comedian for ten years, built up my acting career over that time, and have always been a musician. I've owned a theater in my lifetime, built a career in Brooklyn as a producer, and am a screenwriter. I'm 46 at the time of writing this very sentence, and I've had a full life with many careers. Currently, I'm semi-retired and focused on my author career, slowing things down after losing my parents. You're never too old to start or start over.

Whatever option you choose, make sure it's the one you're most comfortable with. If you believe you must start now because you can't wait ten years, let alone three years, you may be on the wrong track. It's not about getting started at first. You should be thinking about where you are now, then think about the future. Which leads us to the question: how about taking seven years to save up that money? What about five years?

There's always a chance it will take you three years, two years or even one year of full-time work to save that money. You need to figure out which options are best for you and your needs. Do your research and try to gather enough information to make an educated decision.

The truth is, time should not be an issue. This is a time you can take advantage of—a time to fill with tasks and objectives. Besides working, you have other responsibilities to prepare for. If you already know it'll take you X amount of time to save that money, why not do something with that time? You could be setting up your plan of action for when you do step into your first Career Business day. Planning takes time, so take as much time as you need to set up the field for your attack.

START NOW, WORRY LATER MENTALITY

But, Thomas, if I start now, then I could be successful in ten years.

You'd still have to sacrifice a lot of time and more to make it work. Think of all those successful stories of people living in their cars, on the streets, or in shelters. Halle Berry and Chris Pratt are two examples. Are you willing to live homeless? If so, then you could do it.

My guess is that you'd want to be as comfortable as possible. That means you have expenses. Expenses mean you have to make sure money is coming in. Money coming in means you'll have to have a job. Having a job means you'll have less time to devote to your Career Business. Having less time means you'll have less freedom to accept opportunities as they arise.

Living in poverty, always being hungry, and worrying about your bills is not as conducive as living on a budget. A budget that is covered by your startup capital sitting in your Financial Foundation Account. This capital lets you take advantage of opportunities as they come up.

But, Thomas, I can make money in my industry if I start now! Oh, and I'll only take the big paying gigs!

True. You could. Who knows, maybe you'll make big money acting, creating music, drawing pretty images, writing novels, directing, telling jokes on stage as a comedian, etc. However, that's the Artist Brain thinking. And the math is not in your favor. No one makes consistent money at the level they need when first starting out. It just doesn't happen.

As an example, Matt LeBlanc was down to his last $11 when he was cast as Joey Tribbiani on Friends. That's all he had, $11 sitting in his bank account when he got the audition and was hired. He said in an interview, that's too long to hold out for. Because even if he got a job as a waiter, by the time he got a paycheck that $11 would have been gone. He would have starved. I'm paraphrasing.

Getting a job doing what you love to do at the level you want to do it at is not as easy as knocking on a door and handing in your resume. There is The Process that is explored fully throughout this book series. You could potentially get a job within your industry where you're doing something you don't want to do but at least it's in your industry. This is a potential way to approach it for sure. The problem is, most Artist Brain people only want to do the thing they want to do. Rarely do actors want to be an office PA or an assistant. They want to act.

Well, unless you're Bill Hader who was a PA on multiple projects. Nah, that didn't happen. He did nothing with his Career Business. All he did was wait it out until he got "Barry" on HBO.

But, Thomas, he was on SNL.

Yep. Before or after he worked as a PA?

Why am I bringing this up? A career just doesn't happen. You have to put time into it and you have to be able to say yes, and not only when it benefits your needs with a massive reward. And if you don't have that startup capital, then you'll have to work a job to pay your bills.

However, if you *are* working to pay your bills, then you're making choices based on the fear of not eating, not paying your rent, and being without money. This means you're making choices that might not always align with your brand's message and your business plan. No one should live like that while trying to build their Career Business in entertainment.

HOW LONG HAS IT BEEN ALREADY?

Realize that this period of saving your startup capital will require real effort before taking action. Think about this: You're worrying about how long it'll take to save your startup capital; have you considered how long you've already been trying to succeed in your Career Business already?

So let me ask you: how long have you been trying to succeed in your entertainment career? If the answer is one, three, five, seven, or ten years, then you've been working hard at hardly doing anything if the results you see are little to no results at all. *Doing* a lot of stuff that leads to no real reward, or upward mobility, is the same as doing almost nothing.

Time flies by, and how we utilize our time determines where that time takes us. It is better to trade your time to make sure everything you do affects everything you do than it is to work a job you hate while trying to succeed at this thing called a Career Business.

But, Thomas, why?

Because if you work a survival job, you're only putting in "hobby effort" toward your dream career. Hobby efforts are when you can, if you can, and where you can. But "career effort" is because you can, when you want, and where you want.

It's about having control over your Career Business and the choices you make by having the time to make choices. What is the point of trying to succeed with only hope fueling your effort when one, three, five, seven, or ten years fly by with little to no results?

I went through that once. I had a *career* in the music industry for almost five years before I realized I had no career at all. My brain needed to change things up for me to have a chance at success. I chose to give back to myself by saving money so I could invest it back into my Career Business. This is when I began working three jobs. Once I had the money, I was finally able to take action as opportunities came my way instead of waiting around hoping things would happen for me. See, it is better to take action than it is to wait for action to happen.

CHAPTER 2.12
Foundation

2.12 | SACRIFICE

This brings us to the power of sacrifice in a way that will help you get what you really want: a career in the entertainment industry. You want that career in the entertainment industry and sacrificing comfort, among other things, to get that success can be scary. And I know that the thought of giving up your *wants* to afford the Career Business you're working hard for can hold you back. But you can do it. I have faith in you that you can sacrifice your *wants* now. I have that faith in you because I know that you've already made significant sacrifices for things you don't want. So why not go the distance for the things you absolutely want in life?

But, Thomas, what sacrifices have I made for things I don't want?

1. Working at a job you hate.
2. Spending a ton of money to see an agent.
3. Finding reasons to go on a vacation.
4. Absolutely needing a new $2,500 guitar.
5. Paying for editors to edit your book.
6. Buying a new top-of-the line phone.

The list goes on and on. We make excuses to do things we think will give us an instant return on our time, money, and effort. And that *return* is often what people believe are their desired *results*. It's all an illusion.

But, Thomas, what illusions are people seeing?

Working a job they hate equals getting a guaranteed paycheck by the end of the week. This illusion keeps them from taking chances because of the *comfort* of that paycheck. A paycheck that comes from a job they kind of have until something big happens and slowly turns into a job they've been at for ten plus years and now can't leave. If they leave, they'll lose a good-paying position, vacation time, and that 401k.

When actors pay to see an agent, the illusion is that this act will push them to the front of the line of opportunity. Instead of going the long way, they just hopped in front of everyone and got to do a monologue. Makes sense. Paying to see an agent equals getting seen, and when you're so amazing, awesome, and unique, of course they're going to sign you!

The illusion is that people believe the misconception that "if I do A, then B will happen." And it's just simply not how the system works.

If you have, or know someone who has, done these things, you've probably seen little to no results from these sacrifices. And there are many more items on that list when it comes to doing *things* that fuel the Artist Brain's Career Business.

This is why you should ask yourself, "If I've sacrificed for things I hate, why am I not sacrificing for things that will help me obtain the Career Business that I want?"

The solution is to sacrifice now so you can be rewarded later. This mentality involves saving money (your startup capital) by spending less on things you *want* right now and allowing yourself to earn the reward of those *things* later. You need to learn how to respect the wants vs. needs boundaries to strengthen your opportunities in life.

When I talk about success being defined as making a living within your field of interest, a living is not a lifestyle. A living is affording an average monthly overhead. People who fulfill their wants now often let their lifestyle control them, going beyond what they can afford and overindulging in wants over needs. This is why sacrificing wants for needs is difficult, but the long-term return will always pay greater dividends.

If you choose to sacrifice your wants now, you'll be able to live the lifestyle you desire later. Wanting the best car now might not be as helpful to your Career Business as, say, paying for a plane ticket to get to LA for a last-minute opportunity.

Break your spending habits and create new ones now. This is the best way to sacrifice your *wants* and take back control over your life. Instead of buying a new guitar, save money, allocate spending to budgeted caps, and spend less than you save. It sounds easy because it is. Imagine if instead of going on vacation, you changed your spending habits to increase your chances of affording the freedom to take action. These small changes create big results.

> ***A good rule of thumb*** is to take some time and weigh the reality of what you want in your life. Are you content kind of doing this thing on the side as a hobby? If so, then keep doing what you want to do. Do you want to make a living doing what you love? If yes, what are you willing to do to get it?

At the end of the day, you have to come to terms with the following: do you want a career in the entertainment business or that nice car, big apartment, and clothes fit for the wealthy while you "fake it till you make it"? Whatever you choose, you need to figure it out and stand by that choice. You can either use the money to help your dream come true or to make yourself look more successful.

But, Thomas, I'm not trying to make myself look successful. I just want to be comfortable.

I get that. I like being comfortable too. Who doesn't like having a nice car, a warm apartment, or an awesome new PRS? But, honestly, there should never be a choice. Either you want to spend money now or you want to create opportunities to get your Career Business happening.

The hard truth is this: all industries within the entertainment industry are tough. You want to be an actor? Being the best actor is not going to get you through the door. You want to be a writer? Having the greatest book in the world will not get you through the door. You want to be a musician? Recording the greatest album ever will not get you through the door. Don't believe me? How many talented people do you know who've still not been discovered on their talent alone yet? This includes yourself.

If you want that dream career, the hard truth is that you have to be proactive in your choices and protect yourself with your Financial Foundation Account so you can make those choices. A more passive attitude towards success is "if and when it happens, great." I personally like to be proactive with my Career Business by having options, making choices, and having the freedom to take calculated risks.

You are in control of the money earned and the money spent. How you spend it will determine if you are making sacrifices or not. It is, after all, your Career Business and your life. How you choose to run that business is up to you. And this book is me telling you and showing you how to organize your money to take a more proactive approach. An approach that will give you the financial freedom to create opportunities and take calculated risks.

I'll say this much: as your income grows, so will your budget and the caps you have created. As those caps grow, so will your ability to live a more luxurious lifestyle. But the only way those caps and your budget can grow is if you lay the groundwork in the beginning and put in the work to elevate it over time.

SACRIFICE WITHOUT SLEEPING IN YOUR CAR

Tyler Perry lived in his car for years before becoming extremely successful and opening a massive film studio. Am I suggesting you live a poor life in a car? Not at all. What I saw in each and every story involving a successful person was their willingness to sacrifice their *wants* for something bigger.

Yep, every single time.

I'll be Frank with you, even though my name is Thomas; they didn't always know what they were doing. But they did make the hard sacrifices because their Career Business was their dream. As they developed longevity in their Career Business, it generated more opportunities for growth. Each of these people maintained the willingness to sacrifice for their plan, their path, and their choices to have the Career Business they wanted.

Sacrifice is not always about living a poor lifestyle; it's about cutting your desire for wants down because you don't need them right now. Your *wants* are not going to help you succeed.

But, Thomas, I don't want my sacrifices to cause me to struggle.

And you shouldn't have to make that choice. This is why I suggested and wrote these chapters on building a foundation. You need to save your startup capital and place it in a Financial Foundation Account. This account will cover your overhead and support you for the next eighteen months. This money allows you to sacrifice your wants right now so you can afford your needs to get to the next level.

I'll say this much: there are levels of success that can hurt longevity when *wants* take over. When you have money, it doesn't mean you should spend it all. This is why you should always, no matter how much money you have or are making, keep a budget.

But, Thomas, if I have money saved, or coming in, can't I just use it?

You could. However, maybe you heard of Johnny Depp. There was a time when Johnny Depp was reportedly spending two million dollars a month on his overhead. He spent thirty thousand dollars a month on wine alone. That must have been some damn good wine!

When Johnny Depp earned $20 million per film, it only covered ten months of his lifestyle. Sure, that's a lot of money, but earning that kind of money and paying for that kind of lifestyle is why many rich and successful celebrities end up broke. They're not developing wealth nor are they protecting themselves.

Even "successful" people can destroy their opportunities once their *wants* cost more than they can afford. And when you can't afford your *needs*, your wants eat away at your freedom and stability.

But, Thomas, don't they own businesses and property?

Yep. Of course, they do, but when they buy a house as an asset and it costs more to maintain it than to own it, it destroys the investment. Remember, making poor choices on where you spend and invest will lead to loss. This loss means that a rich person is still not wealthy if that money can vanish.

A good rule of thumb is to budget, invest, and organize your money so you do not become your own worst enemy. Sacrificing will play into both your future and present. If you cannot learn to manage your money properly, it'll manage you right into the poorhouse. This is when I'd clear my throat on stage in front of an audience and mumble accountability into the mic.

WHEN SACRIFICE BECOMES A MUST, NOT A CHOICE

There comes a point in a Career Business when you realize you don't have the cash flow to afford your overhead. Without cash flow, overhead is at risk of being compromised. We sacrificed at the beginning to pad our Financial Foundation Account with enough money to support the first full year and a half of our journey. This support allows you the freedom to organize any earned money as it comes in. This is possible because there are at least three or more months in your Financial Foundation Account. This is what I call the safety net threshold. Your safety net threshold informs you if you can activate the 60/40 Split Rule.

This is an important reminder that the beginning stages of a Career Business will also be when you lay the foundation for wealth growth. When money is organized into the 3 Needs of Purpose using the 60/40 Split Rule, money starts working for you and you stop working for it. And you want to generate wealth to continue to protect you and grant you freedom to make more choices.

This process allows money to flow into the system and gives you the next level of strength to make choices. Your Financial Foundation Account's strength is great for the first eighteen months, but after that, you want assets pulling in passive income to maintain the system.

When this happens, you'll have to continue to sacrifice your wants so you can spend money on asset investments instead of liabilities. Don't get me wrong; you do still have your Dream Account money to reward yourself with your wants. The big difference is that your Dream Account rewards you to spend money on your wants before your overhead caps and budget increase.

You have two other *needs* in your 3 Needs of Purpose: Security and Growth. Your Security Accounts are there to protect you in case the day comes when all your money is gone, and your Growth Accounts are designed to allocate money so you can invest in assets.

All of this is done to help the system work while you sacrifice your effort and time to develop these much-needed assets. Assets generate passive income, which in turn develops your wealth. Wealth will always be more than just money. Having wealth generates time, money, and the ability to increase your resources to get involved and help people.

If you work to maintain a lifestyle, you're recouping income to pay your expenses. This makes what you do a job, not a choice, nor a Career Business. You may have heard of celebrities going on a work spree just to pay back the IRS or afford their lifestyle. This is when you see them doing a lot of jobs that have no return on their brand value or life choices. Nor are their choices giving them any kind of joy.

But sure, they're working on a lot of stuff; it's just that now it's cranked out at a lower quality in both their performance and the product itself. This kind of return on their investment destroys their brand's trust with the public. And if this was you, you're taking the fun out of what you choose to do when everything you do is to pay your bills.

By the definition of *success* set forth in this book, if you earn twenty million dollars for a movie, you're not successful if it doesn't cover your budgeted overhead. You're not considered successful if you're trading time for money to pay your bills. Let this sink in and allow it to be something for you to consider when you're enjoying one of your four yachts for the day just because you can afford to buy them.

CHAPTER 2.13

Foundation

2.13 | 5 MISTAKES TO AVOID

Saving up your startup capital can be a blessing and a curse if you're not careful. The reward for having startup capital is that it gives you the freedom to take action, take chances, and reinvest back into the system you've created before starting your Career Business. However, this freedom can backfire if you fall into one of five common mistakes.

But, Thomas, why do people fall into these snafus?

It usually comes down to inexperience and a lack of strong habits. When you've never done something before, it's not easy. As with any new endeavor, there's a learning curve for the skills and knowledge necessary to make the most of your attempt. Taking a leap of faith is a challenging first step that often comes without a clear playbook—until now. This is your playbook, unless it's just another book you purchased, borrowed, or are using as a cup holder.

Instead of doing those things with this book, use the information within to help guide you in establishing a strong Financial Foundation Account to make your Career Business possible. Whether you use this book to advance your career or keep your coffee table from staining, here are five mistakes to avoid once you have a solid Financial Foundation Account filled with your startup capital.

#1—STARTING BEFORE THE MONEY IS SAVED

This is a big one, which is why it's first. One thing I learned early on is that blind ambition can kill success. Those who think they know better than all the people who came before them can back themselves into corners before and after they start. And trust me, an idea won't manifest results simply because someone believes it could, should, or would.

This is one of the biggest lies we tell ourselves as Artist Brains. Most, if not all, who see no results simply continue to pile on effort without any real change in their approach. Doing the same thing over and over isn't going to magically produce new, better results just because you believe you *deserve* said results.

You, like me, or anyone else in this industry, are unlikely to have your book, song, acting reel, comedy set, etc. be seen by one or more people, and then our lives change completely. We often believe that results are all we need to succeed. If I write a book, I'll be successful. If I act in a play, I'll be discovered. If I record a song, it'll be a hit.

But, Thomas, if it's amazing, then the right person would be stupid to pass me up.

Time for an aside: have you ever said or heard someone say, "All we need is for the right person to see us?" Another variation is "all we need is the right person to discover us."

Don't get me wrong, it would be an amazing experience to get that call out of nowhere telling us, "You're in, kid!" But if you've heard the above quote or said it yourself, it's the mindset that is going to destroy your chances at a career in the entertainment industry. Success doesn't just come to us simply because we're awesome, amazing, and unique. You will need a plan and capital to protect you while you take action with that plan.

But, Thomas, are you saying that if I have a plan, I can start earlier?

Well, you could do anything you want, but I wouldn't. No matter how much you tell yourself that you don't need eighteen months of startup capital in your Financial Foundation Account, the truth remains: a business needs money to open its doors. Your Career Business is absolutely the same as a brick-and-mortar business. Which means that if you're a business, you need startup capital. I recommend not starting before you have your startup capital.

But, Thomas, what if I know someone in the industry who can help me now?

That would be great! When these kinds of opportunities arise within your field of interest, take them! What's even more exciting is if you connect the dots to The Process of it all. These are often opportunities that come from people you know (networking), people who have heard about you through a mutual friend (marketing), or through internships (practicing) where people liked you (marketing).

My advice: never turn down the big *ins* when they present themselves. Not everyone gets these opportunities, which is why some of us need a Financial Foundation Account to protect us so we can take calculated risks, giving us the freedom to say *yes* to these opportunities because we want to, not because we have to pay our bills. And some of these *ins* might be one-and-done opportunities. Sure, that's great for getting your foot in the door, but now what? Not having your startup capital would make it difficult to say yes to this.

But, Thomas, it's a great opportunity. I know it's only this one gig, but once they see me, I'll be set. It'll get me more work. Right?

Maybe. Anything is possible in this thing we call life. For me, I'd recommend never saying yes to opportunities you "can't afford." Remember that your Career Business should not be based on "if onlys" and "what ifs." If only I knew the right person, what if I got discovered? These hopes can be career-killing delusions. Be logical about your approach and take proactive action by establishing a Financial Foundation Account to protect you.

> *A good rule of thumb* is that any opportunity from the people you know could be worth it if it offers you consistency. These are jobs at lower to mid-level entry points in the industry where you can work your way up to the position you want. An opportunity should be more than a one-time chance to do what you love. Sure, if a friend offers you a big break in a commercial, a show, or publishing your book, take it for the money, but this isn't worth the leap of faith.

But, Thomas, shouldn't I take a leap of faith and sacrifice my comfort to become successful if I know I'm going to put in the work?

You know, a lot of people have done that. Successful people too. I know this because I did my research, research, research by listening to autobiographies, watching shows on the Biography channel, and studying the journey of these stories to learn how people achieved their success.

One thing I learned is that every success story involves sacrifice, whether living on the street or sharing a small space to focus their resources on starting their career. History shows us the path, and if we can read between the lines, we can adjust and strengthen the methods to best help ourselves.

Again, I'm not saying you should sacrifice by being poor, living in your car, or eating beans every day. A Business Brain sees their Financial Foundation Account as a support system for their freedom to take action. Yes, a Financial Foundation Account comes with a big, scary number you have to save up, especially when you realize you barely earn $25K a year at a survival job. At this rate, it might take you years before you get started on the Career Business of your dreams. So, of course, if your total startup capital is going to be $40K, that's a daunting number.

But, Thomas, what's the payoff of taking time to save that startup capital?

You can sacrifice in style when you set up a system of protection where you're comfortable and able to afford to take action. I promise you, spending five years saving up money versus eating beans in the middle of winter while sleeping in your van is not worth the risk of starting earlier.

But, Thomas, five years is a long time.

Where you work to find solutions, you'll find resolution. Focus not only on the size of your startup capital goal but also on the time it will take to save it. A year flies by as quickly as five years do, but that doesn't mean this time is wasted. Time is only as valuable as you make it. Use this time to create opportunities, ones that ultimately affect everything you do once you start on your path toward success.

Being proactive with your time, efforts, and opportunities is how you make things happen by making things happen.

So stop thinking about how quickly you can get into the game. If you do your job right, you'll get the most out of being in the game when the time comes. And I know that there is almost no way to save that kind of money quickly enough for you to feel motivated. So, let's try a thinking exercise.

Think about what you have been doing for your Career Business over the last year of your life. Now think about the last three years. And finally, think about the last five. Wow, time does fly, but that doesn't mean you are running out of it.

For the Artist Brain, the misconception usually stems from the fear that they have to start right away. I mean, the Artist Brain probably believes that they're so amazing, awesome, and unique that by getting out there, they'll be discovered. And once you get discovered, everything will be fine. But that's not the truth.

Starting now doesn't allow you the freedom to take action if you can't afford your overhead. The brain change here is that this time can be used for more than saving up money. This is time you can utilize for building opportunities through networking and marketing on a small scale. Networking and marketing aren't just about telling people about yourself. They are *needs* that allow you to connect with people on an emotional level, showing them who you are through your actions.

Networking is about meeting new people, even online, through others, or figuring out who you want to know once you start your Career Business. Marketing and networking should be working together to leave a strong impression on the people you meet. The stronger the impression, the more likely they'll be emotionally interested in you. This leads them to be aware of you, think of you, and want to know more about you.

These steps are just two examples of how to use time to set up the foundation of relationships that will build opportunities. When the time comes to take action, these new relationships should know when you'll be one hundred percent available. They should also realize that you would make a strong addition to their team, capable of doing what is needed to lead, follow, and advise.

No matter how long it takes to collect your total startup capital, use this time wisely. If it takes three years to reach your financial goal, that's three years to build and cultivate relationships within your desired field of interest. That's three years to develop a brand that leaves an impression on people within that field of interest. That's three years to be seen as someone with Value Sets and not just your product that does A, B, and C.

Your product is a byproduct of the thing you love to do. But no one cares that someone is an actor who acts, a writer who writes, a musician who records a song, a comedian telling jokes, etc. People within the industry care about themselves being a writer, musician, comedian, and how you can help them. If you make it about you being one or more of those things, you're just another competitor that they need to take down in their mind. This is why you have to be more than what you love to do. You have to be an asset to the potential of the tables you join.

No matter what people tell you in or out of your industry, take your startup capital number seriously. Take your Career Business and business plan seriously. Whether your startup capital goal is $20,000 or $60,000, take it seriously. Save it up, prepare, and get your parachute ready for the jump.

#2—NOT STICKING TO OR EVEN KNOWING YOUR MISSION

Direction leads us to our destination. It drives us with a purpose outlined in an organized method for success. It gives us a plan to take steps each day toward a specific end result. There is a dream inside you that fuels you to work hard as you try to make something of yourself. That something is you accomplishing your goals until you have a career doing what you love. This vision, this dream, this passion has defined you since you could remember.

If you have this belief inside you, then embrace it. Hold it close and let it make your heart beat relentlessly toward the horizon of victory as you proactively work for it. This destination is the fuel that should wake you up in the morning. It should be the deciding factor when it comes to making sacrifices. Passion without action is frail and wasted on daydreaming. Do you want this career? If the answer is yes, then go after it. You deserve it. We all do. We all deserve a chance to live a life that brings us fulfillment and joy. But this passion is only the fuel that keeps you going. It is not your guide to daily tasks that will lead to success.

Your passion is part of the end goal, but it is not the map to your success. Specific actions should be outlined in your business plan as your highway to possibility. This plan is what you should reference for your daily actions. It takes your vision and gives you a clear path through the clouds of uncertainty as you hit multiple milestones.

A business plan of action does not keep your eye on the prize. Far too many people have been told, "It's great to have a hobby as long as you realistically have a Plan B." This saying is meant to protect you in case things don't work out because it's a tough industry. But you know what? All industries are tough. Becoming a doctor, a lawyer, it's all difficult. Imagine if aspiring doctors and lawyers were told, "Hey, I know you want to be a doctor, but make sure you learn a trade, like plumbing, too." Even trades like carpentry take time and effort to master. I should know, I was a carpenter working with my uncle in my youth.

I agree with one part of that statement: you should have a Plan B, but not as a fallback to do something completely different. In life, you need a Plan B to get to your Plan A. You should have Plans A, B, C, D, and all the way up to Z as fallbacks to achieving your dream. If Plan A fails, then try Plan B, which is just another route to the desired results of Plan A.

It's okay to change things up from time to time, and I recommend you do, but you still must maintain focus on your original end results. That end result should be to make a living within your field of interest. Besides, how could you truly give something you love your best shot if you knew you had something to fall back on? If you were spreading your efforts in two directions: your dream and the backup plan?

You should never be okay with a "if it works out then great, but this supermarket job pays well" mentality. Don't go halfway in on your dreams. No person on earth has succeeded by "kind of trying." Life is about giving 110 percent above your 200 percent effort to hold down the fort. Give your full self to what you believe in.

Have you ever seen a person "kind of" work at a job with a desire to become the CEO, and that desire manifested into reality by doing the bare minimum? No, you haven't. The reason is because they had to work for it. They had to sacrifice for it, turning nights into mornings through sleepless days to meet deadlines. No one would ever sacrifice for "maybe" or "if it happens," and neither should you. You owe it to yourself to try.

Your vision is your purpose. This is why I'm asking you: What is it that you want to put your time into? If you "kind of" want to do something, go ahead and enjoy it as a hobby. There is no harm in enjoying a hobby. In that situation, it's okay to embrace the outcome as it finds you. Hobbies are always good for the soul, grounding us during the long days, weeks, and years of life when we're not at the job.

And believe it or not, you will need a job to cover the cost of any hobby. Hobbies cost time and money to do. The cost of that hobby doesn't matter as long as it satisfies the hobbyist's soul. If there is one deep-rooted truth about life, it's that life needs leisure time after long hours of working to recharge who you are.

This hobby lifestyle is for the weekend warrior—those people who are entertainers who love what they do in their spare time and feel it fulfills the artist in them. These are the comedians doing local open-mic nights, actors performing with local troupes, and musicians playing originals or covers in bars on a packed Friday while drunk people watch the Yankees defeat the Mets on television. Even writers who write when they can, hoping their first novel will be their big break, are hobbyists. Who knows, it's always possible to break into the industry with a hit novel, though not highly probable.

If you're a weekend warrior, that's perfectly fine for your life. The moment you want to make a living within your field of interest, you have to drop the weekend warrior mentality and become a business. You have to accept what it takes to bring your vision to reality. You have to learn to sacrifice and make excuses to succeed the same way you sacrificed and made excuses for jobs you hated.

It's true. An Artist Brain finds reasons to pick up that guitar and practice. An Artist Brain makes excuses to get out of bed and go to that open mic night and tell jokes. An Artist Brain finds reasons to audition for local, non-paying acting gigs. And they do these things for a really great reason in their mind: they're getting to do what they love to do. Unfortunately, their business is put on hold during these moments. You can't work on your Career Business when you're being a weekend warrior.

Artist Brains aren't willing to do the stuff they hate for a career they want, unless it's getting to do what they love. And because of that, they neglect the important part of their Career Business: doing their actual job responsibilities outside of the reward to be creative (acting, comedy, etc.).

Who wouldn't want to indulge in only the reward of being creative? Performing, writing, and recording are the fun parts. That's the part that moves the soul and gets a person excited. Sadly, the feeling of excitement from the creative side can destroy a Career Business before it starts. It does this by elevating the return of that feeling of being creative over the value of running their business. If the creative side takes over the majority of time and effort, the business side will falter.

When you find yourself making excuses to do what you *want* to do, you might forget about what you *need* to do. Your Career Business needs you to do your job. And when you're making sacrifices and excuses for a survival job, it shows you can do it, but you're choosing not to do it.

I get it; you want to get paid at the end of the week. You don't want your boss mad at you for being late. You don't want to be reprimanded for doing your duties poorly. This is called accountability, except you're giving that respect to someone else and their business instead of giving it back to yourself and the career you really want.

You need to make a choice and figure out what you want to put your time into. If it's a career in the entertainment industry, then do it. If it's something you're content with kind of doing until something happens, or even if nothing happens, then do that. But you have to choose. Even those who get their one in a million shots still need to be all in when they get that opportunity, or it will fade. You can't be all in if you have a survival job that becomes your career before you get that big shot doing what you love.

I've seen people get their big opportunity and then have to turn it down because they put ten years into a job they hate but now have benefits, a 401k, health insurance, a family, a child, and a house. They have a pension that their old brain tells them to keep working so they can retire at 65.

This is my point. We make excuses for the things we hate because they're right there. The results earned by working a survival job are instant. The people, organizations, and businesses that can afford to pay people have earned the right to hire you to run their business because the owner used their Business Brain and treated their own lives like a business to get there.

Ultimately, the people who own the survival job that you work at benefit from your efforts while they get to stay home and enjoy their lives. You're working for and fueling a company to earn them wealth so they can afford to pay you to recoup your income just so you can pay your bills.

People should be more than a hopeful dream if they want to live that dream. It's okay to be happy while you're *kind of* doing something you love. But the moment you want to make a living doing what you love, you have to put everything on the table to be successful. If you're willing to sacrifice for a job you hate, then why not sacrifice for the career you want? It's easy if you do your job, stay loyal to your vision, and are dedicated to the plan.

#3—ENJOYING YOUR FREEDOM TOO MUCH

You've finally saved up enough startup capital to leave that crappy survival job. Your first official workday of your Career Business starts on Monday. This means you have a weekend to set a full schedule for the week ahead. In this moment, you're in control of your destiny. The only boss around to hold you accountable is yourself, and the first thing you do is take a day to relax, then another, and another...

I get it; you've been working nonstop for years, sacrificing your leisure time to save up that startup capital. Now, you need a moment to catch your breath and recharge. Besides, there's no one to tell you otherwise. It's just one day, right? Okay, maybe two days... or is it more like a week where you get to pause and catch up with yourself?

But, Thomas, there's no harm in a week.

Sure, but that one day, even a wonderful week can quickly turn into a month, then three months, and before you know it, six months have passed.

I've seen it happen before: you become laxed in your effort, and in a few months, you've spent the capital in your Financial Foundation Account with little to no return on your investment. What happens next? You end up back at a survival job before the year's end.

But, Thomas, you said I have six months of overhead in reserve as a backup. What's a month off, or a day here and there? I'm finally free from working a job I hate. Let me enjoy some "me time" so I can recharge and be ready for my new Career Business!

I understand your sentiment; it's tempting for a hobbyist. But you're an adult who's responsible for what you do or do not do. And remember, a person is the total sum of their actions or inactions in life. If others see how you treat your Career Business, it influences how they see you for you and if they want to interact with you.

And I get it; it's easy for one day of rest to turn into six months of inactivity. I've seen many artists and people in the entertainment industry take this path, only to realize they have to save up more money with nothing to show for it, which can be disheartening.

It's not easy to hold yourself accountable or change habits when no one is there to oversee you. Being your own boss takes time to master. This is why

I'm telling you to change your habits now before taking on the responsibility of being the boss.

Most of what I do as a mentor is as simple as helping people find ways to regain control over their lives so they can manage their Career Business. My part begins and ends with the knowledge and guidance I provide, but the moment of truth comes when they find out if they're a doer or a procrastinator. Some clients end up doing little to nothing with their time, while others change their lives one day at a time.

It takes 365 days to find success in the entertainment industry. This means working at least nine hours a day, seven days a week, for twelve months. Sure, you have an extra six months of savings in case something goes wrong, but it's not for vacations—it's there to provide security in case of a bad day, week, or month. Life happens; we get sick, need to take care of someone, or face unexpected challenges. This is the reality we prepare for.

No matter how many bad things happen, your job responsibilities still need to continue. You *need* to consistently work on the five sides of your Triangle of Life, focusing on different aspects of your Career Business that affect your success, longevity, and purpose.

If you choose to do nothing or focus on creating products—albums, filming, books, etc.—you'll find that there is little to no result. What starts as a month of working on a book or comedy routine can turn into months of focusing solely on that "thing," with little to show for it.

Now, if you want to do nothing or focus solely on being creative, you can do that, but your creativity isn't your job. Your workday should be no less than nine hours each day, seven days a week. This time isn't for being creative but for networking, marketing, and practicing. Practicing isn't about your craft or talent; it's about learning the industry, honing your skills, and improving your strengths and weaknesses.

Besides, you wouldn't write a novel during your survival job, would you? No, you wouldn't. You wait until you're home from that job before you start working on your novel. You do this because you're showing respect for your survival job, the job you hate. That, and you probably don't want to get fired. But why not treat your Career Business with the same respect? Leave the *fun* stuff for later, once your work time is complete. Just because you now have time to be creative doesn't mean it's your job.

If you spend your time being creative, then you're not spending time on your 3 Needs of Success—networking, marketing, and practicing. These are crucial *needs* for getting involved in your industry. You need to get involved with others, help elevate their missions, and build relationships.

But, Thomas, what about my personal missions?

Again, I should stress that any mission you do get involved with must have some connection to your personal missions, morals, and purposes in life. This helps you better establish yourself in a way that reflects your true beliefs, or rather, your brand. Of course, if your *missions* are simply to be creative, make money, perform, or win that Oscar, I would recommend rethinking your approach. No one wants to work with people who have selfish missions. Would you really want to put time into someone and their missions if it were for them to make money or win an Oscar?

People will absolutely reach out to you more when you're involved in their missions, show your worth, and develop your Value Sets all with positive experiences. And the system you are building will continue to work and lead to more opportunities. Opportunities where you can showcase your skills, talents, and Value Sets. Whether you're asked to perform or help out their table, remain consistent with your brand's voice.

However, remember that in group projects, your focus should be on the mission of the table, not yourself and showcasing your amazing talent. It's not about being the best actor, comedian, or whatever you are just so you can get noticed. It is about being the best version of yourself to help elevate the mission of that table and make everyone, including yourself, look good.

With all of that said, you can't lay around doing nothing during this time. You're in control of your schedule, so figure out what works for you, either during the day or at night. You need to work nine hours a day minimum, but it doesn't have to be consecutive. Yep, you can split your time up in whatever way works best for you. I've been known to work three hours in the morning, enjoy my afternoon, and then five hours at night. Find what works best for you and stick to it.

Of course, there's an exception to the nine-hours-a-day rule: people come first. Whether it's a meeting, call, or industry event, people will always come first over your office work hours.

But, Thomas, I need to get things done?

People are the ones that will help you make things happen. That's why your first 365 days to success are about relationships. This is time you'll spend building and cultivating them, leaving a lasting impression, and understanding how the entertainment industry works.

But, Thomas, what if someone offers me a job in the industry?

This leads to another exception to the rule: take every opportunity you can that allows you to get involved in your industry (especially if it has something in common with your brand). If people come to you, say yes, even if it's unpaid. That's what your Financial Foundation Account is for—to give you the freedom to always accept opportunities in your industry, especially when you're asked to join specific tables you believe in. The whole point is to say yes to these opportunities to develop your Circle of Influence and grow your career.

> *A good rule of thumb* is to help those who provide the services you want to be involved in. Actors can assist acting schools, comedians can drive comedians to gigs, and writers can work as assistants. Help others achieve their missions, not to elevate your Career Business, but to get involved. You'll waste valuable time if you're trying to get cast, signed to a label, or get your TV show picked up.

#4—FORGETTING ABOUT YOUR 3 NEEDS OF PURPOSE

Startup capital is the total amount needed to cover your average monthly overhead. This total goes into your Financial Foundation Account, which includes a safety net that covers three to six months of your average monthly overhead.

But, Thomas, what's this got to do with my 3 Needs of Purpose?

It has everything to do with it. As long as your Financial Foundation Account meets the safety net threshold, you can activate the 60/40 Split Rule. This rule allocates 60% of your earned income evenly into your 3 Needs of Purpose and 40% back into your Financial Foundation Account.

But, Thomas, how does this help my Career Business?

It helps by building and fueling your financial system, allowing you to make choices because you want to, not because you have to pay your bills.

Many people neglect their 3 Needs of Purpose, which makes no sense when it's there to protect you, invest in you, and reward you. This is the thing: when you start your Career Business, you have eighteen months of startup capital in your FFA. Not only does this capital cover your overhead for the first eighteen months, but it also provides a cushion above your safety net threshold.

But, Thomas, how does this help me?

It helps you by being able to activate the 60/40 Split Rule at the start of your Career Business journey. Every cent earned above that safety net threshold can be placed into both your 3 Needs of Purpose and back into your Financial Foundation Account. This ensures that your accounts are continually growing, allowing your money to work for you.

But, Thomas, how does that allow my money to work for me?

Your Security Account protects you, allowing you to start over with seed money if all your actual money went from some to none. The Growth Account invests in assets, generating passive income and developing wealth. Lastly, your Dream Account is your what the hell money, letting you indulge in whatever you desire, whether it's taking time off, splurging, or burning it like Pablo Escobar to stay warm.

This system ensures you're not just depositing all your earnings into the FFA but growing the stability of your financial system for security, growth, and dreams. Even if you earn only a little over your safety net, the 60/40 Split Rule keeps the machine going and growing. In the long run, these accounts will support you, grow your wealth, and reward your diligence.

People often overlook the value of having a FFA to cover their overhead for the first eighteen months. This setup makes it possible to take advantage of the 60/40 Split Rule. Which means you should be taking advantage of the 60/40 Split Rule as much as possible and organizing your income into your financial system so you can develop wealth. Wealth brings with it freedom, and that freedom starts with you managing your money effectively.

#5—NOT STICKING TO YOUR BUDGET

Having a lot of money in your FFA isn't a license to spend frivolously. You don't have to be overly frugal, but setting up a budget is crucial to making that saved startup capital worthwhile. If you're going to spend the money on whatever you want anyway, then why save it in the first place to support the next eighteen months?

But, Thomas, if I have the money, can't I spend it?

Sure, you're an adult and it's your money. However, there is no reason to buy things just because you have money to spend. Don't get me wrong; I understand that having $30-40,000 in the bank is a lot of money. And spending twenty dollars here and there is nothing compared to the total amount of money in your FFA. But even coffees add up. Breakfast sandwiches add up. Going out to the bar or club to buy drinks adds up.

Stick to the budget you've created. If you really need these things, or if going out on the weekends is essential for you, then budget for them at the start of your journey. Include these extra costs into the original startup capital that you'll need for your Financial Foundation Account.

You're allowed to budget and save for the things you *feel* are necessary. And some of these items are going to be your *wants*, not your *needs*. Especially in the beginning, your budget should focus on essentials, not luxuries. So, save up what you feel you need, but remember, the more you add to that budget, the bigger that number will become.

Having $40,000 can quickly disappear if you have poor spending habits. To prevent this, work on your spending habits while saving up your startup capital. You don't want to be six months in and find that your eighteen-month cushion is already halfway gone when it should only be a third. Focus on spending money on your *needs* so you can live a budgeted lifestyle, not on the whims of your heart's desires.

In the end, you must decide what is more important to you: sacrificing for the sake of building a Career Business in the entertainment industry or indulging in daily breakfast sandwiches? Once you decide, stick with it. One choice could leave your account empty over time, while the other will sustain you throughout your eighteen months as you build your Career Business.

Let your personal budget cover the basics: rent, utilities, phone and internet, groceries, and travel. Business expenses will vary depending on your area in the entertainment industry. These might include travel, meeting costs (occasionally cover lunch and dinner meetings), industry-specific needs like website accounts or union dues, and a 20-40% contingency for emergencies.

The point is, you need to live on a budget; otherwise, what's the point of having one? All I'm saying is that you are in control of what happens— you're the one making the choices. So you can choose to ignore the system, or you can choose to embrace the potential you have within you.

CHAPTER 2.14
Foundation

2.14 | FINAL THOUGHTS

How you set yourself up during the foundational stage will speak volumes about who you are or will be before you ever begin your journey. How much and how well you save your startup capital and get your business needs in place will be a clear indicator of your potential for success. These results are often a direct response to your habits—good or bad. Habits that will reveal themselves during this process of setting the foundational stage.

The foundation you develop is going to be more than just the capital you save; it's a combination of both that startup capital for your Financial Foundation Account and how you organize your business before you take action. This means you'll have to think about who you want to be and how you'll approach The Process and the journey.

When it comes to your Career Business, the chess pieces you start with will set the tone of what's to come for your journey. This is why, during the foundational stage, you need to analyze what will work best for you, gather your information, organize it on paper, and work out the numbers and business plan all before you take a leap out of the plane.

But, Thomas, can't I deal with a lot of that stuff once I'm out there?

No, these are things you need in place before you even begin saving. You have to have a clear understanding of what it will take and whether it's something you're willing to do. There will be a lot of tests that come your way to challenge if this dream career of yours is worth it or even what you really wanted.

I emphasize this so you can be conscious of why you're developing a Financial Foundation Account, why you're setting up your business plan, and why you're doing everything to make sure your foundational stage gives you the best starting point in the first place.

A journey to success should have steps, a purpose, and a clear plan that provides guidance and direction. And since the foundational stage isn't only financial, you'll need to invest time into your 3 Needs of Success to make sure your relationships are going to be there when you start. After all, what good is having money to support yourself for eighteen months if you don't have a strong Circle of Influence, an authentic brand to leave an impression on people, and knowing yourself well enough to get involved with others?

It's not about starting a Career Business as fast as possible. It's about preparing for success in your industry, especially in the entertainment industry, which will literally cast you aside and ignore you if you're not out there networking, marketing, and practicing. The more seriously you take the foundational stage, the more power you'll have to control outcomes. This first step sets your ducks in a row, giving you a chance to take proactive steps into a successful first year.

I'd like to think that we become the change we wish to see in this world, and if our behavior is any indicator of our potential, what's going to change if we're not doing right by ourselves before we start?

SO WHAT NOW?

Think about The Process: startup capital for your Financial Foundation Account, 3 Needs of Success, Longevity, and Purpose. Each of these elements is geared toward ensuring a powerful beginning filled with choice. Choices that lead to freedom. And you need that freedom to have the choice to say yes or no and to be able to commit to things, no matter how small or big.

Remember, relationships are key. Sure, you have to make choices to make things happen, but people have to agree to give you a chance and open those doors of opportunity. So while you need to know people, they also need to remember you, and you need to know yourself well enough to get involved.

And the magic of these relationships: the five people you spend the most time with become the world you live in. This core group of relationships is the starting point of all your opportunities. I must stress that these opportunities are never about taking advantage of people. Opportunities are there to help you get involved to help others also get involved, even when there's no clear return.

To do this, you'll need eighteen months of startup capital in your FFA. This money gives you the freedom to say yes or no when opportunities present themselves. Choose wisely too; you can't just say yes to everything when your limited money, time, and resources are there to protect you to make calculated choices. Choices to get involved with people who fit your brand's values.

When you lack the freedom to say yes or no, you leave your Career Business to the hands of fate. You never want to be in a position where you have to say yes just to pay a bill for something that:

A. Doesn't fulfill your job responsibilities of the Triangle of Life in the first eighteen months of your Career Business.
B. Doesn't help your Career Business in any specific way.
C. Hinders your brand's value, which defines you in the eyes of others.
D. It helps you to develop relationships for your Circle of Influence.

To reiterate, the total value of your startup capital is an investment in yourself, giving you a chance at the dream career you've always wanted. This is the "if only" moment where you are giving yourself the chance to prove yourself. This is the chance to do right by you, sacrificing your wants now for a career and a future.

If someone gave you money, invested in you, or opened the door for your dream to have a chance, how would you repay them in effort? Would you "kind of do it" or tell them that you have a day job and you'll do what you can when you can? No. You would put 100% into whatever it is you have to do to make things happen by making things happen, all while staying true to your brand's missions, morals, and purposes.

But, like all things, you can't just have the money and some inner dream hoping to accomplish your goals one day, some day. No, you have to actually take action. You have to do your job responsibilities while you're saving up that startup capital, accomplishing certain tasks, and setting up your business plan to get the most out of your first eighteen months of your Career Business.

THINGS TO SET UP DURING THIS TIME

1. Create relationship opportunities that will allow you to get involved.

- Make calls, send emails, and text people to build relationships.
- Organize your Circle of Influence and do your research on people.
- Introduce people to one another in a way that benefits *them* both.
- Follow and interact with people on social media.
- Support people's endeavors where and when you can.

2. Design a brand for representation through presentation.

- Present your brand to leave an emotional impression on people.
- Set the tone of your brand through your social media accounts.
- Create a website to represent your brand, not to sell things (at first).
- Research annual free or affordable events you can get involved with.
- Figure out who in your Circle of Influence has a similar brand.

3. Learn about your industry beyond what you think you know.

- Check your sources (Uncle Harold on the couch doesn't count).
- If you think you know what you're doing, before you take action, stop and ask yourself, "How do I know what I'm doing if I haven't researched it or been involved in this industry yet?"
- Trust your instincts to guide you on what's right and wrong, take accountability when you are wrong, and be humble when right.
- "Research, research, research" to better understand the things you know before letting new information guide your actions.
- Explore and break down the nuances of The Process over results.

CHAPTER 3.1
Triangle of Life

3.1 | HOW MANY SIDES TO A TRIANGLE

A triangle is one of the strongest shapes in the world. You'll find it in designs for buildings, structures, and bridges. The reason this shape is considered so strong is that any force applied to it is evenly distributed through all its sides. This is why my system for success, longevity, and fueling one's purpose is dedicated to the shape of a triangle. Therefore, when you see the words Triangle of Life, you'll understand why I decided to call it that.

Each side of the Triangle of Life represents different responsibilities that will strengthen your Career Business overall. The better you understand each side and their responsibilities, the stronger your Triangle of Life will be. And you'll need a strong Triangle of Life to get the most out of your Career Business.

As you learn about each side, you'll start to see the value of your triangle and the benefits of each of those sides. Sure, there are multiple sides, but they all serve an important role in The Process. No matter how different they are from one another, they are all equally important.

Unfortunately, it's not uncommon for people to put more effort into one side over another. Or, in some cases, they focus on some areas of each side of their Triangle of Life and ignore the rest. Usually, the fun Needs of those sides get the most attention: practice, talent, and dream.

The secret to success is to maintain a balance between each side, allowing you to have more control over the path leading you to that success. For the Artist Brain, they believe practicing their craft or creative endeavors is always going to be what gives them their best shot.

This is why they love putting the most time into getting better at the creative part, which is another reason talent fuels their motivation. They want their talent to be the key to success in their careers. It validates their efforts, and it makes all their hard work at becoming talented worth it.

That mentality is the dream. If I practice, I'll be talented enough to get discovered. Or better: I'll be so good they can't ignore me. And the problem with this dream is that you have to be asleep to witness it come to life. And this whole book series is about being proactive, not reactive.

It's common for an ambitious Artist Brain to get caught up in the reward of being creative and ignore the unfun Needs of the Triangle of Life. But this isn't how it works. As you'll discover, these three Needs are last on their respective sides. They're three smaller parts of a much bigger system. If you focus too much on any one side or Need of your Triangle of Life, you won't see any significant progress in your Career Business.

But, Thomas, how many sides are there to a Triangle of Life?

Traditionally, when looking at a triangle on paper, you would not be judged for only seeing three sides. But here's one of the first lessons in living your life as if it were a business: you have to look beyond what your eyes show you. To gain a good perspective on life, you need to breakdown The Process of how things work, do your research on what you discover for that process, and keep learning to enhance your understanding of The Process.

Most people see what's in front of them and accept that as the whole truth without putting the time or care into researching or asking a follow-up question. This is the moment that separates those who make choices just to pay their bills from those who take action to change their lives. Those who take proactive steps to look beyond what they see open doors that aren't visible to the reactive eye. There are more than three sides to a triangle, and your Triangle of Life is complete when you learn about, understand, and utilize these other hidden sides.

A "▲" is, for all intents and purposes, three-sided. I mean, look at that triangle. It has three sides: left, right, and bottom. Unless you decide to dig a little deeper. If you pay attention to another dimension (that rhymed), you'll see the front side.

What some see, others might not acknowledge until it's pointed out. The front is easy to find if you just look for a little while. Now consider what few others ever notice without a nudge: the side hidden on the back. This makes the front and back the fourth and fifth sides of your Triangle of Life.

That's right; there are five sides to the Triangle of Life: left, right, bottom, front, and the ever-elusive back. These two sides, front and back, make a huge difference in your Triangle of Life. Alone, all sides are useless without the interaction of the left, right, and bottom sides working together with the front and back. Additionally, the back and front sides add greater value to your left, right, and bottom sides. As each side develops, they protect and strengthen the whole triangle.

Now it's time to explain what each side is.

CHAPTER 3.2
Triangle of Life

3.2 | THE SIDES OF A TRIANGLE

So what are these sides? Before we get into it, here's a quick overview of each side, and keep in mind that this is a series of five books. Each one allows me to dedicate entire books to a side of the Triangle of Life. For now, here are the quick reference names for each side:

- 3 Needs of Success—Relationships
- 3 Needs of Longevity—Business
- 3 Needs of Purpose—Financial
- The Assets of Life—Wealth
- Treat Your Life Like A Business—Philosophy

This book and the next will focus on all of the 3 Needs of Longevity. Showing you how to develop both a foundation of wealth and a plan of attack for your Career Business. Books three and four expand on the 3 Needs of Success and TAC: The Art of Conversation. They'll give you the tools to grow your Circle of Influence, be remembered, and develop yourself. Book five will tackle the 3 Needs of Purpose, Assets of Life, and Treating Your Life Like A Business.

This book touches on your 3 Needs of Longevity before the other sides of the Triangle of Life. The reason: you need to know how to generate longevity by first learning how to run your business. I lay out the triangle when I first sit down with a client to show them the big picture of what's to come. It's better to have the map laid out than to travel blindly into the unknown.

SIDE ONE: 3 NEEDS OF SUCCESS

The 3 Needs of Success are divided into three main Needs: networking, marketing, and practicing. This side is about establishing relationships. Each relationship you develop will help create opportunities for you and your Circle of Influence.

But, Thomas, what relationships are you talking about?

I'm talking about the relationships of who you know (networking), who knows you (marketing), and how well you know yourself (practicing). The majority of your efforts in your first full year will be dedicated to taking action on building each of these relationships.

Networking: You want to know people so you can explore who's right for your bus and potential candidates for your Circle of Influence. At the beginning of your Career Business, people won't know you, so you need to take action to get to know them first. People become friends with those who remember them first. Remember, networking is not about people calling you; it's about you calling them.

Marketing: People will form an impression of you based on your actions. Actions speak louder than words. The more aware you are of your brand's message, the easier it is to establish your brand's message among your Circle of Influence. You want people to remember you for your brand, not just because you're one of hundreds who does what you do—whether that's acting, writing, comedy, etc.

Practicing: The most important person in your life is you. Success depends on the relationship you develop with yourself. You have to be honest with who you are and what you're capable of doing. When it comes to who you are, you need to know your strengths and weaknesses so you can improve on yourself, learn more, and remind yourself how important you are in your Circle of Influence.

SIDE TWO: 3 NEEDS OF LONGEVITY

The 3 Needs of Longevity establish your foundation, giving you stability to take command of your business so you can organize it (management), find solutions (entrepreneurial brain), and add Value Sets to the tables you join (talent).

Longevity is having the power and freedom to say yes or no to opportunities that best align with your brand's mission. The stronger your 3 Needs of Longevity are, the more control you'll have over what you do or don't do to influence your Career Business forward.

Management: If you don't pay attention to the resources that fuel your opportunities, it can end up taking control over you. We have limited time that we trade for money at the request of people pulling us in multiple directions. The first step to taking back that control is managing your time, money, and the people around you.

Entrepreneurial Brain: A Business Brain knows this all too well: there are no walls, only solutions. They try to find those solutions by thinking outside the box in a proactive way. It's a superpower that sets them apart from Artist Brains. The shift from Artist Brain to Business Brian influences your longevity. It enlightens the potential to find a yes to any no that comes your way.

Talent: When you've put the work in and are called to the table—and it will happen—you'll need to prove you belong there. The truth is, if you get called up, you deserve to be there. But talent is more than just your craft and what you do. It's the Value Sets you bring with you that will benefit everyone involved and the missions of those tables you join. The secret is doing it without making it about you. Talent ultimately allows you to best lead, follow, and advise.

SIDE THREE: 3 NEEDS OF PURPOSE

Your 3 Needs of Purpose give you power over the financial aspect of your life and the Career Business you're growing. You can fuel your purpose when you know how to organize your money to protect you, invest in assets, and reward you.

It's one thing to earn money, but it's another to learn and then understand how to turn that money into a wealth-generating system. The goal is to establish these Needs to create a system where your money gives you the freedom to say yes because you want to, not because you have to pay a bill.

Security Account: This account protects you when all else fails. It's the money that sits in interest-bearing accounts, untouched, waiting in reserves. You should never touch this money unless something catastrophic happens, where all your capital is lost and your Career Business falls apart. This money is going to help you start over.

Growth Account: You need to invest in assets. Most people don't have that kind of extra money sitting around. Your Growth Account is that money. It's allocated to give you the option to do just that: invest. This account, along with the 60/40 Split Rule, gives you the means to invest. Investing leads to wealth. Wealth leads to options, choices, and freedom.

Dream Account: Everyone deserves a reward from time to time. And there'll come a day when you've saved up enough funds in your Dream Account, to reward yourself. When this money reaches a specific number, you've earned the right to have some fun. Don't waste your overhead money sitting in your Financial Foundation Account. Use your Dream Account to earn the reward.

SIDE FOUR: THE ASSETS OF LIFE

There are liabilities; then there are assets. Liabilities cost money to maintain and assets generate passive income to accumulate wealth. Passive income also gives you some control over your resources, as they work twenty-four hours a day and you don't or can't.

SIDE FIVE: TREAT YOUR LIFE LIKE A BUSINESS

This side is the glue that holds your Triangle of Life together. It's what keeps everything working. This side makes you think about The Process and rewards you by allowing you to do the enjoyable part, which is the thing you do. And remember, what you "do" is not your job. Your "job" rewards you financially to do the thing you do passionately. And that "job" is treating your life like a business.

CHAPTER 3.3
Triangle of Life

3.3 | A JOB VS A CAREER BUSINESS

The main difference between a job and a Career Business is that a job is there for you to pay your bills, while a Career Business is something you dedicate time and passion to. You need to be more than a job; you need to be making choices that influence your Career Business.

But, Thomas, work is work. Does it matter what job I take as long as I'm making money?

It does matter for the long game. Remember, everything you do must affect everything you do. When you take a gig just to cover your overhead, those gigs become jobs. A Career Business, on the other hand, is taking gigs to create and expand on opportunities in your field of interest for longevity.

What matters most is you shifting your mindset from Artist Brain to Business Brain. When an actor takes a gig to pay their bills, it becomes a job; when an actor takes a gig that allows them to get involved and network, market, and practice or to lead, follow, and advise, they're making Career Business moves.

But, Thomas, I don't understand the difference.

The difference comes down to the *why* of taking the gig in the first place. For a Business Brain, every gig should align in some way with your brand. It's less about the craft or simply saying yes to a gig just to do the thing you love to do or pay your bills; it's about making choices that lead to opportunities for your Career Business.

What I'm saying is that when you're in desperate need of money, you're saying yes to a gig because you have to, not because you want to. And that means you're taking the choice out of your own hands to *pay your bills*. You're now there for the money, not the opportunities.

Sure, not all acting gigs are going to be fun for you. And I know, I've played many gigs with my band, performed theater productions, got hired to ghostwrite scripts, and was asked to perform on comedy shows that were all not fun. But the purpose of a gig, especially at the beginning of your Career Business, is to make purposeful moves for the trajectory of your future. It's not about acting, doing comedy, or even writing. It's about taking advantage of your Financial Foundation Account to build upon your success so you have opportunities for longevity.

I'm trying to make the point that we, as career-driven individuals, should never be in a position where our choices are taken out of our hands because we need to pay rent on the first. This book, and the series itself, is all about the need for generating a Financial Foundation Account to support your first eighteen months of overhead. That capital gives you the freedom to make certain moves that benefit your Career Business.

THE REALITY OF THE LONG GAME

And you know what? Your choices might lead to small results, but all opportunities made with your brand in mind lead to much bigger payoffs down the road. That's right, every move you make is about the long game, not the short game. Even when you experience immediate results, you need to allow the residuals of that success to influence ten years from now.

One thing you should really try to learn and understand is that you are more than a job. It's not about getting work so you can act, play your guitar, tell jokes on a stage, etc. It's about getting involved, even as a runner where you fetch coffee, copies, etc.

Of course, the Artist Brain would happily take the time to get the next gig, practice for that gig, and perform on that gig at the expense of their overhead and time. Artist Brains want to perform.

But you have to be a Business Brain and look at gig opportunities that will influence your Career Business. Treating your life like a business is doing just that: making smart choices that allow you to build your Career Business. It's you fulfilling each side of your job responsibilities for your Triangle of Life. Because what you "do" is not your job. Your "job" rewards you financially to do the thing you do passionately.

But, Thomas, I want to do what I do passionately for a living.

I know that you want to live your dream of making a living in the entertainment industry doing what you do passionately—comedy, writing, music, acting—but the truth is, we never truly do what we do passionately for a living. I know, that sounds weird. So let me explain it directly.

HOW IT REALLY WORKS

If acting got you work, then you would only have to do monologues in the mirror, and people would knock on your door and cast you. If writing got you paid, sold your books, or got you hired to write scripts, all you would have to do is write and hide it in the closet until someone knocked on your door. If music got you signed to record labels, then all you would have to do is record albums and wait for them to come to you as soon as you finish recording.

In reality, you have to do the boring stuff. But it's the boring stuff that leads to success, longevity, and fueling your purpose. These are the things that will give you the opportunity to do what you do passionately.

You have to meet people (network), they have to like you (market), and you have to be capable (practice) when they call you to get involved. And the Triangle of Life gives you that option; it teaches you to find success, create longevity, and fuel your purpose by doing your actual job, which is putting time into the Needs of each side of that triangle.

I'm not saying don't put time into your craft. Keep doing what you do passionately. After all, you love doing what you do, so don't stop acting, comedy, writing, etc. What I'm saying for you to do is put your time into your job responsibilities instead of wasting time to reward yourself with a gig. There is a difference between putting time into getting a gig so you can "perform" your craft and putting time into your Triangle of Life to create opportunities for success and longevity.

But, Thomas, what's the difference? It seems all the same to me.

Take an actor, for example. If an actor is just acting to act, they're a hobbyist, right? We've explained that in earlier chapters. Now, take an actor who wants to act so they can make a living doing it. Well, this makes them a business first and a performer second.

As a company, this business would take steps to do what every other business does to succeed: expand, grow, and evolve. And since they're considered Actors, Inc. now, they should have a plan to expand. The next logical choice for Actors, Inc. depends on their needs.

A small step could be doing some coaching on the side, being available for readings, or helping people with self-tape auditions. A big step would be starting a production company.

You might do all three: acting, coaching, and producing. As a result, your production company is now able to produce any project that you work on for your Career Business. Or, even more logically, whenever you work on a project. You might be hired as an actor and/or an acting coach for the other performers. Those are services your business provides.

You are essentially getting two paychecks for thinking beyond what you do as a craft. Which in that example is only acting. But you do more than just act. More importantly, a production company brings in additional money even when you are not working on that project. You own the production company, helping to get other projects off the ground. This means you get paid for having the business because the business makes money.

In this situation, you can now act in one movie as an actor while your production company works on another project, making you a producer.

But, Thomas, that seems like a lot of work. I just want to focus on the thing I do passionately.

You have to think beyond what you do and think beyond the next job if you want to be successful. You have to be smarter than trying to get a gig and then another gig, and so on, and so on. Success is all about creating opportunities where you can take proactive steps to open doors for those opportunities. Not only for yourself, but for those around you. This is an example of being more than what you do.

This is how you get involved, create opportunities for yourself and others, and truly bring more value to the tables you join than just being great at acting, comedy, writing, or whatever you just do passionately.

If any of this sounds familiar, you can look at Brad Pitt, who is an actor himself and owns Plan B Entertainment, which is his production company. Another example is someone you've probably never heard of: George Lucas, who was originally an independent director. This is a man who eventually created an empire (no pun intended).

I'm not saying you or anyone else has to create an empire, but the road to success is about studying the paths of others and turning them into your own path through the forest. And George Lucas' path is an amazing one to study. It's about a person who got told no, so he built his yes.

When it came time to film Star Wars, Mr. Lucas created several businesses that all changed cinema. Industrial Light & Magic is known for its innovative visual effects, computer graphics, feature animation, and TV animation. This company has and continues to work with major studios. It's been involved with some of the most famous films in history, a majority of which George had no direct link to at the time. This particular business and others were a mixture of subsidiaries under the Lucasfilm brand, from Skywalker Sound to LucasArts.

Another illustration of diversifying your brand, assets, etc., is Walt Disney Studios, which owns all of these (at the time of this book).

This brings us to Walt Disney Studios. This empire did not start with all of its assets. Today, they own theme parks, major animation studios, toys, television stations, music, probably your soul, definitely your childhood, and more. This company began as an animation studio on the edge of failing, and yet they created a rat, which turned into a mouse, and the rest is history.

All great stories come with growth and change. I know you love acting, or possibly being a musician or director, a writer, or maybe you love the sound of laughter while doing standup. I get it, because I do too. I love performing, creating, and making my imagination a reality. But, at the end of the day, you must create diversity in your wealth, opportunities, and ability to make choices to grow an empire of possibilities just so you can have the freedom to do what you do passionately.

CHAPTER 3.4
Triangle of Life

3.4 | EVERYTHING YOU DO MUST...

Everything you do must affect everything you do. This way of thinking is the basis for running your life like a business. This brain change is all about getting the most out of your time, money, and the people around you. This is no small task, and it will take time for you to figure out what you need to do and what you want to do.

But, Thomas, isn't what I want to do the same as what I need to do?

Not necessarily. The real issue is when you waste time trying to get the most out of one specific thing—like only networking, marketing, or focusing on your craft. In reality, you should be trying to get a little out of each side of your Triangle of Life so everything elevates together.

The purpose of this approach is to allow many little things to influence the bigger picture. Sure, it's great to get a performance opportunity or finally publish your book as a personal victory. But how does this affect your larger goals as a Career Business?

This leads us to the "getting the most out of your first year" concept. Before you start that year, you should already have your Financial Foundation Account set up. Since that account supports you for the first 365 days, each day should influence the next day, week, month, and year. You don't have time to waste doing just one thing a day. Instead, several smaller aspects of many things will build up over time.

Does this mean you have to overload every little thing you do? Not at all. It means you have to look at the big picture first. Ask yourself: Is what I'm doing helping with my overall business plan? Will this one action influence other opportunities that affect my end goal?

Either of these questions is a useful guideline for moving forward.

But, Thomas, what would the answer even look like?

Here's an example plan and goal: "I have an idea to get a group of writers together to work on a project."

Now, break the idea down into sections of action based on the Triangle of Life to see how, or even if, this project can affect everything you do. As you'll notice, this example isn't about the "project" or the resulting "product." It's about the effect it has on your overall goals and plan to influence your Career Business.

IDEAS BROKEN DOWN INTO SECTIONS OF ACTION

Networking:

1. Bring people together, build & cultivate relationships to establish a strong Circle of Influence.
2. Create lasting relationships that help develop future opportunities for all those involved.
3. The end goal isn't to sell the product; it's about giving people a chance to work together so they can get to know and learn from one another.

Marketing:

1. Create opportunities to prove yourself through actions, Value Sets, skills, and real-time demonstrations of what you're capable of.
2. Use The Process to identify who excels at specific skills—head writer, joke person, idea person, etc.
3. Observe how people interact, add to, and elevate the group's mission and overall goals

Practicing:

1. Develop your writing skills.
2. Manage the people in your Circle of Influence.
3. Handle time and money management: purchasing food, renting space for writing sessions, and scheduling meetings.
4. Think outside the box to find solutions in a proactive way.

Management:

1. Manage time to conduct writing sessions efficiently.
2. Manage money within a budget by not overspending.
3. Select the right people while learning when to remove them, where to place them, and how they contribute.

Entrepreneurial Brain:

1. Develop solutions for managing your time, money, and the people involved to keep writing sessions productive.
2. Provide opportunities for people to showcase their talents, cultivate relationships, and prove their Value Sets.

Talent:

1. Actively bring people to the table to lead, follow, and advise.
2. Lead: take initiative by bringing people together.
3. Follow: open new collaborative doors with a growing team.
4. Advise: share writing knowledge with each other.

When it comes to your 3 Needs of Purpose and your Assets of Life, you won't be able to influence these sides in this particular situation. But you're still treating your life like a business by getting the most out of one action: writing together with others.

This goal isn't about getting every single side to work together at all times. It's about affecting everything the best you can, and it's a victory to influence six of the ten sides of your Triangle of Life. In this example, you're getting a lot out of one *thing*. This is what thinking outside the box in a proactive way looks like.

One more thing: you're able to see that simple things actually affect the bigger picture. Of course, when a person goes in with the goal of "getting something" out of it or thinking, "How's this going to help only me?" they're wasting their time. Leave selfish agendas at the door.

For example, "writing together with others" for the sole purpose of getting a script or novel out of it is a waste of time. Not only is there an agenda in the action, but you're doing nothing by focusing on the resulting "product" as the end goal. Great, you have the "product," but what about the people involved? No one wants to work with selfish people again.

But, Thomas, why?

When your goal is to get a book or script out of it, the end result is a *thing*. A thing ends at its creation. You can't even sell a thing on its own without doing the work to build a brand and network to establish potential sales avenues. Which means, now that you have a *thing*, you're going to have to dedicate time to selling it. Time away from growing your Career Business is always going to be a bad move.

This is why you put energy and effort into the six elements explained above. You'll get the most out of these elements by putting time and effort into them for your Career Business first. This means giving effort to networking, marketing, and practicing; paying attention to your management of time, money, and people; and finding solutions in a proactive way as you get the most out of your time to lead, follow, and advise.

The more time you put into these elements to establish relationships, build your brand, understand the industry, and so on, the greater the reward for your efforts will be. A reward that leads to opportunities to be paid to do the thing you love—acting, writing, comedy, and more. Putting time into selling a *thing* isn't worth the return for the bigger, longer picture of a Career Business.

CHAPTER 3.5
Triangle of Life

3.5 | YOU TIME

You time is as important as work time. When building a Career Business, your mind, body, and spirit (the energy to keep going) need to be recharged. I'll say it often: make sure your Financial Foundation Account can cover your overhead for anything and everything you need and want. Once you start, you're living on a budget. Smart money should be allocated for the fun stuff too. It's harder to reward yourself with leisure activities if you're broke or living on a tight budget. After all, all work and no play makes... Well, you know the rest.

When it comes down to it, you need to know your limits and prioritize your work. This is the key to your success, especially in those first 365 days. You're putting everything into making something happen during this time. But life/work balance is absolutely important too. And sure, even though you *should* be working a minimum of nine hours a day, seven days a week, you still need to make time for yourself after work.

So yes, you need to work. And not just a little, but a lot. I mean, like more than you would for a job job working for someone else. This is your Career Business that you're building. Every ounce of your sweat and tears is going into creating an empire that starts with baby steps.

If you don't take time off from work, you'll become overworked, overwhelmed, and overextended. Of course, if the opposite is true, where all you do is work a few hours here and there, and enjoy the fun stuff, you may end up falling into bad habits that will never reward you for your effort. So give yourself a strong habit-driven work week and reward yourself after hours so you can recharge your mind, body, and soul.

But, Thomas, is there such a thing as too much leisure?

If hanging out with your friends on a Friday night is fun, go for it. People come first. People always come first. They're the ones holding the keepers of the seven keys that open the doors to your future. Always give your time to others—unless they're the kind who drain you from the inside out. Your mental health and well-being always come before anyone else.

But, Thomas, you just said that people come first.

Yes. You are a *people*. In fact, you are the most important *people* in your life. Without you, nothing can happen. Not only can you not take the key from someone who is giving it to you, but if you don't exist, then you don't have the capability to do so. So yes, people come first, and you're the most important *people* in your life.

Just a heads up: if you're spending every Friday and Saturday night out with friends or hitting the town, you're probably not focusing on the big picture. Unless, of course, you're spending that time with people in your field of interest—because people come first, especially in your industry. Networking is all about being with others in your field of interest. And no, networking isn't just handing out a business card and moving on to another person. It's about genuinely giving your time to cultivate those relationships. There's a big difference between going out to drink and going out to connect with others.

The truth is, you're a grown up. You have to take responsibility for what you are willing to do, want to do, and have to do. And somewhere in there, you have to take accountability when it comes to how you spend your time, and when too much leisure time is too much.

Look, I like playing video games with my friends, but when the majority of my time has vanished, I need to take accountability for my actions and change things up. I can't keep beating them in Call of Duty all day and night. I mean, I could, and I can, and I have, but a strong indicator that these friends might not be right for my Circle of Influence comes in the form of their response. If they're upset with me for not playing video games every night all night, they might not have my best interests in mind.

No one should judge you for how you use your time except for you. You need to judge how you use your time, and often, if not harshly. Because you don't have a parent or a boss standing over you, and telling you when to go to bed. You know why? Because you're an adult now.

A good rule of thumb is that the more time you devote to your Career Business in the beginning, the more time you'll receive as a bonus on the other side of your results. When you start out, you have to make sacrifices that'll pay off after you've built your business, brand, and created financial stability with wealth.

CHAPTER 3.6
Triangle of Life

3.6 | FINAL THOUGHTS

You'll only get so far believing in yourself and having a deep passion for what you feel you desire. Time and action. That's the difference. You have to put time in and take action to achieve your goals. Your Triangle of Life is there as the literal outline of what to put your time into and how to take action to create real results.

This means that you have to take back control over your life by approaching your Triangle of Life correctly and letting your responsibilities guide you in treating your life like a business. A business that is about investing your time into relationships, managing and organizing your life, and controlling your finances. These things will create the freedom of choice.

Having the "choice" to say yes or no is what will change your life. The whole purpose of this book is to show you how to create the power to make those choices so you can have control over *things* instead of *things* controlling you.

I created the Triangle of Life to give people a framework for organizing their approach on how to achieve their dreams. Whether you're aiming for a career in the entertainment industry or just want more control over your life, the Triangle of Life has room for flexibility in the variables that come with your specific life and needs. Keep in mind, it's not about sticking to a bunch of strict rules. Like the pirate laws, they're more like guidelines.

Each side of the Triangle of Life focuses on key aspects of building a Career Business. But it's also designed to be flexible, so you can adjust it as you go—finding what works best for you. That's why you should use it as a tool for reference and guidance, and less "this way or the highway."

If you regularly compare your progress to where you want to be in your Career Business, you'll be able to make better, smarter choices. And if you're not happy with how things are playing out, take a moment to ask yourself:

"Am I using the sides of my Triangle of Life in a way that adds value to my actions so that everything I do affects everything I do?"

If the answer is no, then you might see why things aren't going your way. If the answer is yes, but you're still not where you want to be, it might be time to reevaluate and change how you're utilizing the sides. Always be ready to adjust when things aren't working. You never want to be that person who keeps doing the same thing expecting a different result. I assure you, the results will not change.

Remember, you have to network, but how you network is the variable that is up to you. You'll have to figure out what method works best for you through trial and error and by knowing yourself. Networking is about building and cultivating relationships to establish a strong Circle of Influence. If you feel you don't have that, ask yourself:

"Have I been regularly meeting new people and putting time into the relationships of these new people to build a strong Circle of Influence?"

If you have, then look at who's in your Circle of Influence, because you want to have people around you who influence stronger, smarter habits. You want to surround yourself with people who share similar goals and missions. And this includes the things that matter to you and your brand's messages that are compiled with your missions, morals, and purposes.

It's crucial to regularly analyze your Triangle of Life and compare it to your circumstances. When it comes to your Career Business, it's essential to be aware of what you're doing, how you're doing it, and what's coming from those actions. Part of your job is not just enjoying the results but ensuring that you're running your life like a business. You'll be surprised how often things slow down when you think you're in a groove.

The truth is, the success of your Career Business is in your hands. When it comes down to it, a well-analyzed Career Business gives you the ability to take calculated risks and take that leap with a prepared parachute. And guess what? You're allowed to fail—and fail often. The Process is about learning. No one is perfect at the beginning, middle, or even at the end of their career. You should always be learning.

Failing isn't losing. Failing doesn't make you any less valuable in this life. Failing is the secret to success, but only if you take accountability, reevaluate, and learn from it. The next level of your Career Business is the difference between not changing things up and being willing to try new things when something isn't working.

I've known plenty of people who insist on doing things their way, and even when it's not working, there's no other way but theirs. These are people who have to always be right. And I'll tell you—it can be amusing to watch someone run headfirst into a wall over and over, but it's also sad when the popcorn runs out.

You don't always need to be right every single time. But you do need to be willing to adjust and change things up when things are not working. Oddly enough, even when things are working, it's wise to mix things up from time to time. This keeps your Career Business growing, especially when it starts to plateau, even after years of success.

CHAPTER 4.1
Needs of Longevity

4.1 | THE 3 NEEDS OF LONGEVITY

Once you achieve success within your field of interest, maintaining it can be exciting! So why not begin with the 3 Needs of Success? The simple answer is that you need to be able to run the business side of your Career Business correctly before you can ever find success.

Besides, what's the point of success if you can't generate longevity? You don't want to put all that work into succeeding and then realize you don't know how to maintain it. Each side is important, and there are different rules for different sides of the Triangle of Life and different levels of your Career Business. So you have to have each side under control before jumping out of the plane.

The 3 Needs of Longevity are designed to give you the tools to organize and maintain your success. And it all starts with the foundation of how to run a business. See, a Career Business in the entertainment industry is no different than running a donut shop. And if you're going to open up a donut shop, wouldn't it be better if you knew how to handle the business side of running that shop?

This side of your triangle will teach you how to take back control over *things* instead of *things* controlling you. Being able to manage your resources, find solutions outside the box, and utilize your talents to best lead, follow, and advise the tables you join is the key to gaining control over *things*.

I'm sure you've heard that old cliché about celebrities and athletes alike losing everything. They get millions upon millions of dollars from a huge paycheck, and the next thing you know, they are broke. This can be attributed to many reasons that ultimately come down to mishandling any part of their 3 Needs of Longevity.

A common example is the mismanagement of money. Unorganized money will surely turn into spent capital that can't be reclaimed; this is when you buy big houses, maybe a castle or two, cars, and the next thing you know, you owe the I.R.S. for not paying your taxes.

To this day, the number of absurd tales of people who neglected to pay their taxes continues to astound me. An even worse situation is how the mind can play tricks on an Artist Brain's reality. It's when they believe there's more money coming in when the cash is not in hand. This leads to spending money before you have it.

You have to always take accountability for the results that come your way. Whether the consequences are good or bad, you're the one who will be responsible. You can't expect others to live up to their commitments, whether that's to pay what they agreed to pay, be where they agreed to be, etc. Expecting them to do anything is bad money, time, and people management.

It's bad business to rely on money coming in, having *enough* time, or people doing what you asked. So, when it comes to these things, like money, you can't live dollar by dollar. This way of life is going to get you caught in a recouping loop. Never rely on money that isn't in your hands as much as you can't rely on people who didn't do the thing they said they would do. This will become a prison that eats away at your freedom to do what you want to.

> *A good rule of thumb* is that you have zero dollars until the money is in the bank, and a promise isn't kept until a person makes good on it.

WE CAN LEARN A LOT FROM THE FRESH PRINCE OF BEL-AIR

Will Smith has an amazing story about his rise and fall at the beginning of his rap career. Of course, he tells it better than I could ever write it, so if you want to watch it, check it out on his YouTube channel and search for the video titled "How I Became the Fresh Prince of Bel-Air."

I'll paraphrase what happened. In the video, Will Smith said that he won triple Grammys for his hit single "Parents Just Don't Understand." That success led to him and DJ Jazzy Jeff earning massive paydays. From there, Will bought all kinds of big-ticket items, and with their newfound success and celebrity, the two felt unstoppable.

Then they released their second album. An album that did nothing but flop. Which meant no money for fun was coming in. That's the problem he hadn't accounted for: he thought an album equaled money, but when an album doesn't sell, you don't get paid.

Another problem hit when the IRS came calling for the money he owed. He had forgotten about paying his taxes. See, kids, you have to pay your taxes. What's interesting is that at this point, he was broke-broke, and yet, he was still a massive celebrity. He recalls riding on a bus next to someone and signing an autograph for him. The fan was happy, but all Will could think about was how he knew that the kid had more money than he did at that moment. All that fame and success and no money in his bank.

This is a classic example of not knowing how your business works before getting involved. Will Smith had no idea how money worked, but his Artist Brain motivated him to enjoy creating music and performing. After all, his art would make him money because, to him, it already had. And in his mind, he was a great musician, but, as we already know, being great isn't what brings a person success or money.

Ultimately, he didn't understand the value of being a business because he wasn't using his Business Brain, at least not enough to understand tax breaks, how to organize money, or how to generate wealth by investing in assets for passive income. In the end, his lack of knowledge cost him opportunities, peace of mind, and the chance to grow his business. Sure, he eventually became the Will Smith we know today, but only after starting over, being guided by mentors, and learning the industry.

But, Thomas, Will Smith starting over, and me starting over are not the same thing. He had celebrity, some money, and people helping him.

Ah, yes, well, let's look at that a bit closer and compare it to what we've been learning in this book.

Will Smith literally sold his stuff to pay for his taxes, so that money went straight to Uncle Sam. This left him with no money. Now we get to the learning part: Will Smith starting over meant he needed money and people, just like you said. His goal was to move away from Philadelphia to the West Coast. Sounds like a great idea: new people, new location, new life. But how did he get out there?

Will Smith had to borrow money to move and support himself (financial foundation). He could have worked a job, but instead, he asked a drug dealer friend for cash. That man gave him about $10k. sadly, that man passed away a short time later. I recommend reading Will Smith's autobiography. Amazing stuff.

Having that money allowed Will Smith to move out west and live with a friend (networking). He knew he wanted to try his hand at acting (business plan). To do this, he had to be proactive and start over (sacrifice) in a new place (entrepreneurial brain). This meant he didn't have the same pull as he had as a musician. Sure, he had a reputation, and people did want to help him (marketing), but he still needed to rebuild himself.

Now we know he didn't live on a responsible budget at home in West Philadelphia. However, after moving west, he lived on a small budget that allowed him to build and cultivate relationships that would eventually lead him to a little television show you might have heard of.

This is why the Artist Brain and Business Brain can't play together. An Artist Brain can have all the fun it wants during the creative process, but the Business Brain is what leads ideas to the summit. Give your Artist Brain the creative freedom, and let your Business Brain take on the responsibility of guiding your Career Business. As an aside, I'll say this: you should be wary of the *me perspective*, which can give the Artist Brain too much power. The me perspective makes an artist think of themselves, their talent, and what they'll get out of it first.

Will Smith relied on this method of thinking when he started, believing that his talent was the key to his success. And before learning about the business of his industry, his Artist Brain led to him mismanaging his money, his time, and the people in his Circle of Influence.

The greatest chance for success happens near the beginning of your career by being proactive and taking calculated risks that are afforded to you by having a Financial Foundation Account. When that success does hit, it's all about managing your responsibilities to maintain longevity for that success. Success can come out of nowhere, but there's still a process to longevity that takes effort.

And when you rely on talent, as Will Smith did, you can fall into holes of consequence. Such as when Will Smith believed he would have record sales coming in for his second album before he ever had cash in hand. He believed this because he'd done well with the first album, and his second album was going to hit big, or so he thought. Spoiler alert, it didn't. Though one could argue that he needed this failure to find himself in LA to become the big star he is today.

I'd push back and argue that it takes a Business Brain to accept failure and turn it into an opportunity. Remember, success doesn't come to those who passively wait; it takes a proactive individual willing to (a) make sacrifices and (b) find solutions by thinking outside the box.

No one is immune to this truth. It can happen to anyone if they're not careful and don't learn how to grow their Career Business. Not everyone is as lucky as Will Smith to have certain mentors around them who will slap reality across their face. And by reality, I mean that they assisted him in rebuilding his Career Business and advised him on what he needed to do to stay in the game. People literally gave Will Smith their time to teach him about managing his money, his time, and the people around him. They taught Will how to find solutions by being proactive with the "there's no better time than right now" mentality.

Case in point: when he was in a full room of people and Quincy Jones asked him to read the script for a little TV show that blew up. Yeah, his talent was there, but he wanted to *be perfect* and come back another time after going over the script. His Artist Brain guided him with his talent until Quincy told him that there's no better time than right now.

This pearl of wisdom pushed Will Smith to embrace his truth and lead, follow, and advise those around him when the time called for it. This new mindset had developed a stronger team for Will Smith, and over time, he was able to help the dreams of those around him.

DEFINING THE 3 NEEDS OF LONGEVITY

Before I break down what the 3 Needs of Longevity are, I need to define what longevity is in this book. I define longevity as having the ability to maintain and grow your resources to afford your average monthly overhead, create opportunities, and have the freedom to say yes or no within your field of interest.

As you take action in your Career Business, there will be clear signs that you have created longevity for yourself. Some of these signs will be having more freedom, opportunities, and the people around are willing to listen to what you have to say. Essentially, someone with longevity becomes the person who can make things happen by making things happen. When you can do this, people will want to be around you, have you around, or refer you to others.

Another sign of longevity is that moment when you realize people are coming to you as an authority in your field, and others are reaching out simply because you have the valuable resources of time, money, and people at your disposal. And thus, you have proof that you've created longevity for your success.

> *A fun side note* is that generating longevity in your Career Business happens when your overhead increase periodically, you're generating opportunities through proactiveness, and being called to tables without asking to join.

There is another form of proof that you're creating longevity in your Career Business. That proof is when you finally take action to expand your businesses beyond what you do creatively. I'll expand on this later, but for now, I want to get your mind thinking. Expanding beyond what you do creatively is when new businesses are created that give you the opportunity to do more than what you *do* and help you to ingrain your brand within your field of interest.

This is the George Lucas effect: He can write, direct, and produce the projects he wants after developing his production company and more. And his businesses were able to handle different elements of The Process. Furthermore, his companies worked with others while George got a chance to enjoy what he does passionately.

WHAT ARE THE 3 NEEDS OF LONGEVITY?

The Needs of Longevity are divided into three specific areas: management, entrepreneurial brain, and talent. Each Need has a specific responsibility for operating the business side of your Career Business.

To truly run your Career Business properly, you need to manage your time, money, and the people around. This is how you take back control over *things* instead of things controlling you. Time is limited, and you'll need to know how to manage your time, when to give it to others, and how to stay on schedule. What good are opportunities if you don't have the time or know how to stay on time?

This goes for money and people too. You need to be able to manage your money so it works for you, and you're not working for it. When it comes to people, you want to know how to manage the people in your life. This doesn't mean controlling them or ordering them around. Managing people in your life is more about how much time and money you give to them. It has to do with knowing when to cut people out and when to give people more of your time and money.

An entrepreneurial brain is the Need that leads to true longevity. Honing the skill to think beyond your problems is a huge resource to have. Especially when you're at the table with other people and their problems. Problems are not just about consequences, issues, and when things go wrong. Oh no, see, this Need not only runs your Career Business, but it fuels ideas and finds solutions by thinking outside the box in a proactive way. A strong entrepreneurial brain will never see a wall because there are no walls.

Talent is more than what makes you special. Yeah, there are the talents that you've honed by having a passion for what you do (craft), but talent is more than that. It's what you bring to the tables you join. It's the things you can do beyond the creative. It's how you solve problems, get investors, or maybe you're the guy who knows a guy. These talents are your Value Sets. And I assure you, Value Sets are what will get you called to the tables and keep you there. Your craft might occasionally get you to the tables, but what you bring to those tables to better lead, follow, and advise will get you called back.

The more established you are with your 3 Needs of Longevity, the more of an asset you'll become to any table you join or build. People want to work with others who have multiple Value Sets and can bring movement to the table.

If we look at the difference between being unknown and known, we get a pretty straight answer: the greatest unknown actor in the world at the beginning of their Career Business will not get a lot of work. The actor who gets the most work will always be the subpar, but known, actor in the middle of their Career Business.

This is the result of relationships, marketability, and knowing how their industry works by being involved. When a Career Business starts out, no one wants to work with people they don't know. If people do not know you, then they don't care about you.

Longevity is there because you worked hard to create a successful Career Business in your field of interest by being known, getting involved, and leaving an impression on others. The 3 Needs of Success are about relationships. Those Needs contribute to who you know, who knows you, and how well you know yourself. The more effort you put into relationships, the more doors will open as your Career Business develops.

See, people want to work with those they know, will get along with, and who can make things happen by making things happen. Longevity happens when people care about you. Once they care about you, they'll want you around.

Don't believe me? Do you hang out with strangers all day? Do you knock on random houses and ask to hang out with them? No. You reach out to people you know. And the more you know them, like them, or care about them, the more comfortable you are around them. And the more comfortable you are around them, the more you want to work with them. Especially when they are people who work within your field of interest. You know, like minded people.

CHAPTER 5.1
Time Management

5.1 | MANAGEMENT OF TIME

If time can control our limitations, then time management is the act of taking back control over those limitations. We allow time to take the lead in our lives when, in reality, we have the power to control how we use it. We create the illusion that the tasks before us become our *needs*. These *needs* propel our anxiety and trick our brain into believing that *things* need to get done. They tell us we have to finish every task jotted down on that evil little (or sometimes big) to-do list.

This way of thinking is what could lead to a circle of inaction pushing back against proactiveness. Essentially, we become so overwhelmed by what it would take to even finish something that we end up not starting at all.

> *A fun side note* about the reality of time and things. When we do *things*, this doesn't mean *things* are actually getting accomplished. In fact, doing a lot of things doesn't mean a lot of things are getting done. It's not about getting stuff done; it's about starting things and consistently working on them. As the saying goes, *"Don't work too hard, but be productive."*

Traditionally, time management has been The Process of organizing a schedule of tasks and sticking with it. What I want to present to you is something slightly different. I think of time management as having the power to say *no* to things and *yes* to yourself. Should we get things accomplished? Yes, but not at the cost of our time. Things get done. They really do, and no matter how much time we put into getting *things* done, they will eventually be completed. So why not try to have control over the time we put into things?

When I talk about time management, I picture it as having a loosely structured schedule that we are free to work around. Time management should be about controlling time so *things* don't control us. As you develop control over your time, you'll notice how you have more power to say *no* to *things* and *yes* to life. One of the secrets to this power is knowing that nothing will be set in stone except the ability to take charge of our needs and say no. Adaptation is the key to making time work for us instead of us working for it.

Now that I've presented the foundation of the mind shift and how I approach time management in this book, think about the following:

- Not everyone has the same to-do lists (it's all our own choices).
- 30 minutes per task will accomplish more than eight hours on one.
- People come first, things come second, and you're people too.
- Time isn't limited by what you can do; it's limited by how you use it.
- Our time is limited and unknown, so focus on today instead of tomorrow.

"Yesterday is history, tomorrow is a mystery, and today is a gift, that's why it is called the present." ~ Eleanor Roosevelt

CHAPTER 5.2
Time Management

5.2 | TIME AUDITING

First and foremost, you have to be aware of how much time you use for your personal, business, and survival jobs. Knowing what you're using between the three is going to give you a bit more control over the results you create.

Right now, I want to focus on your personal time and your survival job—the job you should be working to save up your Financial Foundation Account so you can begin your first 365 days to success.

We begin here because there's really only so much time in a day. When you're not working at your survival job, you have usable time to play with. That time can get away from you if you're not managing it. How you use that time will determine how prepared you'll be once you quit your job and start your Career Business.

Your first step is to block out all the time for your survival job. These hours are already dedicated to something specific: saving your startup capital.

The easy part is over. Now, your personal time. Ah, yes, the leisure of it all. You put so much time into your survival job over the past week, and now it's the weekend. You want to relax, maybe go to a movie, and hang out with friends. And you know what? You can do that. You've earned it. But…

Your personal leisure is going to cost you your business time. And it's your business time that increases your opportunities for your Career Business, specifically when you're starting out and what you do for your preparation.

Preparation is important because no one can magically have startup capital, quit their job, and step into their field of interest with tons of opportunities awaiting them. You have to set those up, and your startup capital is important for covering your overhead for the first 365 days. Sure, you have the extra six months in reserves, so eighteen months altogether. But…

That first year can fly by, and if you're using it to just *now* do the preparation you need to create opportunities, you're already failing. The time to start your preparation is before you start your Career Business.

But, Thomas, isn't relaxing and resting a great way to stay energized?

Absolutely! And this is why we have to manage our personal time and allocate the majority of it to business time.

But, Thomas, what would I even do for my business time that I couldn't do when I started my Career Business?

Before you quit your job and take one step into your new Career Business life, you need to prepare the foundation of your actual Career Business. This is where your Triangle of Life comes in.

Here's a question for you: How serious are you about your Career Business and making a living within your field of interest? Think about the question; let it settle inside of you. Are you happy kind of doing music on the side, or do you want to be a musician making a living with music? Do you kind of want to be a comedian, writer, actor, etc., or is this the dream you want to make a reality? If the answer is yes, then look at your business time through these lenses:

Your available time isn't about fun; it's about sacrificing for a greater future. And you have to embrace it as work time, dedicating yourself to preparing for your next steps into your Career Business, which you've wanted since forever. So use this time for things like relationships, developing your brand, and crossing the T's in your business plan. And, of course, this is the time to learn the industry of your interest.

TIME IS LIMITED

Mathematically speaking, time is limited. If there are 7 days a week at 24 hours a day, this leaves you with only 168 hours to play with every week. You should also figure out practical things, like the fact that you sleep eight hours a night, right? Sleep is important, which means you need sleep. Basically, I'm saying to you that sleep is important, so get those 8 hours of sleep—not five or six, but eight hours of much-needed sleep, totaling 56 hours a week, and totally worth it.

This leaves you with 112 hours in your week, besides the little things we all do, like some of us want to eat, shower (please shower), do bathroom stuff, and get dressed. Assuming you are average at doing these things, this will be another 2 hours a day all together. 14 more hours you lost, leaving only 98 hours to play with.

98 hours seems like a lot when it's in a lump like that. Wait, you're working 40 hours a week at your survival job at this point. We have to subtract that from the remaining total, which leaves you with 58 hours.

But, Thomas, what about dinner?

You didn't eat on your break at work? Okay, add another hour for driving to and from work and another hour for din din each day. 37 hours remain. That leaves you with just around 5 hours a day for personal time. Or…

It's five hours a day for you to dedicate to your business time so you can handle your Career Business responsibilities. Even if you go out on Friday nights, you're still left with 32 hours, or six days of five hours each. This is a good amount of time to play with.

In reality, once you quit your survival job and step in the direction of your new Career Business, you'll want to work a 40-hour work week. The mental shift is now that those hours are for your personal Career Business.

With that said, in this situation, you should still be working to save up your startup capital and allow yourself five hours a day, six days a week, to get your business foundation in place.

A good rule of thumb is that you should never trade your time at the expense of your mind, body, and soul. You need to be alive to enjoy living. There you have it; please get your sleep, work on your responsibilities, and give yourself personal time to go to that movie and hang out with your friend.

CHAPTER 5.3
Time Management

5.3 | BUDGET YOUR TIME

You can begin working on your time budget once you've completed the time audit of your three areas of activity: personal leisure, survival job, and business. You'll want to budget your time so you can get the most out of your days between all three of these activities. As you budget your time, you'll reinforce how in control you can be of your time, especially when you realize the power of saying no to things.

You'll need to prioritize your time to best effect what tasks are most important to you and your future. Prioritizing what's important to you is not code for being rude to people, ignoring others, or choosing what responsibilities you like the most. But you do have the power to rearrange the life you want, from the people you spend time with to the jobs you agree to and the boundaries you're absolutely allowed to set.

There will come a time when you're giving too much to people and to the jobs you agreed to, and those boundaries will be pushed back further and further. These pushbacks will potentially turn productive days into moments when nothing gets done or worse, even get started.

But, Thomas, you said people come first.

Yes, yes, I did. I also said you are people. Your mind, body, and soul are more important than anything else. People come first, but never at the cost of depleting your resources, internally and externally. This leads to the "there is never enough time" anxieties.

When you're being overwhelmed by those anxieties, you'll have to sit back, reevaluate, and budget your time properly. In reality, there is only so much time to spend. As we talked about in the last chapter, you need to be in control of how you use your time.

And yes, I'll be the first to tell you that people do come first, so network and build those relationships. But you still need to say no when you've said yes to far too many people or things.

But, Thomas, how do I make it all work and figure out who to say yes to and who to say no to?

Always say yes to you. This rule allows you to find solutions to all your problems. And trust me, there are solutions to every problem in life. This is why you should exercise your entrepreneurial brain; because a strong entrepreneurial brain focuses on finding solutions by thinking outside the box in a proactive way. When you find solutions, you find ways to make things happen by making things happen.

Some of your solutions will be defined by those you say yes to. By how much they influence the same missions or behave with similar morals. See, the reality of your success is based on those you surround yourself with. When you give time to people who are so far outside of your missions, morals, and purposes, it'll cost you your potential.

Does this mean to use people? No, not at all. It means that with limited time, get involved with people of similar mindsets. Not an echo chamber, but people who believe in similar things.

I believe in people helping one another, but I won't work with people who help others for their own gain. There is a fine line between what we believe in and what others believe in. Sure, they're helping other people, but with the expectation of gaining from it. To me, that doesn't fit my morals. So I say no to those people.

A WEEK OF WORK

Time to figure out what matters most to you and your Career Business. As an aside, we're basing this on you having your weeks freed up. Considering that by this time, you finally quit your survival jobs and are now able to put everything into your Career Business. Additionally, you should have your overhead covered with your startup capital, and you're ready to take action. Which means you need to know how much time you'll dedicate to your career during each week.

But, Thomas, what if I get an opportunity to work in my field when I start my Career Business because I had built relationships before taking action?

That would be amazing. And that means while you're at work, you need to continue to utilize the sides of your Triangle of Life and absolutely network, market, and practice in and around your job within the industry of your choice. However, when you're not working at that job, you'll still need to put time into your Career Business. Remember, that job within your field of interest isn't the end goal.

Whether you're working a job and only have thirty minutes to play with at the end of the day or you don't have a job and you have eight hours, put time into your Career Business.

For this specific example, base my notes on having eight hours a day, seven days a week, to dedicate to your Career Business. This is a time when you'll need to be productive for eight hours minimum. I personally work ten to twelve hours a day, but I'm also crazy. So gift yourself an eight-hour workday when it comes to your Career Business—unless you can handle more.

Whatever you organize into your work week, make sure that you're always working on your Career Business tasks associated with your Triangle of Life. The secret is to do a little for a lot of things each day, but never only focus your full efforts on one thing. That becomes the trap.

You need to give each side of your Triangle of Life some time, even a little, here and there, by spreading out your efforts across your work days. You can do this in many different ways, one being that you give each task or responsibility a set amount of time, or you break things up into goals.

Personally, I like to organize my tasks into boxes—which we'll get more into in another chapter. For now, know that your goal is not to work on one single thing for the whole day, week, month, or year. A little every day leads to a lot throughout the year. Besides, if you're giving a little time to everything, you're going to get more accomplished in the long run.

And your craft has nothing to do with your business. If you believe that becoming the greatest actor, comedian, writer, director, musician, etc., is going to get you to the top of the mountain, you're forgetting everything you've read up to this point. Skill might get you noticed. Talent might keep you in the game a little longer. But when it comes down to it, if people don't see you, remember you, or know that you know what you're doing beyond your craft, it will all last for that amazing fifteen minutes of fame.

People hire talent, but they work with capable people that bring more to the table than "I can write the greatest script ever!" So don't put your Career Business responsibilities off to the side so you can work on your craft. When you're free and living off your startup capital, think of your time like this: personal, business, and craft (craft has replaced the time you put into your survival jobs).

Let's be honest for a moment: if you're having trouble finding the time to put into your Career Business, this is less of a "there is no time" and more of an "I don't feel like it right now." We all find ways to practice our craft for a few minutes here and there. You don't believe me? In school, did you draw in books while the teacher taught or work on your assignment? How often did you forget to eat because you were practicing an instrument?

My point is, we all make time for the things we want to do. Time management is about making time for the things we don't want to do so we can earn the right to do the things we love doing. In time, your effort will lead you to put more time into your craft and be rewarded to do what it is you love to do. But right now, you have to put time into establishing your Career Business so people see the value in you and what you bring to the tables to best lead, follow, and advise.

CHAPTER 5.4
Time Management

5.4 | 40-HOUR WORK WEEK

Giving anything less than forty hours a week toward your Career Business is irresponsible. With the effort and sacrifice it took to get to this point, it would be an insult to yourself to not take it seriously. And taking it seriously doesn't mean you *feel* or *believe* you're taking it seriously. There are clear indicators when and where your efforts are showing real results. And those results are proof that you've been taking all of this seriously.

But, Thomas, what I feel is true.

True. No one can tell you that you don't *feel* serious about what you're doing. I get it, but your actions *will* determine if you're taking it seriously. Actions outweigh our feelings. I can feel motivated and, deep inside, believe that I want to make things happen, but what am I physically doing to make it happen?

What I'm saying is that you need to connect your feelings to your actions, which should lead to calculable results. Because this is the time to take accountability and responsibility for what you want in life. You must remember that you are the boss who tells you when you're messing things up or doing a great job. And since you're viewing your progress through a biased lens you'll have to know the difference between sitting in your feelings of accomplishment and actually taking action that shows real results.

> ***A good rule of thumb*** is to have your business plan and Triangle of Life guide you. You have to physically put effort into two things: achieving your 1, 3, 5, 7, and 10 year business goals, and putting real effort into your Triangle of Life. Only then will you see real, well-earned results.

LIFE IS A LEARNING CURVE

Effort leads to results; good or bad, the goal is to motivate yourself to take action. Whether the results lead to success or failure, any result is positive. The reason for this is that failure can lead to learning, adjusting, and adapting to do better next time. Especially when learning or doing a new thing.

And don't worry if you fail. Life has a learning curve, and trust me, that's okay. Since, honestly, most successful people have stood on a massive mountain of failure over the course of their journey to success. And when it comes to your success, you're the only one holding you back or driving you forward. So how you react to your successes and failures will determine a great deal about the consequences of your response. Are you someone who will learn or someone who will keep doing the same thing expecting different results?

It is your responsibility to give your Career Business the attention it needs. And to gain your intended results, there are certain things you'll have to do. But, remember, you have to make things happen by making things happen—this includes changing things up when things are not happening.

This is not the time to fall back on old habits or to allow the "I can't be wrong" mentality or selfish intentions to lead you down the road of intelligent choices. Just because you now have the money in the bank and the freedom to do what you want doesn't give you the freedom to waste opportunities away. Getting to this point, where you have money in the bank covering your overhead, was no doubt a challenge. Now challenge yourself to be responsible for the next steps you take.

All I'm saying is that you need to be prepared to be wrong, listen to others, and know that you don't know everything. More importantly, you don't know everything about the industry you're walking into. Sure, if you're a musician, you know music is involved. But do you know the inner workings of a record label, from the interns to legal? Maybe you're an actor who studied Meisner, but do you truly know what goes into casting, directing, or payroll?

But, Thomas, why would I have to know anything outside my craft?

Knowledge is power. That's first. The second is that the more you know, the more opportunities you can create. Just knowing the casting process would change your approach to trying to get cast in a project. Knowing how a record label works will change your approach. The system of how things operate is another way to get the most out of your actions.

And honestly, right now, that's neither here nor there, because what you should be getting out of this is that you're always going to be learning while building your Career Business. And if you rely solely on what you believe is the right way and refuse to ask questions or try new things, especially when someone more versed in the field educates you, then you're destroying the results of your opportunities.

CLEAR INDICATORS OF RESULTS

This is the step you've been waiting for—that chance to prove you belong here. This is where you get a chance to take a calculated risk and leap into the entertainment industry. Your dream of being here is now a reality. To make this reality a lifelong truth, you have to give it forty hours a week. That's forty hours a week dedicated to your Career Business, without question. And the reward for giving your Career Business forty hours a week will pay a massive ROI as your value becomes bullish in your industry.

And each return on your investments should have specific indicators that your results are moving you in the right direction.

If you look at your Triangle of Life, each side represents something specific, from relationships to organizing your business and even investing. Before you can take any results as a true sign of your success, you must understand your business goals and your responsibilities pertaining to your Career Business.

You can set your business goals to whatever you want, although my advice is to link them to the Needs of your Triangle of Life. For example, your 3 Needs of Success consist of networking, marketing, and practicing. Look at the definitions of each and allow that to guide you. For now, we'll examine networking.

Networking is building and cultivating relationships to establish a strong Circle of Influence. A Circle of Influence is not there to influence your Career Business but to influence stronger, better habits.

Now that we can see the definition of networking, let's break it down into business goals we can physically compare ourselves to as we take action.

Building means to meet new people and add them to your Circle of Influence. Connecting this to your business goals, you might want to meet three new people a week. How you do this is up to you. You can interact on social media, go to events, spend time around the community of your industry, etc.

Cultivating means to put time into the people you know within your Circle of Influence. How many people are you keeping in touch with each week? Are you spending time with them, elevating them, or doing what you can to help them? You might have three people a week set as your business goals.

I can continue to do this for each Need of your Triangle of Life, but the point of this is to show you how to connect things and create a line of action. If you need to meet three new people a week and interact with three people you're already established with, you have a baseline.

Are you meeting three new people a week or interacting with established people? If the answer is yes, then you're taking your Career Business seriously. If the answer is no, then you just have a business plan and a dream sitting around in your head, *feeling* like you're taking things seriously.

Ultimately, what are the results of your actions? Are the people you're putting time into asking you to hang out with them, work with them, or refer you to others? If the answer is yes, then you're again showing results to your actions and taking your Career Business seriously.

Your clear indicators will come when you have goals mapped out, take action to achieve those goals, and are seeing a return on putting time into your Career Business, Triangle of Life, and your business goals.

A fun side note is that opportunities will come when you get involved, are remembered by others, and know what you're doing. You never want to just be someone who is awesome, amazing, and unique at your craft (others are just as great). Get involved beyond *only* your craft, and you'll establish a reputation, your brand, and the Value Sets to develop movement and influence.

CHAPTER 5.5
Time Management

5.5 | TIME BLOCKS

I've already gone over how you need to work a forty hour week. Every hour will help you succeed once you begin your Career Business journey. To get the most out of those forty hours, you'll need to manage your time efficiently. Time blocks are a tool that has helped me organize my time the most.

Generally speaking, time blocks are nothing new. You might have heard of them or use them yourself. Whether you're familiar or not, this chapter will go over how I utilize time blocks to get the most out of my business time.

With that said, these are my specific methods that have served me well over the years. Do you have to use these time blocks? No, not really. Could they be helpful? Yes, yes, they could be. For now, let this chapter be a guide to help you best use time blocks. And even if you have a method that works best for you, it's always nice to have alternative options.

WHAT'S SO SPECIAL ABOUT TIME BLOCKS

Time blocks have a malleable quality to them, making them easy to adjust as needed, as they are a system for managing time, not a set of rules to restrain you.

The only aspects of time blocks that adhere to a structured process are their rules. These rules give time blocks a sense of purpose so you can develop influential habits for other aspects of your Career Business. And what makes time blocks useful is how they give you structure. Their true strength is in how they bring focus to your day and the tasks within that day.

The time block rules were created to give a person control over time instead of time controlling them. When a person has difficulty saying no to things, time blocks give back that control when used correctly.

> *A good rule of thumb* is to always say *yes* to life and *no* to things. Nothing will ever have more value than your time. Remember this precious truth: You're not just another person running around *having* to do things because you *feel* you must. *Things* are simply nothing more than choices we place weight on, when the real weight should be on ourselves and what we want to do the most.

THE TYPES OF TIME BLOCKS

Each time block has a particular quality relative to the sides of your Triangle of Life. Does this mean you can't add new qualities to time blocks? No. These are qualities that have helped me organize my work hours to get the most out of my Career Business. Figure out what's important to you and designate specific time blocks for each of your needs. As you read through what works for me, you'll get a better understanding of what you might have to adjust for yourself.

Before going deeper, here's an example: I had a dog. This meant that alongside my traditional Triangle of Life time blocks, I needed an additional time block for my dog. This time block was specific to my life and needs. The pupper needed to go for walks, play time, snuggles (let's face it, we all need them), and I had to feed the whittle furbaby. Sorry, where was I? Oh, yes. When scheduling my work days, I made sure to include time blocks for my dog.

Keep that in mind with your time blocks and schedule. Your life will delegate what and how your time blocks should be scheduled based on your needs. In the end, you will always have control over what goes into your time blocks, what they are dedicated to, and where they go in your schedule.

With that said, here is a breakdown of the essential time blocks that I use that are associated with the Triangle of Life.

BRAINSTORMING TIME BLOCKS

Without fail, I begin and end my days with a brainstorming time block. First and foremost, there are benefits to brainstorming that get the brain active and thinking. Secondly, by getting my brain thinking, I allow myself to truly wake up before tackling any tasks. There's nothing off the table during my brainstorming time blocks. Sometimes I give it direction, but most often I begin with a blank slate to see where it goes.

For me, I'll think about how to get the most out of my day and what I need to accomplish that specific day within other time blocks. For example, I might add and subtract items from my to-do list to figure out my workday. Additionally, I might look ahead and set up my work week or work months to get an idea of what is coming.

This time block is never about physically taking action on a task. Brainstorming should always be dedicated to brainstorming. To me, it's all about setting up my schedule, tasks, and the microtasks that are specific to each time block.

> *A fun side note* is that you should start and end your day with a brainstorming time block. The benefit to brainstorming at the end of any workday is that at the start of the day it wakes the brain up and at the end of the day cools it down. It gives you a chance to ease your mind and see what you did or didn't get to.

NETWORKING TIME BLOCKS

Since networking is all about "who you know," it's my responsibility to schedule time specifically for it. This is where I can put real time into building and cultivating relationships.

Mentors taught me early on that friends love to work with friends; I realized how right they were as I grew my Career Business within my industry of interest. And since I'm always working to strengthen my Circle of Influence, I need to dedicate time to these people. Over the course of time, my Circle of Influence will weaken if I neglect, ignore, or rarely put myself out there for others to see me.

A networking time block literally gives me a chunk of time to reach out to my friends, family, and associates. Giving people your time is the secret to building and cultivating relationships. People love getting attention from others, and when it's filled with pure, authentic interest, it grows a relationship.

Believe it or not, if you want to be on the radar of specific people, you actually have to put yourself out there. Your job is to put in the effort.

But, Thomas, I don't see other people going out of their way to put themselves in front of the right people.

Well, see, the thing is this: people want to succeed, but they're going to break the rules. And you have to remember that they can break the rules, but you can't. If they don't want to make new friends, that's okay. But you *need* to make new friends. Friends lead to opportunities.

This is why I have a minimum of two networking time blocks a week, and at most three. One networking time block is placed at the beginning of my day and the other for after lunch. The first part of my morning is dedicated to me sending emails, texts, or calls to say good morning, follow up, maybe set up meetings, etc. My afternoon time block is when I try to connect people I know to other people I know.

I might even use my networking time block to research, organize, and clean up my Circle of Influence file. If I recently met someone, I'll do research during this time, jot notes down about them into my phone, and see what they have going on. When I have enough information, it gives me an idea of how I can get involved, help them out, or who I know who could be introduced to them where they can benefit from each other.

The more attention I can give my Circle of Influence, the better organized my strategy can be. Overall, my networking time blocks are going to be for me to keep in touch with people, introduce people to others, and figure out where and when I can help others.

Keep in mind that hanging out in person does not count as a task. Networking time blocks are dedicated to in-office tasks for relationship development. In-person interactions are not considered office hours. However, you'll learn throughout this series that when you hang out with people, these interactions have their own set of rules.

Besides that, keep your networking time blocks for proactive tasks that help you build and cultivate relationships, organize your Circle of Influence, and figure out ways to add your Value Sets to the tables you join.

MARKETING TIME BLOCKS

What is your brand? You need to know that, and a marketing time block is a great time to spend on figuring that out. When I'm working on a new venture or even adjusting my older ones, I need to know what my brand stands for, represents, and how to present it authentically.

With that said, my marketing time block is there to analyze what I'm doing and not doing to represent my brand and how to get involved to properly present my brand physically.

And when it comes to that, it's all about getting more involved. Which means I need to figure out how I can get involved with others (or organizations) who have something in common with my brand's missions, morals, and purposes.

Additionally, I schedule my social media posts for the week, the month, and sometimes the quarter. These social media posts could end up being brand or adventure posts. I want my social presence to be an accurate representation of me and my goals.

This list is small compared to what is possible. For you and your brand, I'd allow the actions to benefit your course of action and what you feel comfortable doing. You'll have to figure out what works for you and how it best represents your brand's message.

PRACTICE TIME BLOCKS

Practice time blocks might seem like the perfect time to work on your craft, write a song, or practice drawing eyes. Those damn eyes are so hard to draw—wait, or is it hands? I know, how about eyes on a person's hands? That's where the real challenge lies. Anyway, my point is that practice time blocks are not for craft. Working on one's craft will always be something you do after workday hours.

These practice time blocks are where I would personally check in on myself. I take inventory of my current position, my strengths and weaknesses, and what has and has not been working for me lately. I list out my strengths and weaknesses, check through it, and see where I need to improve or how I'm doing in general.

Items on that list would include my knowledge of the industry. If I don't know how the industry works, that's a weakness and something I need to work on. Whether it's systems within my industry of choice or adjacent industries, I need to know and learn these things. For me, there's always going to be information I could discover, might feel I know (but don't understand), need to know, kind of know, or wish I could know and be better at. A dedicated time block for figuring out how it all comes together is a benefit that pays off in the long run.

What I end up learning about myself during this practice time block gives me insight into where and when I can get involved. This is how I discover what I'm capable of doing, so when I join certain tables, my addition will both benefit my involvement and the table's missions.

The more I know about myself, the more confident I'll feel in saying yes or no to opportunities. When I organize my strengths and weaknesses, it gives me a chance to visualize my skill level and any Value Sets I bring to the table. From there, I know who and how I could get involved.

> *A fun side note* is that to me, this is not a chance for me to say, "Hey, I act, so let me call my friend, who I haven't spoken with in a long while, and see if I can be the lead in their new film that they mentioned on social media." Never do that. For me, it's a chance to see how I can help the missions of others and how I can elevate their tables with my involvement.

TIME MANAGEMENT TIME BLOCKS

But, Thomas, time management time blocks are the same as brainstorming.

I can understand why you'd think that. However, brainstorming is about jotting down brief ideas, goals, and to-dos. Time management, on the other hand, is about planning, organizing actions, and breaking down SMART goals into smaller, actionable tasks.

I often tell people, "Don't work too hard, but be productive." And that's why the whole point of time management is to find ways to work smarter, not harder. You want to be productive by doing a little at a time so that a lot can be accomplished over a specific amount of time.

Additionally, I use this time to think about what The Process of something is. Every result has a process. And I think about The Process, the steps needed to achieve my end results. Each step is a smaller objective I need to put time into. Once I know those steps within The Process, I lay them out and organize them into other time blocks and my work schedule.

MONEY MANAGEMENT TIME BLOCKS

Money management time blocks allow me to see where and what I've earned and spent against my budget. It's important that I stay within my budget to keep from falling into debt. What good is a budget if I'm not keeping track of what I am or am not spending?

Dedicating time to this part of my Triangle of Life gives me a chance to keep up with my spending habits against what I'm earning. Sure, earning an income is great, but spending money faster than it's earned is not. It's my job, as much as it is your job, to be aware of the budget. This is a great way of holding myself accountable.

I'd use this time to adjust my budget as needed too. My initial figures might not be holding up, or I may have miscalculated. It's okay to get things wrong as long as you don't take them personally. Change things up when it's not working out. There will come a time when I'll have to clean up my budget; it happens. This is where I would adjust caps, subtract or add caps, columns, or other elements to my budget.

When I look at those things, it gives me a chance to pay attention to how my money is moving around or standing still. I can zero in on things without them coming out of nowhere. Yes, I can make sure I'm not coming close to my financial cap, but I can also see where my money is going, pay my bills on time, or place money into one of my 3 Needs of Purpose to develop wealth.

Once it's placed into my 3 Needs of Purpose accounts, I need to know how it's being spent, allocated, or generally utilized. The big looksee is to make sure my investments are yielding a return. Ultimately, this time block is here to figure out what my money is doing or could be doing, and, of course, how to get the most out of it.

The rule about money management is not "I have money," but "how I'm organizing that money to work for me." Lots of people have some form of money, but fewer people have a crap ton of cash in their banks. Having money and being in control of your money are not the same thing.

I've seen people with almost no money afford their lives better than those who earn six figures a year but end up with almost zero dollars to their name at the end of each week, month, or year. It's a matter of controlling how you use money, save it, and invest it. Because your job is to determine how to transform it from bill-paying currency into wealth-generating passive income.

> *A good rule of thumb* is that auto payments should be given attention too. When money leaves an account, it is better to make sure the amount is as recorded, has come out, or will come out. Set alert dates on your calendar for each month to keep an eye on your bills.

PEOPLE MANAGEMENT TIME BLOCKS

I use this specific time block to determine *who* is in my Circle of Influence and *how* we affect each other. We never want to take time away from people as much as we don't want our time to be wasted. One thing I look for in a person is to see if they have an Artist Brain mentality. And trust me, they're everywhere in the entertainment industry. As a quick aside, it's okay to have a few Artist Brain people around you. However, it's never productive to let them join the tables you create or lead the tables you join.

I want to be around people who possess particular qualities. And these qualities should be standards I personally live up to as well. If I want people to be honest with me, I have to be honest with them. And since I know some people lean more toward the Artist Brain mentality than the Business Brain, I don't want to isolate everyone. However, if I find myself surrounded by people who live and die by the Artist Brain, I might want to make sure we have similar qualities at minimum.

This is where I pay attention to my Circle of Influence to see if our personalities have been working well together or clashing. This is how you take inventory of yourself and the relationships you invested in.

There is no reason to move forward in a relationship if they're using you as a stepping stone. I'm a we perspective person who loves groups, teams, and working together. Rarely can I see myself in a group filled with those who survive on the me perspective, fueling their personal needs to achieve goals of validation or achieve a result.

Since I know what my missions, morals, and purposes are, I use those truths to see where and how I connect with people in my life. When it turns out that the majority of our beliefs don't line up, I know it's time to manage who I'm spending time with.

If my plan is to elevate the mission of a table I joined by adding value to XYZ, I want to know others care a bit about that. If I'm at a table with people mostly interested in "leaving their legacy," "being the best," or their desire is to "make money performing," then I know we don't align.

And again, these missions for them are all fine, but you want to work with people who are on the same page. Do all people have to be on the same page completely? No. But the majority of all involved at the table should be at least on the same page.

But, Thomas, what if I want a specific *thing* that they themselves don't desire?

Individuals can want anything that drives them. It's their approach that defines them. Wanting to win an Oscar doesn't mean they are going to use you to get their Oscar. When I try to figure out who's right for my bus, I use my list of qualities, my brand, and any Value Sets to organize people in my Circle of Influence.

Keep in mind that a good person can still be selfish and not realize it. Our minds don't always know why we're doing what we do, but our behavior and the habits driving those behaviors control our instincts. Think of your morning routine. Do you really put a lot of thought into your morning process or how you shower?

When I sit down to work on my people management time block, I want to think about who they are, what they have been doing, and how I feel about them. Always take inventory of both them and yourself and how you feel about the relationship.

Once I know who they are and have put some thought into them, I like to figure out how much time I've been putting into them. Because, on average,

I might only get seventy summers in my lifetime! And that's okay for me. But think about that for a moment. We find ourselves enjoying certain people around us: people who make us laugh, smile, think, and challenge us at times. And you know what? It's amazing to be around people who stir up these feelings.

Sure, these might be the people for you in the long run, or they might not be. It's not just how people make us feel that's important to our Circle of Influence. It must have a purpose. That purpose is to influence better and stronger habits that motivate, inspire, and give us a chance to do the same for them.

If you have a best friend who makes you laugh but is not in the same industry as you, has almost nothing really happening in their life, and is completely unmotivated, they might not be right for your Career Business and Circle of Influence. This individual is ideal for your personal time but not during your Career Business time. What you do in your personal time has nothing to do with your Career Business time.

> *A good rule of thumb* is to invest your limited time in the people who truly add value to you and those around you. People who have great habits and can motivate you, inspire you, and elevate you simply by watching them be themselves are a beautiful gift and return on your time. Be that for others, and you'll see a Circle of Influence flourish.

ENTREPRENEURIAL BRAIN TIME BLOCKS

An entrepreneurial brain finds solutions by thinking outside the box in a proactive way. And there are always two ways of approaching a situation: I can't and I can. When something seems impossible, the entrepreneurial brain finds ways to make it possible, even if the first thousand attempts fail.

Use the entrepreneurial brain time block as an opportunity to do just that: find solutions by thinking outside the box in a proactive way.

If I'm having trouble networking, I use this time block to specifically brainstorm and research ways to improve myself. If I have certain goals I'd like to accomplish with networking but I'm not achieving them, it's time to find new ways to approach them.

This is not a to-do list or SMART goal list. This is the time block for me to specifically put time into finding solutions. So, here is an example of how I might find solutions for networking during this time block.

I want to meet three new people a month. I also want to put them on a rotating list of 10 people to grow a relationship with. The thing is, I can't find the time to get the most out of my relationships. This lack of time also affects my ability to meet new people.

My brain finds the first solution: figure out how to make it possible for me to hang out with ten people a month. Also, everything I do must affect everything I do. And since my mission is to bring people together so we can work, grow, and rise together, I need to fit that in as well. And right there, my brand's mission gave me an idea to help me find a solution, since my mission should be represented in my actions.

I could hold networking events once a month. Wait a minute, a networking event makes it possible for me to do several different things. This event would allow me to hang out with the same ten people each month. The first goal is completed, but I can also bring in new people to the events. This is my second goal. By having new people come in and meet my already established friends, I'm accomplishing a third thing: my friends can build relationships with the new people who show up. A fourth solution is in the return I get for my brand as it's represented through my actions: bringing people together to work, grow, and rise together. A fifth solution is that I've opened up more time for myself.

I usually have one or maybe two entrepreneurial brain time blocks available each month. If I find myself falling behind or my goals are not being met, I'll increase this to once a week. You should use these more at the beginning of your journey and less as you find your groove.

If you end up finding yourself needing to use more of these time blocks per week, it doesn't devalue your worth. Being amazing, awesome, and unique at something takes time, mistakes, and practice. You'll find your groove, and over time, you might slip or become too comfortable with what you're doing. This could lead to a slow plateau or a failure to notice things have changed or not changed.

Overall, be good to yourself even when you fear you're appearing weak in one way or another. Accountability is the key to finding solutions by not taking failure, adjustments, change, or being wrong too personally.

TALENT TIME BLOCKS

What can I bring to the tables I join? That's a great question I ask myself often. My talent time block is my chance to do just that and evaluate my Value Sets, skills, contributions, etc. A few rules to this time block would be A) that I am more than what I *do* creatively, and B) how I can be an asset to any table I join where I can best lead, follow, or advise.

And what I do end up discovering about myself shouldn't be a list of what makes me great or how I can showcase my creative talents. No. The talent time block is a mixture of time I get to dedicate to knowing myself better, researching what people need, and deciding how I can personally help them or recommend others to do it.

One way I might benefit from this time block is by breaking down what I really do as a writer. So here's a general list of what I can do as a writer: outline, edit, format, develop characters, create natural dialogue, etc. These are the tools that allow me to be a writer.

Once I have my list together, I try to figure out where I could best use them. That's right, it is time to research, research, research others in my field to see what they need. My goal isn't to be hired; it's to see if they need help. Helping my friends does more than open doors to more opportunities; it gives me a chance to work with people I care about.

When making this list, I try to include the people I'm interested in building and cultivating deeper relationships with. This is a chance to say, "How do I get involved with these individuals?" Talent is not always about what you want to do, but how you can help others.

> *A good rule of thumb* is to volunteer your time in any way that *they* need, not what you *want*. How can you elevate their missions? And you're there for their best interests, not yours. So never help with an agenda or selfish goal. We help people to be involved, and if being involved helps their mission, so be it.

So jot down your talents and connect them to who might be in need of those talents. If your list of talents is short or you feel you don't have any talents in general, try breaking down one talent into multiple parts, like I did for being a writer.

If you still feel you lack certain *talents*, list out what you would like to learn or improve. This third list gets pushed over to your practice time block so you can work on it at a later time. Let this time block be a chance to focus your efforts more on what you can do, how you can do it, and who you can help by being able to do these things.

REST TIME BLOCKS

Every human needs several things in their life: food, water, emotion, protection, air, and rest. And resting gives me a chance to reconnect with myself. My mind and body need rest. This gives me a chance to give my mind a moment to breathe.

Rest time blocks are scheduled pause moments throughout my workday. This is the time when I check in on the things that are important to me, which is myself. That's right, I am more important than anything else. Just as you're more important than anything else. The thing is, you have to put the oxygen mask on yourself before you help the person to your side. So this means I need to make sure I'm healthy, capable, rested, and so on.

I need food, water, emotion, protection, air, and rest. Without those things, my workday suffers, as does my health. This is why you need to schedule a time block that is dedicated to food, water, emotion, protection, air, and rest. Pause your workday for a chance to eat, drink, and check in on your mental health. You need to protect yourself.

Self-love is part of protecting the core of who you are. So, get outside and sit in the warm weather. Take a deep breath. Do what you can to ensure you are being kind to yourself. This includes getting enough sleep each night. Because without you, nothing can happen at all.

Remember, you don't have to finish things; you just need to work on them consistently. If you work on it today, tomorrow, or the next day, it'll get started, and you can always work a little on it each day. But never work on things at the cost of your health.

The few rest time blocks I have are specific to my needs. First, I make sure to have time set aside every morning for my breakfast. This is my wake-up time. This time is as long as it needs to be. The reason: I take my time waking up, getting ready, and making sure I'm mentally prepared for my day.

Now, second, there's no way I'm going a full day without eating lunch, and by lunch, I mean pizza. A good pizza hour is filled with eating, breathing, and resting my brain. At the end of my workday, I'll eat again, because dinner wants to be eaten.

You need to rest, but everyone has a different day filled with specific needs for them. Some workout their bodies; others have children, dogs, cats that won't stop lying on your keyboard; a day is going to be a day. Figure out what works for you and adjust your schedule as needed.

Make sure you have those pauses throughout your day for food, rest, and breathing. It's not about how much work you can get done; it's about how well you can keep those eyes open and that brain focused on the joy of what you are doing. We can't enjoy the day if our bellies hurt, our heads are pounding, or we keep falling asleep at the desk.

You, like me, might be a workaholic. And you and I both deserve rest. Without rest, we are no good to ourselves or our mission. The truth is that we are not getting more done by not resting. By not resting, we are only turning great work into half-assed work due to a mushy brain that absolutely needs rest and food.

Please, for the love of life, do yourself a huge favor and listen to your body, love your body, and take care of your body. Work, as it should always be, will be there tomorrow.

If there is one thing I have learned over the years, it is that nothing ever gets done. There is always more to get started. And you know what? That's the point. You should always have something to do or something to start. If your to-do list ends, then you're doing something wrong.

Forget about getting things done by the end of one day. Sit down, breathe, and jump back into the grind tomorrow. We both know that a rested, healthier version of you will lead you down the path to success without falling asleep.

CHAPTER 5.6
Time Management

5.6 | TIME BLOCK RULES

Like anything in life, there are rules we apply to what we do. And rules are there to help a person get the most out of what they do. Time blocks are no different than anything else. Therefore, they also have rules, rules that should guide you to stay in control. Which means, if you break these rules, it could lead to things controlling you instead of you controlling things.

Keep in mind that you can add rules to these blocks, ignore rules altogether, or toss out the time blocks if they don't work for you. After all, these are suggestions to better help you. But there are many ways to do things. For me, these associated rules and time blocks are what helped me regain control over my time and the things I put time into.

Ultimately, if you choose to use the time blocks, the rules should help you develop habits; habits that will teach your mind to start and stop things when the allotted time ends. Yes, stopping gives you control. This is one of the hardest habits to break. It's breaking the anxiety that pushes you to believe that you must finish what you started.

As you know by now, this book is all about taking back control from things and changing the brain to change the game. The brain change here is to remember that you'll finish it in time. But that does not have to happen in one long sitting. You can do it over the course of a few days, weeks, months, or years. The idea is that when you work on a task, you consistently work on it when it comes up in your schedule.

Time blocks are designed to give you a chance to work a little on a lot over time. Doing a little here and there opens the door to working on multiple things over the course of your week. Time management is not about getting things done. It is about starting, stopping, and consistency.

1. THERE IS ALWAYS TOMORROW

Why put pressure on yourself today when there's always tomorrow waiting for you? By mastering this rule, we can relieve the unnecessary stress that our own fears typically cause. If you work on something for an hour each day, that is seven hours a week, which will give you a better return on your investment of time and effort. Working on the same thing for seven hours in one day takes away both the quality of that time and the ability to do multiple things.

But, Thomas, why do I need to do multiple things when I can get one thing done now and then focus on the next thing?

Imagine you worked on six things a day and gave each task about an hour. That's six things you're working on seven hours a week. Productivity isn't about finishing one thing. It's about working on many little things. So, a little now for an hour, stop, then a little later.

But, Thomas, I have a deadline.

I love deadlines, but they won't change the reality of your time. What you should be worrying about are your boundaries and accountability.

Accountability is when you give yourself a reasonable amount of time with realistic expectations. If a deadline is given to you with one week's notice, you can't start working on it the day before it's due, or even two days before it's due. That approach would be on you.

Time management begins with making the right choices at the right time. Rarely do we ever have a deadline for the next day, but whatever the deadline is, it will come down to being able to say no to things.

But, Thomas, I get acting auditions that are due the next day.

Great. An audition is not office hours. Time blocks are dedicated to working your business hours in the home office. You have things you need to do to keep your business growing. Auditions have nothing to do with your business, even as an actor. Auditions are rewards for putting time into your Career Business and the job responsibilities of that business.

So you have to look at auditions differently than you did in the past. Auditions fall under another reality of your schedule—work. And your Career Business is not work; it's about running your company. Which means you need to look at work as what you earn in return for *you* doing your job.

One of the most satisfying aspects of this rule is that there is always tomorrow. Which means that you can leave everything for tomorrow if something does come up. Remember, people come first, but so do the work opportunities you've earned.

So, yes, if a self-tape pops up, do it. If you are hired to perform, do it. If you are going to record with a band, do it. Worst case scenario: leave your Career Business tasks for tomorrow. If you end up getting booked on a show, you can't do your office hours while working that show. Put your effort into doing the show, networking at the show, and leaving a great impression on people.

Working falls outside of your office hours. If you have to stop your office hours to work on an audition, fine, do it. But what I wouldn't do is only work on trying to get auditions all day while working within my office hours. Because the truth is, when you put time into getting auditions, you're not putting time into your Career Business responsibilities. Trying to get work falls outside of the responsibilities for your Triangle of Life.

With that said, you need to take accountability and set boundaries to be able to push things off until tomorrow. One of those boundaries you should set is knowing that you don't have to take everything that's offered your way.

When people ask you to do things and you have too much on your plate, say no. Maybe you do have the time, but it's limited. If your time is limited, tell them you can do it, but you will need X amount of time and clearly explain your needs. See what I just did there? I set boundaries with clear communication with the parties involved. Because you need to be able to say, "Yes, I can do it, but these are my stipulations." If they cannot accept them, then they will have to find someone else.

To put it in perspective: communicate clear boundaries to others, work opportunities have nothing to do with your office schedule, and take accountability when it comes to time management. And, it's always going to be your responsibility to approach opportunities or deadlines with respect to yourself and those opportunities or deadlines.

As an aside, did you know that the writers of Saturday Night Live are given Monday through Wednesday to come up with solid sketch ideas? On Thursday, Friday, and Saturday, they're cleaning up scripts for the live performances. They can't wait.

They have to take accountability for their deadlines. But they're working an earned job, which came from running their Career Business. It is your responsibility to not allow procrastination to be the cause of your issues. When you do not get things done, it's because you did not start them in an appropriate amount of time.

There are other aspects to it, but it always has to come back to you and your accountability. Excuses make terrible additions to any Circle of Influence. One cannot lead, follow, or advise if they're trying to justify their value or actions. Your value is based on what you do and what others see you doing or not doing.

And honestly, talking only makes it worse when you try to qualify your behavior, or rather, the intent of your behavior. The old, "I was going to do it; that's why it was on my list because it was extremely important to me, but I ended up having to throw out the garbage, eat lunch, work on my music, and then there was this video online, add another excuse here," will only turn your words against you. You are the quality of your word through your actions.

Do not be this person.

2. SAY NO TO THINGS AND YES TO LIFE

When you work on an objective and all these outside forces come in and distract you, it tends to cause you stress. Truth be told, life comes first. As the first rule implies, things can always wait until tomorrow.

The second rule is a simple choice to choose life over things. People and your life come first. When life and people come your way, stop what you're doing and go be with them. Yes, tomorrow you'll be able to work on your job responsibilities again, but today people are reaching out to you, or something in your life has come up and needs your attention.

Here's an example of rule two in practice using a telephone call. Your time block is sixty minutes long, and there you are, chugging along on your task, and thirty minutes in, the phone rings. It's Bob, your local so-and-so from blah-blah-blah, and so you pick it up.

Time flies when speaking with Bob. He's interesting and provocative with his ideas about expanding his garden. By mere chance, you realize that forty-five minutes have flown by when your call with Bob ends. You're officially fifteen minutes past your time block schedule. What do you do? Do you work for another thirty minutes on that time block, or do you move on? You move on.

The second rule is clear: say yes to life and no to things, and those you know are considered part of your life. It was the right thing to do to talk with Bob. All it means is that now you have to reallocate your time blocks.

If you worked for thirty minutes before you spoke with Bob, his forty-five-minute conversation places you fifteen minutes into your *next* time block. Which is fine. Why? Because time blocks are scheduled, you're working on things that can be moved to tomorrow. Your new sixty-minute time block has forty-five minutes remaining.

People and life come first, and they have the right of way when it comes to your schedule. This includes when people come over or invite you out from out of nowhere. Say yes to life and no to things—your job responsibilities will be there tomorrow (or later that day).

The point is to speak with people and meet up with them. When you do meet with people, relax and enjoy your time out. Try not to look at the clock every other minute because you feel you have to get back and work.

There are such things as boundaries. If you're on the phone for two hours, you might want to cut that call short. Unless it's been forever since you've spoken with them. But if your buddy calls you every other day or messages you throughout the day, shut that down. It's okay to give them some of your time, but not all of it, and not at the expense of your sanity. And by sanity, I mean that there's a point when people are taking your time, and you're no longer giving it.

A good rule of thumb is to respect your time. An hour-long call is fine, but you have the right to say, "Hey, I'm glad you called; let's get lunch next week; right now, I need to get back to work." Then set that meeting up and have lunch for as long as you want.

3. START THINGS

I'll always stand by the idea that you're not here to *finish* things but start them. Because a little goes a long way, as the old saying goes. So work on things at a reasonable rate without overwhelming yourself or going above and beyond at the cost of your health and peace. When in doubt, remember: consistency, consistency, consistency.

The purpose of your time blocks is to help you take back control of both your *time* and *things*. You need to change the brain to change the game. Instead of worrying about finishing things, worry about starting things each day. This will help you accomplish much more by doing less.

But, Thomas, that doesn't even make sense. If I'm doing a lot of little things, how am I accomplishing much more?

I know it sounds counterproductive to think that a little becomes a lot, but one thing per hour in an eight-hour day leads to eight different things getting worked on. That's more than if you put eight hours into one thing.

But, Thomas, what if I could finish one thing in eight hours?

What if you could? Eight hours on one thing. What happens with those other things you need to work on and get done? Let's say you have eight things, and you work on each one for eight hours a day. A few things are going to happen:

- You're going to get burnt out.
- Quality fades after hours of working on the same thing.
- You're not allowing your brain a chance to rest.
- By switching things up, you keep your brain active.

Okay, what if you worked on one thing at a time for eight hours a day over the long run? What are you trying to accomplish? Are you working this hard to get the task finished? What is the outcome worth to you? Is it worth ignoring other tasks? Are you going to work on one thing per day for eight hours a day?

You will burn yourself out. Working on multiple things each day for shorter periods allows for rest and motivation; plus, more is getting worked on, and therefore you see progress across the board. You have to work smarter, not harder. As I've always said, "Don't work too hard, but be productive."

4. NO MORE THAN THE ALLOTTED TIME

What good are rules if we don't hold ourselves accountable to them? We must remain beholden to the allotted time of our time blocks. That allotted time is still in our hands when it comes to setting the alarm. I'd recommend setting a time block for no less than fifteen minutes for a fast-paced stretch and no more than two hours for a focused time block.

The goal of this rule is to keep things moving along and start them. This rule helps you develop habits for taking back control over your anxiety and training yourself to let go of things. You must make the choice to stop doing things instead of continuing to work on things because you feel you have to. The truth is, you don't have to do anything; you choose to do things. That means you're always the one in control. Remember that.

And with that control in your hands, set the clock to a time block, and when the alarm goes off, making that loud, annoying sound, stop and move on to the next task. This will help take the pressure off of the task.

Before you ask, there's nothing wrong with finishing the last action out. Writing a sentence? Finish your sentence or thought. Adding a name to a column, go on and add that name. Just don't start up another name or sentence. I usually write "Ended Here" so I can search for it when I come back.

That alarm is your friend. Well, okay, more like a drill sergeant working alongside you to build discipline. Keep in mind that there is no drill sergeant, and this means that you'll actually have to watch yourself. You have to take responsibility and hold yourself accountable to the rules and times you have chosen. You're the boss, so take charge and be your own boss by running your company, but also be your own boss as if you were an employee too.

But, Thomas, what if I finish a task within a time block?

If you finish a task and have time remaining, keep going. Your time block isn't finished. If you have time remaining in that time block, then work on another task. If you're working on your networking time block and have finished organizing your Circle of Influence, then start on emails or follow-ups. Take advantage of your time within the time blocks.

But, Thomas, can I stop if something comes up?

Absolutely. People come first. Family comes first. You come first. There is always a good reason to stop. People and your relationships to people.

This means your relationship with yourself. Tired? Relax. Overworked? Slow down. *Things* will always be there tomorrow.

Listen to your mind, body, and soul when it talks with you. There will be moments when you must stop due to exhausting your resources, or you just need to stop for the day. And sure, your days might be shorter from time to time, and trust me, that's okay. Extra rest for you is not a bad thing (this is coming from the mouth of a workaholic).

As a workaholic, I get it. The time will come when you might be revved up to keep going. You're in the zone, and you've found your motivation. Therefore, the hell with it. Let's bypass the rule to stop when the alarm goes off and keep on going.

My advice to you is to not do that. You will do more damage to your progress than not. The goal is to have a rested, productive mind when working on anything. It's not about how much you can get done, finish, or prove to yourself. Being productive is about managing your time first and tasks second.

5. WORK HOURS ARE OFFICE HOURS

The inevitable moment will happen when people come over or call out of nowhere. Yes, the rule that people come first is always in effect. They are allowed to interrupt you, and you should always stop what you are doing so you can give them your time. But…

This doesn't mean you should give them all your time.

Your work hours are your office hours for a reason. There is a difference between people showing up or calling out of nowhere and you hanging out with people who are doing nothing. Being lazy around the house because you invited people over is not a loophole. Imagine doing that at a job? And your boss is wondering why you're not packing out the aisles and you're over here chilling with your buddies for the day.

You're on the clock. So be on the clock.

Managing your time and the people around you keeps you in control of your life by giving you the power to say *no* to *things* and *yes* to *life*. Again, if they show up out of nowhere, give them your time. Limit that time, if you can, and get back to work. But don't fall into the trap of thinking, "I have the money in the bank, which means I can relax a little and enjoy the sun."

You need to be responsible for your Career Business. You have to treat your Career Business just like a job because it is a job. A job for a business you own and are trying to build. Sure, it's in the entertainment industry, and you're trying to be an actor, musician, comedian, or whatever your dream is. But if you worked a survival job, would you disrespect it by being lazy?

But, Thomas, I don't care about my survival job, or any job for that matter. I want to be successful in my entertainment career.

Okay, so what you're saying is that you want to be here working your ass off to be successful in your career of choice? If that's the case, then give yourself the respect of taking your Career Business seriously.

Work hours are there so you can concentrate on your Career Business responsibilities. No one else is going to set up meetings for you, market your brand, learn the industry for you, etc.

And before you ask, remember, meeting people in person is considered *active time* because you're outside of your office and placing time into the earned reward for your work. Which means that *work hours* are any time you spend at home (or in your office) putting time into your responsibilities to earn more opportunities in your field of interest.

However, when you do interviews in person or online, you are using active time. This is simply because interviews give you a chance to build relationships with the people in real time. Yes, you are marketing your brand, but in this case, you are representing your brand physically in an interview. Thus, active time.

Work hours are for working, setting up, and getting the machine of your Career Business in motion in a way that benefits your active time.

Active hours are when you *work* in the field, meet with people, get involved with projects, do interviews, attend events or gatherings, etc. And well, you should be doing these things too. It's important to be active with others.

The whole point of office hours is to set up opportunities to get involved, find ways to best represent your brand, learn the industry, and organize the inner workings of your Career Business.

But Thomas, that sounds like a lot of work.

It is a lot of work. You're running a business. And how else are you going to make things happen by making things happen if you don't do the work? The work helps you increase your chances of earning opportunities to get involved.

When you're able to get involved, you can finally leave your office to demonstrate to others that you are A) alive, B) engaged in what you love doing, and C) demonstrating that you are more than the sum of your words, but proof through action.

Think of it this way: if you are never seen around comedy clubs, how will people know you are interested in being a comedian? How will they know you want to get involved with the scene and help out when and where you can?

Performing comedy is not the same as being involved. Performing is an advertisement for your services, especially when you have no demand for that service. Performances are the "hey, look at me, I do this thing. Do you like it?" And when you do have an audience and demand, then shows are a reward for the audience to experience the brand they bought into.

To get to this level, you need to put time into your office hours so you can earn opportunities to be seen, get involved, and work with others that will eventually consider you a friend. Friends work with friends. Which means they'll want you around as they start rising up. This also means you need to think about your friends when you're rising up too.

As one rises (whether it's you or them), all rise up. This is what building a future looks like. Build your team or grow within one.

6. ONE THING AT A TIME

No multitasking. This is a big rule to stand by, and I mean it. And you don't have to tell me; I know you can do a lot because you're amazing! We're all amazing, and we all know you're amazing. But time management is about doing as much as you can to prove you can, or to get everything on your list accomplished in one day. No, no, no.

Time management is about staying in control and focused. Limit your tasks to one per time block. Allow yourself a chance to give a hundred percent of your brain to starting a task (or continuing a task).

But, Thomas, I can do more than one thing at a time. Trust me.

I trust that you can't write the best email if you speak with people on the phone at the same time while also making sure you're editing a YouTube video for upload. And oddly enough, the person on the other end of your email or phone call won't like it either.

Imagine writing an email, interacting on social media, and texting multiple people at once. All these tasks will suffer from mental overload. This behavior takes away the chance to get the most out of what you are doing. Stay focused on one thing at a time to get the most out of it.

Sixty minutes fly by quickly when you have a timer keeping track of your effort. It is not about doing as much as possible during that hour. It's about doing one specific thing during each hour-long time block. If you work on more than one thing at a time, you won't get much accomplished. When you devote your full attention to a single task, you are rewarded with high-quality results. There is never a rush to finish a multitude of tasks or to overcomplicate things by multitasking.

The secret is to maintain a steady work ethic to get a lot of *things* started over the course of a week, month, or year. And from there, *things* will come to a natural conclusion, but like all *things*, there should always be more to do. And if you don't finish something, you'll have an opportunity to work on that task tomorrow.

One thing at a time is a way to show yourself and your Career Business journey the respect you and it deserve. There is no reason for you to do more than one thing at a time.

Besides, why do you have to do everything right now? Are you in a race? Do you have a deadline for every single thing you are working on? If so, you need to reschedule, realign, and reorganize your life. This kind of backup, stress, and ridiculousness tells me one thing: you have trouble saying *no* to people (or *things*) and *yes* to your life.

This problem can be adjusted with ease by taking back control over your time and the things around you.

A good rule of thumb is that you're in control of what you choose to do.

CHAPTER 5.7
Time Management

5.7 | TO-DO LISTS

A to-do list is a vital tool for organizing and scheduling your time blocks with detailed objectives. A to-do list is a centralized collection of objectives for that day, week, month, or year. These objectives should be placed within each specific time block. A strong to-do list prioritizes time-sensitive objectives, maintenance tasks, and the broken-down elements of your SMART goals.

But, Thomas, what are objectives?

Think of your objectives as goalposts that you set up. Goalpost objectives are going to be your desired end results. And you should have goalposts for many things. For example, finding an agent, building your Circle of Influence to thirty people, and establishing your brand's message on social media.

But, Thomas, what's the difference between an objective I'm trying to reach and a SMART goal?

SMART goals break down The Process of your objective goals, where you map out and outline a plan of attack. Ultimately, SMART goals will lead you one step at a time toward accomplishing your end results. These goals can be as complex as mapping out your full week or as simple as setting up maintenance tasks and a weekly schedule.

But, Thomas, what are maintenance tasks?

Certain tasks are going to be ongoing. Tasks where you need to build lists by collecting data, maybe clean those lists up, post on social media daily, or website updates. Maintenance tasks are busy work, but important work. You will always have to organize your finances. You will always have to keep your social media up. You will, or at least should, always be following up with people.

I'll say this much: a to-do list is going to be filled with everything from objective goals to SMART goals and even those maintenance tasks, but what a to-do list is not is a "what I need to finish" list.

It's called a to-do list because you need to begin doing *things*, and this is the list to keep you going. Remember, it's all about starting *things*, consistency, and when something is finished, it doesn't mean you're done.

After all, a to-do list is not only about deleting items from it. You never want to have an empty to-do list. You're not trying to clear out the list so you can sit back with a deep sigh of relief. Nope. You never want to be finished. Besides, if a to-do list is empty, then what is there to do?

The trick is that you should always be doing something. It is a career and not a competition to clean a to-do list of all its items. It should never be empty. In some cases, those maintenance tasks will stay on your to-do list forever.

There will be daily maintenance to-do items that will supersede your bigger objective goals. This is why you alternate days, even weeks, and, as I said, a website needs to be updated. This means there needs to be a day of the week where this task is settled in for eternity, or until you hire someone to do it for you.

And when one thing vanishes from the list, it means you get to move other things up. And sure, there will be times when one thing takes precedence over another, and once that thing is accomplished, you can move the other one into its place.

You might have several to-do lists that are designated for specific time periods. For me, I have on my whiteboards a few lists, each with a different purpose. One to-do list is for maintenance, another for priorities, and another for personal tasks.

On the other hand, I have my company's lists too. Client to-do lists come in two forms: maintenance and urgent. These are things I know I'll have to do weekly for them, and the other is when tasks come up that need urgency.

My goal with these lists is not to overwhelm myself but to map out my action plan, organize my week, and keep myself on track. During my brainstorming time blocks, I might rearrange items on any one of my to-do lists. I can do this because I am in control of *things*, and not the other way around.

To get the most out of my lists, I'll prioritize items with deadlines. These items will always get worked on first. Be in control of your lists, and remember that you do not need one massive list of to-dos. You need as many lists as you will need based on certain criteria that fit your needs. Then take those many lists and map out your time blocks as needed with tasks.

There will come a time when your to-do lists have one-and-done items on them. Probably more often than not, you'll have singular tasks that have to be attacked in a timely manner.

You might brainstorm at the start of your day and realize, "I've not spoken to so-and-so in a long time." Place that person in your networking time block to email, call, or schedule a hangout. This is not a repeatable task, but reaching out to people would be.

My point is this: use your to-do list for placing all items together, then take that list and organize your items into your actionable time blocks. Attack them as they come up in your schedule, and sooner or later you'll create a habit to be in control of *things* while seeing progress over time. Additionally, this is all malleable for your needs too. Don't think that this is the only way. Figure out what works best for you by trying things, adjusting where needed, and being aware of what's showing real, tangible results for you.

CHAPTER 5.8
Time Management

5.8 | LAST MINUTE CAN WAIT

Some of the best lessons I've learned came from the *touch it once* and *do it now* mentalities. Remember, you can't change the game if you don't change the brain—and changing the brain begins with you. This adapted mindset helps pave the way from an inactive personality to a proactive one.

I learned a long time ago that the cost of waiting till the last minute was too high. For some reason, I believed that I could bull rush through a day and finish any task. Hey, I was young and dumb. Wait, no, not dumb, just young. That, and I was ill-informed by my own limited understanding of The Process.

See, that kind of thinking did not help my productivity. It forced me to stop everything else and put all my energy into one thing. That approach cost me too much time—time I could've spent being productive from the start. I'm telling you, just fold the laundry, otherwise laundry takes two hours to do and three weeks to fold while you're going through the clean pile searching for socks.

My point is that I had not realized yet that it's not about finishing things; it's about starting things. Thus, the list of two essential rules to live by when it comes to time management. You need to start understanding the value of time-sensitive objectives, how important your commodity of time is, and how truly powerful saying *yes* and *no* can be.

1. TOUCH IT ONCE

There's no better time to start than now. "Touch it once" primarily refers to one-and-done tasks that can be completed in one go. Such as emails—see it, read it, respond. A text? Just respond. It's anything that takes less than ten minutes to do.

The rule tells you to take action once you look at it. Did you open an email? Respond to it. Don't have time? Don't open the email. But if you opened it already, there's no reason to let it linger.

But, Thomas, I don't really like answering emails. What if I see it, and I know I'm going to have to put real time into it?

This is why we have networking time blocks. You place the bulk of your emails for a later time block in your day. If you know you don't want to answer emails right away, save that for later. You are not responsible for answering any email, text, or phone call instantly. You're busy but organized. So you can get to it later. BUT... If you do open it, just respond.

However, if your brand is about being available, like mine, then it's important to respond in a timely manner. I keep my mailbox open at all times so I can see the notifications right away. This tells people that I'm reachable, I'm available, and I'm someone they can get a response from quickly.

I do this with texts, calls, and emails alike. Mostly because telling people I'm available is not the same as actually being available.

But, Thomas, what are other things I could use this rule for?

Here's a quick list of small, quick tasks:

- Email, text, phone call
- Paying a bill
- Filing or organizing a document
- Adding an event to the calendar
- Cleaning up your workspace
- Home chores: dishes, laundry, vacuum

The list goes on, but ultimately, knocking these small, quick tasks out eliminates the cycle of revisiting small tasks that can easily multiply and overwhelm and unclutters the mind for bigger tasks.

2. DO IT NOW

Start right now. Okay, maybe not right this second; you're reading this book. The mind shift to "do it now" affects your time blocks and tasks. When one comes up, even if you're not mentally ready, do it now. Get started on what your next objective is. The reason for this is because you're responsible for doing it now and not waiting until later. The time block is here. Open up the document, pick up your phone, get that program going—whatever it is, just do it now.

You're training your brain to operate at a different capacity than you're used to. That's right, you have trained your brain in the past to hold off on doing things. The old, "I'll get to it tomorrow, after I get home from XYZ." Whatever the reason, we train ourselves to behave in certain ways. We actively train ourselves to avoid tasks and create excuses when we train ourselves to not pick up the phone, to not answer an email, and to be trapped in the mindset that we have to get this thing done right now.

And that can be overwhelming. But remember, you don't have to get it done right now; you need only start it now. The rule still applies to the time blocks: there's always tomorrow.

When I learned this rule, it changed everything for me. I had to work at it since I live with anxiety, but at the same time, I also wanted to be successful at what I do. When I feel my anxiety coming on, I try to talk myself out of it, take a breath, and remind myself to do it now. This is how I write novels, books, and scripts. It's on my to-do list, organized into time blocks, all so I can do it right now. A little each day leads to a ridiculous number of words.

Approach your time blocks with a sense of action, and you'll see a reaction once the results start coming in. You need to do things for things to happen in your life. Whether you're interested in being an actor, writer, musician, or even comedian, you need to put time into your Career Business and the Triangle of Life to see real results leading to opportunities. So why wait? Just do it now and get started.

3. A BONUS RULE: PROCRASTINATE LATER

Raise your hand if you're a procrastinator. Feel free to raise your hand later if it makes you feel more comfortable. I'll say it again: procrastination is a saboteur of results. To get things started, it takes a proactive mind filled with motivation.

As an artist myself, I'm fully aware that inspiration from outside sources is occasionally necessary. But the thing is, your Career Business is not based on when you can be inspired. It's based on finding ways to inspire yourself to be motivated. If you follow the rules to touch it once by doing it now, then this rule becomes a natural next step.

Motivation will better develop in you as these rules merge into one, creating a sense of urgency. This sense of urgency becomes your motivation to start it now. And since you've been training your brain by actually starting your tasks, you're developing better habits.

But, Thomas, how does this really help me?

Want to work with people? Well, if they ask you to do something, and you do it right away (or damn near right away), they'll remember you. That's marketing. You're leaving an impression of your value on them. They'll call you back because they can rely on you.

See, the thing is, when people hire you, or if you're working on something, you don't get paid to eventually be inspired—you're paid to be inspired now, to be motivated now, to get things started now. And whether you're working with a team, hired by a company, or running the tables you've built, it's your job to start now.

This is all important because when you're hired to work, volunteer, or choose to do something for yourself, there are deadlines. Every aspect of your life has a deadline. Some deadlines could be a year from now while others could be tomorrow.

TOMORROW!?

Yes, it happens. Not often, but it happens. A common deadline situation is a month. That isn't too bad unless you start the night before it's due. Why would you do that!? Oh, that's right, there inside of you lives the evil procrastination monster, and it hates you getting things done.

Some deadlines are invisible. They're this way because we place no value on their urgency. If you truly value a task, start it as soon as you can by placing urgency on it. If you don't, and it doesn't get done...

Well, when either happens, it's your job to accept responsibility for doing it or not doing it. And when you don't do it, you shouldn't try to justify why you didn't do it in the first place. Justifying or making excuses only damages your reputation for not following through when you commit to things.

Consider this: when things don't matter to us, we don't prioritize them, even if there's a small voice inside our head telling us that we care about it. Maybe we justify it to ourselves by saying that things came up.

The problem with that is this: people can see through our actions (or rather, inactions) and get to the truth. If we care about something and we want people to know we care about it, then we have to put time into it and get started (especially the things we committed to, along with the deadline).

But, Thomas, what if I get behind?

Communicate. I'll repeat that. Communicate. You need to tell people when and where you're at when you're working with them. And absolutely tell them when you need help, will be late on it, or if you're not reaching the deadlines that were agreed upon.

Communication cancels out poor results. Poor communication cancels you out. They're not expecting you to fail if you're communicating that you're having trouble or are backed up. They care when you don't let them know, and then when the day of the deadline hits, you have excuses.

I'll say it a thousand times: we're the total sum of our actions, or lack thereof, despite what we feel inside. If we don't like how people are recognizing our behaviors (through continued patterns), then it is up to us to change those behaviors to reflect our intentions. We might believe we're doing or not doing something, but what we feel is only one side of the story. Truly successful people listen, observe, recalibrate, and take accountability for their actions (or lack of).

All I'm saying is that you control whether you get started or not. No one else is holding you back except for you when you're choosing to not do things.

Ultimately, these rules are about being in control of your time and the tasks that come your way. The reality is this: you have to create a sense of urgency. Develop habits of change. Start now. Be proactive to become active in getting things started.

CHAPTER 5.9
Time Management

5.9 | FINAL THOUGHTS

Control. In a single word, time management is about *control*, about controlling *things* instead of *things* controlling you. Which means it's all about making choices; good or bad, you have to take proactive steps to make the choices that will best influence the bigger picture, even if in smaller steps.

But, Thomas, how do I know if my choices are affecting the bigger picture?

Choices have consequences. And the results of those choices will guide you in answering that question. If you stop going to work, you'll probably be fired. If you stop eating, you will absolutely feel hungry at some point, so please eat some pizza. And the right choices come with rewarding results. You want to build your Circle of Influence? Put time into people: meeting, helping, referring. Getting involved with others leads to positive results.

If you want to be successful and you choose to use people… not so much. Your time should be spent on elevating your Circle of Influence, marketing your brand, and learning the industry. Beyond that, put time into each side of your Triangle of Life. Making choices to spend time on this will reward you over the course of Career Business.

And if you think of time management as a finite resource you cannot replenish (which it is), you'll start to respect your time and others. Sure, you can earn more money if it runs out, meet new people when your Circle of Influence shrinks, but time, yeah, once it passes, that's it. Gone. But luckily for you, how you use your time is up to you, and how you use it will determine what comes from it.

In the long run, your future is the product of your present choices. The past is gone, and all you have done can't be changed. But you can influence where, when, and how you take steps toward your future. This potential reality is possible, and the outcome will be influenced by how you manage your time now.

The truth is, right now, you have to choose your needs over your wants before you start your Career Business and after you jump into the first one, three, five, seven, and ten years of it. It's not about what you want; it's about what needs to get done.

Put the work in right now and reward yourself later when the results start piling in. As your Career Business opportunities come, your wants will become more accessible (you'll earn them). This is why you need to learn how to sacrifice now while you manage your time to do what is needed.

But, Thomas, what's needed?

Your Triangle of Life responsibilities. Listen, you want a career in the entertainment industry, right? So, make choices that get you there. You need startup capital, so work the survival job or two and save it up. It's all about who you know, so put time into building and cultivating the relationships within your Circle of Influence. People need to remember you, and people need to know you're out there, so put time into marketing your brand.

If you don't know where to start, or you feel lost, then look at your Triangle of Life. The sides of your TOL are there to guide you. Organize these sides into daily tasks, separating them into smaller to-do list items, and you will start seeing a return on your investment of time.

A fun side note is that no one ever has to do anything unless they truly want to. We think we have to do *things*, but the truth is, we choose to do *things*. The ideas in this book, what people advise, or the *things* you believe must be done are not real. They're constructs of your *wants*, and you're in control.

CHOOSE ONE: CAREER BUSINESS OR SURVIVAL JOB

That investment of time can be spread thin if you don't save up your startup capital or if you choose to work a survival job while trying to make something happen with your Career Business. Don't believe me? Let me prove it to you with this example: Imagine you're a comedian.

But, Thomas, I am a comedian. And a musician, and a—

Um, yes, I know. Just hear me out as I paint the whole picture first. You're a comedian and all that other stuff, but as a comedian, you want to get on stage, tell jokes, and see your name on the marquee.

But, Thomas, who wouldn't want that as a comedian?

I know. You're jumping ahead. But that's great; you want those things. And you should want those things. However, they're not your needs... (I'll get back to that). But, since you want those things, why would you ever get involved with the supermarket industry?

But, Thomas, that's my job right now. I have to get involved.

And yet, you have friends at the job, go to the company picnics, and have elevated your ten-year career at the supermarket, but... You're still nowhere near having a career in entertainment.

Which is interesting, because you're not interested in a career in the supermarket industry. In fact, you hate having to call managers, hang out at supermarkets, or go to bars after work with the upper management team to build your supermarket career.

But, Thomas—

Before you say anything, let's reverse it and assume you're a cashier at some supermarket with actual dreams and aspirations to be the next store manager or CEO of a specific chain. In that situation, you would put all that time into it. You would go to the picnics, hang out after work, and text or call your managers. You'd want to get involved as much as you can.

Would it make sense if you wanted all that for your career within a supermarket but also got involved with the comedy scene on the side? Hell, you don't even have an interest in doing stand-up comedy, not even as a hobby. In fact, you can't wait until you're not doing comedy anymore. Because you hate going there.

See, in this situation you'd have no interest in being a comedian, a PA, a bartender at a comedy club, or a runner at a publishing company. So why put time into it?

But, Thomas, I *do* want to be a comedian.

Exactly! So why put the time into a job you hate? How does growing a career at a supermarket, or an accounting firm, or your local Subway restaurant help your Career Business goals? You choose to work a job because you choose to not save up startup capital.

But, Thomas, it'll take too long.

How long will it take to not do it? Ever? Like, at all? Everything we *need* to do comes down to what we really *want* to do in life. And we must learn to make the choices to sacrifice for the bigger picture. But, as an aside, know that nothing has to get done or be done. You don't have to do anything you don't want to.

Here's the reality of it all: if you want to be successful in any field of interest, you do have job responsibilities. These responsibilities are there to guide you and lead you to success, longevity, and the ability to fuel your purpose. It comes down to prioritizing what is important to you and what is not. When you prioritize your responsibilities, you need to prioritize your health, wealth, and soul (mental state) first, or else you'll never be able to enjoy the fruits of your labor.

There is a lot you can do, should do, and *need* to do for a Career Business to prosper. Think of yourself as a machine ready to be consistent in developing habits, skills, Value Sets, and the ability to control your time, money, and the people around you.

This is the real talent that will take you places—not your craft, not your passion, not your hopes and dreams. Those things have nothing to do with your success. Being good at your craft will absolutely help you with longevity, but without success first, you will never be able to reach the level needed to activate your longevity. Don't believe me? Just ask the musician blowing everyone away with their playing as they busk on the street for like thirty dollars every couple of days.

Develop your skills to run your Career Business, take control of your resources, and learn how to control *things* instead of *things* controlling you. Every *yes* and every *no* is going to be another step toward or away from your success. And you literally control where you end up by what you say yes and no to.

The advantage of managing your time is how it can create habits for other aspects of your life and career. I know it can be tough to get started, as starting is the hardest part, but the skill of summoning the motivation to *start* and get to work is developed through habit. The power of *doing* leads to getting stuff going.

Right now, you might have the passion to do something but no motivation to do it. You love writing, but you can't find inspiration to get the words out into the white void of nothing. You set up a meeting to go get pizza with people at a local place, but you lack the energy to get out of bed, and these things hold you back. As you get better at managing your time, you'll also elevate other skills to motivate, inspire, and get your butt out of bed.

People ask me how I find motivation to write when I'm hired to. I tell them, "When I'm hired to write, I'm hired to be inspired." I can't tell a client, "Hey, thanks for the gig, and just so you know, I'll get this back to you in like four months; maybe, if, well, let's see if inspiration hits!" You have to train yourself to do things—to get to work and make things happen by making things happen. And yeah, a lot of stuff will be crap. But your skill should be to turn crap into gold on your second, third, or fourth pass as you *start it* and work on *things* consistently.

Imagine being a musician or a writer and relying on your first draft of anything. You would have a short career. And besides, if you work longer than your allotted time, *things* will get backed up, and you will fall behind. You can't keep up with your tasks if you leave them on the side and ignore them for the sake of doing the *things* you'd rather be doing.

Honestly, the most advantageous tasks of a Career Business, and the responsibilities of it, will usually fall into the "I don't want to be doing this" pile. We don't get to choose our success by only doing what we like to do. We do, however, have the right to choose what we do or do not do. To get the most out of all of this, you have to make the choice to do things you don't want to do so you can earn the right to do the things you love doing.

CHAPTER 6.1
Money Management

6.1 | MONEY MANAGEMENT

Any venture, business or otherwise, has a fundamental need for capital, and that capital needs to be managed properly. Money management is a Need that provides the tools to best support, fuel, and elevate a Career Business. These tools will help you afford your overhead, save capital, and develop wealth.

And I know that not everyone is aware of the ins and outs of taking back control of their financial situations. Life happens, things get in the way, and sometimes the walls are too damn high. Also, not everyone has disposable money; I get that. And when they do finally have some money to play with, not everyone knows how to budget, invest, or save capital to get the most out of it.

This is why you need to look at money management in stages, with each stage having their own rules. These next few chapters on money management will help guide you to understand what money management is. Once you have a grasp on managing your money, you'll know how to organize it, control your overhead, and how to take advantage of your investments. And you guessed it, you'll have to make sacrifices.

You want to make a living within your field of interest, right? Whether you want to be a comedian, musician, actor, or writer, you can't rely on being so awesome people will knock on your door. Instead, to approach your Career

Business using your Business Brain, you'll have to make proactive adjustments to how you approach every aspect of your life, including money management.

As I've said earlier in this book, you'll need a strong Financial Foundation Account to support the first eighteen months of your Career Business. Having that startup capital is proactive, and this proactive approach, when consistent, will reward your Career Business with a certain level of success.

Whatever the level of success, it can falter and fall by the wayside for any Career Business with poor planning and execution. Success gets a person to the party, but it's still their responsibility to establish longevity. And money management is one aspect of securing longevity.

Money management will influence each side of your Triangle of Life—from your networking and marketing budget to the cost of learning and understanding the industry of your interest. It'll afford you the right to have a return on your 3 Needs of Purpose accounts: security, growth, and the dream account.

Like each side of your TOL, each of these accounts has a purpose. The money in your Security Account protects you, so you can take calculated risks. Your Growth Account allows you to invest allocated money into assets. And your Dream Account earns you the right to spend extra money on things you want.

But none of that means anything if your money management skills are not in order or you don't put the time into developing them. Remember, money management comes down to choices. You either choose to buy things you *want* or you resist the urge to spend irresponsibly so you can afford what you *need*.

But, Thomas, sometimes I *need* the things I *want*.

Do you? Okay, maybe you feel you have to look the part so you're concerned with appearances, and you want to show up to a location looking wealthy. The issue is, smart money management begins with logical choices, not emotional ones. Mentors taught me very early on that "a car is a car if it works." Anything more than that is about you and not the bigger picture.

This is true for any status purchases: cars, clothes, sneakers, jewelry, or anything meant to elevate your status. You don't need a fancy car, but you do need to get places. These choices mean that you're no longer managing money. This behavior falls into *things* are controlling you instead of you controlling *things*.

But, Thomas, a BMW opens doors for me! I'll fake it till I make it!

A Toyota Corolla will get you to your appointments, auditions, and meetings the same way a BMW would. Now, I'll say this: every wealthy mentor I've ever known has had a crappy car. When they do need a nice car, they end up renting a car and driver for events. Not only do they not have to drive, but they also don't have a monthly bill.

What's always been interesting to me is that their day-to-day cars are usually extremely affordable in comparison to their wealth. I asked them why they don't have really nice cars, and usually the response is that they only need to get from point A to point B. Anything else is a waste of money.

Wealthy people know that it's not about status, as per any billionaire you see; Bill Gates or Warren Buffett don't necessarily dress the part. They don't need status approval through appearance. Look how they dress.

Personally, I've owned several crappy cars over my lifetime. Each one cost me anywhere between $1,000 and $3,500. I have only purchased two vehicles in my life outright and both were used through a dealer. Both were for business: a cargo van for the band and a car for a long-distance drive across the country. If I purchase two cars that each last me three years over the course of six years, I'm still spending less than one car at $25k.

Whatever your experience with money management has been up to this point, remember that you can always change your habits. If you feel broke all the time, it's not because you don't make enough money. It comes down to the effort you put into changing the brain to change the game. That game is how you manage the money you do earn vs. your expenses.

These chapters are going to give you a chance to review The Process of managing your money better. Each new rule, tool, or habit will give you a chance to change your approach so you can take back control over your spending and saving behaviors.

And yes, saving money is going to be part of the solution in giving you a chance to get back on track and ultimately out of debt. This includes paying off (or staying away from) negative debt. And when it comes down to actual wealth, I'll show you how investing capital into assets is a game changer. If you don't invest in assets, you'll never become wealthy. And wealth is going to pay you back by giving you more time to do things. Because, if you're spending time to earn money, you're not spending time to make things happen.

Oh, sure, you could work your butt off until you get promoted and finally make six figures a year; that's always an option. But that breaks a rule when it comes to money: if it's not in your hand, you don't have it. Additionally, you want assets earning money twenty-four hours a day so you can take action on things that matter to you in the long run.

> ***A good rule of thumb*** is to never make choices based on the potential of money flow but on the actual money you have in hand. There's nothing more worthless than spending money that doesn't yet exist. What's meant to come in is not the same as what's able to be utilized.

The whole point of money management is to get to a point where you can take back control over your time. How you manage your money is what makes this possible. You'll know when you're actually creating capital to fuel your purpose when your time is no longer traded for money. The term "recoup income" is the first step to imprisoning yourself in a cycle of never-ending insanity: work to earn at the cost of your time, spend your money, and repeat.

So you're going to have to learn to control your money so you can afford the time to do what you want because you choose to, not because you have to pay the bills. No one should make choices based on outside forces throwing them into impossible decisions. Imagine having to take gigs based on needing that money to afford your rent for the month. If that's the case, then you're not in control at that moment, but do you know who is? Your bills are, and they're controlling you.

Financial advice comes in many shapes and sizes, and everyone claims to have the secret to wealth. I should make it clear that I'm not a financial advisor, and you really should speak with one. I'm a consultant who has found success in the entertainment industry and earned enough wealth to live comfortably on.

All advice from all people is based on knowledge obtained through discovery and trial and error with that information. In these chapters, I'll show you how I made what I've learned work for me. And remember to research, research, research what I show you so you can figure out what works and doesn't work for you. At the end of the day, it's all about choices. I've seen poor people make a fortune from nothing and rich people lose it all due to poor money management in both scenarios.

CHAPTER 6.2
Money Management

6.2 | WHAT IS MONEY MANAGEMENT

As always, we need to define and understand what money management actually is before we can actively manage our money. So, let's define it first: Money management refers to the multiple processes of budgeting your overhead, saving any surplus, investing in assets, and creating spending caps to control the overall flow of money out. To oversimplify the definition, it means to oversee the capital usage of an individual or business.

That didn't seem simple. How about we manage that definition and trim off the fat: it's watching where and how your money is coming, going, and growing.

How you manage your earned capital, spend it, or invest it are all important aspects of becoming an expert at money management. This leads us to understanding how it all works. Money management starts by creating a system and having control over that system. A system helps you regulate how money works for you so you can take back control over having to say *yes* because you want to, not because you have to pay bills.

To help you gain an upper hand on your approach to managing your money, let me break down the four main money management habits: being consistent, being timely, justifying a purchase, and keeping detailed records.

1. BEING CONSISTENT

What good is money management if you're not consistently putting in the effort toward developing habits and keeping to the rules of your system? A system without habits is going to lead to financial chaos. That sounded a bit dramatic. How about this: you want to go on vacation, but you never have enough money, so you're forced to choose between bills and a vacation?

In reality, you need a system that is given love and attention. Your habits should be guiding you to do your due diligence to manage your financial responsibilities. How you budget and keep track of your spending can ultimately lead to you being better protected, given a chance to invest in assets for wealth generation, and reward yourself. All of which should consistently be happening *because* of your habits.

Honestly, having a budget that you kind of do once in a while is just as useless as not having one at all. Keeping track of what you spend, what you can spend, and where your money is organized requires consistency for your money management behavior to improve. This improvement will help you go on vacation and still be able to afford your bills.

But, Thomas, as long as I can afford my bills, what does it matter?

Great question. As an example, think about how wealth is created. A person, in this case, you, wants to grow their wealth. This happens when you develop passive income through asset investments. But if you're not consistently allocating money to protect yourself so you *can* invest, then you'll find yourself wasting money you don't have to invest. I say this because people might see a great investment opportunity and jump on it without having money protecting them or affording their overhead. If that investment goes south, it won't be fun.

Money management begins with getting your finances in order, then maintaining that order while you develop a system that will eventually protect you, allocate money outside your overhead for investing, and place some cash on the side so you can reward yourself. However, if each part of that system isn't shown love constantly, it won't love you back.

2. TIMELY | DOING THINGS ON TIME

Being financially timely helps keep your money management from getting out of hand. Being late on bills, forgetting about autopayments, or the coming tax season all contribute to a bigger mess that could have been avoided. Bills that could have been placed in your calendar, an alarm for a bill to be paid, or maybe you need to send information to your accountant.

The truth is, a late bill creates a late charge, and honestly, they can pile up if you don't stay ahead of it. So pay your bills on time, get your reports together, file your receipts as they come in, and, of course, always make sure your accountant gets what they need on time to do their job.

As an aside, there are federal agencies out there, laws, and, in some cases, investors who want their money now. Paying things on time is a beautiful habit to create for the little things. This habit will also become a reflection of who you are for the bigger things. It builds character that represents your brand. You get things started, consistently work on them, and finish them in a timely manner.

For me, I set calendar notifications for all my bills. However, I also make sure to pay all my bills on the first of every month to stay ahead of any bills. I'd rather pay it all in one moment than worry about it later. Though, I'm aware that not all people can do this. It would behoove you to think about your future plans now so you can prepare to be in a position to take action like that or any action you feel will best work for you.

A good rule of thumb is to get it done now. If you expect to keep getting money and ignore those bills, taxes, and other responsibilities, you'll end up like the majority of all those other celebrities who learned the hard way. Stay on top of your expenses, bills, and responsibilities, and you'll stay ahead of the curve.

3. JUSTIFYING A PURCHASE

Wanting something is not the same as needing it. We want nice things; I want nice things, but we need to eat, stay warm, and drink that water. It's no secret that I want and need pizza. However, I created an actual budget for eating pizza.

See, my pizza addiction has its own column in my budget plan. I justified eating pizza by creating a responsibility to control it. There are rules when it comes to justifying the cost of spending X number of dollars on anything. This rule applies to everything, including the desire to buy stuff you truly, without a doubt, believe you need because you want it more than air—even if you don't *really* need it.

But, Thomas, when is something I feel I *need* a *want*?

You have to analyze that *want* and your financial situation. If anything, try asking yourself these two questions:

"Is this in my budget?"

"Can I afford five of these and still afford my annual overhead?"

You're allowed anything you want in life; you're a grownup. The trick is to be responsible with those choices. Your first responsibility is to be able to afford your new venture: your Career Business within the entertainment industry. And your *want* might not be worth it if it takes away from your Financial Foundation Account.

To keep your budget in order, give yourself safeguards that help justify purchases that fall into the *want* category. The things you might not have thought of while organizing your budget in the first place. All you need to do is weigh out the needs vs. wants of what expenses will be accrued by spending money on item XYZ.

You're always going to be in control of what you choose to spend, save, or invest in. No one can take that choice away from you. At the end of the day, what is money management? It's about controlling your behavior.

If you want that new $500 game system or those $300 sneakers, all you have to do is justify it within your budget, the long game, and whether you had placed a contingency cost into your overhead. I'll always be the first person to tell a client to figure out their overhead and add 10 to 25% to it as a random expense contingency.

You can never go wrong with extra protection.

4. KEEPING DETAILED RECORDS

Documentation, documentation, documentation. Documentation is a great tool for managing your capital. Any effort to keep detailed records will benefit your progress and give you more control over your money. Data equals control. The more you know, the more information you have to make an educated choice, the better off you'll be.

At the end of the day, you need to keep an eye on how your money flows in and, more importantly, out. Make sure you have or obtain proof of what, where, and when you've spent money, saved it, or invested it. This will give you a chance to monitor your capital responsibility.

Numbers need to line up and when they don't during a self-audit, you need that documentation to track charges. As you are an actual business, it's wise to keep bank statements, receipts for big-ticket items, and absolutely all documentation for any investment you partake in.

Documentation gives you access to information for your own observations and the ability to present data to interested parties. Being ahead of any investigation by knowing how your month moves is a responsibility, one that gives you an upper hand over inquiring minds who might investigate your financial situations, i.e., accountants, IRS, and potential investors.

I know that it's possible to look at a bank account and say, "I have more money than yesterday." But the truth is, your bank statements are only a small part of a much bigger picture. It doesn't tell you how you're growing or by what margins. In fact, keeping a checkbook alone isn't smart money management. It's up to you to keep track of your accounts in a way where you can make educated decisions if needed.

A good rule of thumb is that even if you have an accountant, you should understand The Process of how your money is moving around and what it can and cannot do. Not that you should have the education of an accountant, but that you're in the know of how things work, even in a general sense.

A fun side note is that it's not uncommon to hear the term money management also referred to as investment management and/or portfolio management.

CHAPTER 6.3
Money Management

6.3 | THE PATH TO MONEY MANAGEMENT

The path to money management has many steps and tools. It includes goals and milestones that require your attention. Based on the previous chapters, you should have a general idea of what your financial responsibilities are to take back control over your finances. That general understanding should help you approach the following list to build your money management system.

This chapter breaks down The Process of managing your money to develop your Financial Foundation Accounts, budget an overhead, organize money flows, and invest in assets. I've pulled previous information into this chapter and organized The Process in a way that should help you establish order in the chaos of bills, debt, savings, and investing.

However, as always, I do recommend that you take whatever ideas I present to you and research, research, research. Knowing something is not the same as understanding it, and understanding these techniques will give you better control over your capital.

You might find that the order doesn't work for you, and that's okay. As you read through The Process, you might discover a new way of looking at your money management system. If you realize there's a different way, try it. After all, my advice is to find what works best for you.

> *A good rule of thumb* is to remember that you are always in control of what you do, how you do it, and why you do it. So figure out what works best for you to get the best outcome that you're looking for.

1. CREATE A BUDGET

First, the major difference between a budget and budgeting is the action it represents. These definitions will get us on the same page (no pun intended).

Budgeting: The act of sticking to financial cap limits, organizing capital, and keeping a record of any spending, saving, and investing moves.

Budget: A strict set of rules, guidelines, and organized methods to maintain an overhead and its costs through budgeting.

> *A fun side note* is that a budget is useless if you're not going to do your part by actively budgeting. It's your first line of defense, which, coincidentally, is also the first step to taking back control of your capital.

     It's not hard to shoot yourself in the foot if you're not in control of what you're spending, saving, or investing in. And if you don't have feet, then you're shooting yourself in the leg. If you don't have legs—my point is, a budget keeps you in a position to make moves that'll give your Career Business a fighting chance.
     But, Thomas, what does that equate to?
     It equates to what this book is teaching you about: control. Having control to say *yes* because you want to, not because you have to. When you have the money to afford your overhead, you're able to say *yes* for one very important reason: you're not trading time for money anymore, nor are you making emotional decisions to direct your life where you don't want to be.

> *A good rule of thumb* is to be accountable for your spending. There's a liveable budget, and then there's a lifestyle budget. The key is to understand when and where you can spend money and treat yourself. You'll always have the final say in how and where your money is spent. Be in control of your spending habits.

When you do finally create a budget, you have to organize expenses into these groups: fixed, savings, irregular, and variable expenses.

Fixed expenses are any expense that doesn't change from period to period. These could include a mortgage, rent, utility bill, bank fee, and loan payments. The control you have over these expenses comes in the form of lifestyle choices, from wanting a super fancy car to a vehicle that gets you from A to B. So watch what fixed expenses you add to your overhead.

Saving expenses are the money you take out of your paycheck each week and place into a special account or accounts. My method takes a different approach to this. As you'll read later in this book, there is a way to *earn* the right to save money, and then there is saving money. I consider saving money from your check the same as going on a vacation because you want to, not because you've earned it through the allocation of your funds. Basically, don't just save money to save money; have a plan.

However, as there should be options, if you are going to save money from each check, there are several acceptable ways. One is deducting 10% of each paycheck you earn, and another is the Jay Leno method: having two jobs, where money from one job covers his overhead while the other goes straight to savings.

I recommend researching each method you find and weighing out what would work best for you. For those that didn't know, Jay Leno has always worked at least two jobs at a time. When he hosted the Tonight Show, that was his spending money, and he said his stand-up comedy gigs went right into his savings accounts.

Irregular expenses come up randomly throughout the year. These expenses will occur, no matter how much you think they won't. You need to plan for these expenses. To do so, you'll have to set aside smaller amounts per month in your budget. This is different from an emergency account. These expenses can add up if you're not prepared for them. We're not always prepared for a random vet bill, vehicle maintenance, replacing damaged clothing or shoes, or, the big one, any health issues.

But, Thomas, how do you prepare for these expenses?

Set up a yearly expense in your budget to be proactive against these irregular expenses, then divide it into twelve months. This is your monthly expense for each. So set money aside in a separate bank account dedicated to irregular expenses. The plus side is that, even if you end up not having to spend the money, you're always prepared for it.

There's nothing like having a massive bill come from nowhere. Think of this as spending money on an expense you know will come up eventually. An example would be a car accident. You didn't plan for it, but it happened. And insurance won't cover it. Think smart, think ahead, and be prepared.

Variable expenses are defined by purchases within your control. Who doesn't like entertainment? Or how about eating at a restaurant with friends? However, these expenses do pile up: personal care items, groceries, entertainment items like alcohol, and lottery tickets. Ultimately, these are expenses that you choose to pay for but don't have a fixed cost. Budgeting for these items is your second line of defense.

This second line of defense makes it easier to identify where cuts can be made. And variable expenses are usually the easiest to reduce. Eating out can be reduced to once a week; groceries can focus on long-term meals like lasagna; or maybe you can start buying in bulk for shampoos and other items. Remember, it's about what you *need* and not what you *want*.

> *A fun side note* is that the variable expense columns you create will usually end up being the most expensive totals in your budget overall when you're finished. The cost that piles up just from eating out, enjoying any form of entertainment, or getting that weekly haircut is a killer experience.

HOW TO CREATE A BUDGET

The rules for organizing your initial budget are explained in two Foundation chapters: Chapter 2.9 Startup Capital and 2.10 Calculate Your Overhead. This will get your physical budget together and show you how to make sense of it. Keep in mind, it'll take a good amount of time.

Honestly, the more details you have, the better equipped you'll be to make educated decisions about what to cut, what to keep, and how to plan your future finances.

To save you time flipping back through those chapters, I've summarized the seven key rules below; you're welcome:

STEP 1: 12 MONTHS OF BANK AND CREDIT CARD STATEMENTS

The purpose of this step is to figure out what you've been spending your money on in a twelve-month period. To do this, simply print out the past twelve months of both bank and credit card statements.

But, Thomas, I'm a cash person.

Great! If you happen to be a cash person, then keep the receipts as you purchase items.

But, Thomas, I never kept any receipts before buying your book.

Moving forward, keep receipts if you're a cash person. You'll need twelve months of data to really get a clear sense of your expenses, so start marking down your spending in real time.

But, Thomas, I want to start now but don't have any information.

If you have zero ways of looking back at the last twelve months of your spending history (not your earning history), find solutions by thinking outside the box. There will be some expenses, like rent, utilities, phone, and similar fixed expenses you can write down. What about food? How much do you spend on groceries? The idea is to think about what you do spend money on and then write it down. But, honestly, you should take the next year and write down, save, and keep meticulous track of it moving forward.

But, Thomas, I don't have a book?

You don't have a book? Okay, download a spending tracker app (some are free, others are not). The point is that you're going to have a year or longer to save up your startup capital to start your Career Business venture. So while you're doing that, start changing your budget and budgeting habits now.

Once you have twelve months of data, you're officially on your way to figuring out your average monthly overhead.

A good rule of thumb is that moving forward, I highly recommend you use credit cards to make purchases, pay your bills, and cover costs. Afterwards, pay it off monthly. With that said, don't spend what you don't have.

A fun side note is that when you use credit cards, it's safer than when you use debit cards or cash. Credit cards have rewards when used responsibly.

STEP 2: USE EXPENSES TO CREATE COLUMNS

Go through each bank statement and allow the expenses to dictate what columns you need to create. If the first expense is gas for your car, the column would be added to your budget and labeled "transportation."

If I were you, I'd lump together any form of transportation under this column: gas, insurance, fluids, etc. But you might want a separate column for car maintenance that includes tires, wipers, and batteries.

However, if you're trying to keep track of gas specifically, feel free to have a column dedicated to gas. Let your budget be designed for your own needs. Afterall, you have control over the columns you create.

If you live in New York City, there's a high chance you might have an MTA card for transportation. This column might be labeled "metro," and your car might be labeled "transportation," which might be its own column too. Again, it's all up to you.

Once you have the first expense marked down in its new column, the next expense item on your bank statement might be a repeat of that first expense. A repeat expense goes in the same column you just created. If it's a new expense, create a new column. As you can see, spending habits slowly appear right before your eyes.

Keep in mind that if there are items that aren't on your statements, you're able to add new columns whenever you want. Yes, these things won't have expense totals yet, but you know they'll come up in the first year of your Career Business.

For example, actors, for instance, will need columns for headshots, reels, and audition websites. Personally, I'd figure out what it would cost for headshots and add that number (plus 20%) to its own column.

If you're like me, I have a pizza addiction. As stated earlier, that's my *want*. So I created a column for my *want* too. I need my pizza!

It sounds like a joke, but I made my budget and overhead reflect my choices. I knew it would increase my budget, but I was willing to take the hit. For me, being able to eat breakfast, lunch, and dinner out was part of what made me tick. I like cooking, but I found that eating out cost less than buying groceries. So I prepared for the cost to be covered.

Additionally, you should know that there are never too many columns at first. It's all about working out your regular spending habits from the last year, then adding any potential Career Business expenses, followed by the expenses you feel you can't live without. This process is mostly to get a general idea of what expenses you had over the last year.

STEP 3: COMBINE THE TOTAL EXPENSES IN EACH COLUMN

Once you're finished with Step 2, you can now add the items up within each individual column. Next, take a good look at the total accumulated values for each of those columns. Are they higher than you expected, about where you expected, or lower than you expected? It's fun looking at your numbers a bit closer, isn't it? When you see your spending patterns laid out, it truly begins to make sense. That's the thing about taking back control. It starts with information, and the more you know and understand, the more choices you can plan for.

STEP 4: DIVIDE THE TOTAL OF EACH COLUMN BY 12 MONTHS

Now divide each column total by twelve months to get its average monthly total for each column. This figure shows how much you've spent on average per month on that expense. For annual expenses like Amazon Prime, divide the total annual cost by twelve months and add that into your monthly expense. For example, a $139 annual Prime membership breaks down to about $11.58 per month. This monthly perspective helps you better grasp the true impact of both regular and annual expenses on your budget.

STEP 5: IF NECESSARY, REDUCE THESE COLUMNS

If you find that the average monthly figure is far higher than you expected, you might want to adjust your spending habits for that specific expense. I assure you that there will be a sweet spot that affords you a chance to enjoy a comfortable lifestyle based on your personal *wants* and *needs*.

You'll have expenses that make up the majority of your average monthly costs that need to be chopped down—not just reduced, but chopped down by half, a third, or altogether deleted from your budget. Days add up, and so do expenses when you look at them through the long lens of cost.

This part of the technique is vital to controlling what you spend. You have a chance to really reduce what you give to your *wants* and take back control of your finances to afford your *needs*.

> *A fun side note* is that what you cut now can come back later. It's about sacrificing your *wants* and rewarding your *needs* so you can afford opportunities to build your Career Business. Earn the right to raise your average monthly overhead by first accepting the discipline it takes to live on a budget, let alone a tight budget.

But, Thomas, how can I reduce my expenses?

Drastic actions create drastic results. Right away, you could cut your drinking and bar expenses every Friday or Saturday in half or one-third. The best action is to cut your budget drastically and take out all the unneeded expenses for now.

But, Thomas, I love going out to drink on the weekends!

Generally speaking, how much money is traditionally spent on going out to drink? Depending on what state you are in, the average cost of a beer, not even a harder drink, is about $5 to $15. So, why don't we go with $8? These drink prices reflect restaurants' standard pricing model: a 20% pour cost with an 80% margin on liquor sales. Wait, remember to add a 20% tip ($1 to $5). Usually, if you get an $8 drink, you leave a $2 tip. This brings the price of each beer to $10 per glass (or bottle).

Assuming you get three drinks, that $30 tab for one night becomes $120 when you go out every weekend ($30 × 4 weeks). And we haven't even factored in food, travel, or the dreaded door charges yet. What about the cost to get there—multiple days out drinking with friends? Now think about your own habits: Do you buy rounds for friends? Drink more than three beers? Go out multiple times per week? Each *yes* multiplies that $120 monthly figure significantly. These are things to think about.

But, Thomas, I don't go to bars. I eat at restaurants with my friends.

I see. I also would rather go out eating. Remember, I hate cooking and cleaning. However, restaurants are a big expense. This is another area in your budget where you can aggressively cut your average monthly cost by a third or even half. The reason we do not delete this column completely is the fact that you need a restaurant budget to do a few things: network to build and cultivate those relationships; and have meetings to make things happen.

And again, I'd say this much: eating at a restaurant is better than being at a bar. You can at least speak clearly with people. You need to hear the other person to make deals while you're both sober and focused. You're trying to build a relationship, not scream in someone's ear so they can hear you over the loud music, a large group of people, or the game blasting on the television.

However, cut where it makes sense for you and your *needs*, not your *wants*. One of the main reasons I have a pizza column, as I'm sure you're wondering about, is because I've earned the right to increase my overhead. And you will too, but for now, think about what your *needs* are for your personal and Career Business overheads to survive while you sacrifice those *wants* of yours.

Whatever you choose to add or subtract, this part of The Process gives you a deeper insight into your spending habits. Give yourself permission to look at these numbers with a non-biased approach. Let your spending patterns show you where your budget needs cleaning up and trimming down. Then allocate your necessary expenses to fit within your month so you can afford a *living*.

STEP 6: CREATE REASONABLE CAPS ON COLUMNS

It's time to cap your columns with realistic numbers. Realistic caps will alert you when you've reached your limit or are getting close to it. And once you've figured out a realistic financial cap for a specific expense, you'll need to stay on top of what you do spend so you don't go over realistic caps.

But, Thomas, what would a realistic cap look like?

Let's look at your average monthly grocery spending as an example. Capping it at $250 a month might seem like a good target, but is it realistic? For a single person, grocery costs typically range between $75 and $125 per week, and that's if you stick to coupons and smart purchases. $75 a week is $300 a month, and $125 comes to $500 a month.

Yes, you might want to only spend $250, but it comes down to being honest with yourself. Be wiser than your *wants* and give caps some wiggle room. For example, if your average monthly grocery cost is $500, consider setting a cap of $600. This buffer gives you flexibility while maintaining control.

When you spend less than your cap, you create a surplus—extra money you can reallocate to other columns that need it.

The good news is that you can review and adjust your caps quarterly based on your actual spending patterns. If you consistently spend less than a cap in one column while another column needs more funding, you can adjust both by lowering one and raising the other to better match your real needs.

A good rule of thumb when it comes to saving: go with bulk and long-term solutions. For food, think of prep meals, bagged lunches for travel, or three-day meals (like a casserole). Also, spread a dollar when you can; those "buy one, get one free" moments: a tube of toothpaste will not go bad when you stock up.

STEP 7: DOCUMENT EXPENSES BASED ON THESE COLUMNS

Now that you have an idea of your budget, have set your caps, and are on track to live on said budget, it's time for the fun part. I say that sarcastically since most people do not like this part. This is where you have to accept accountability.

See, part of having a budget is budgeting. You need to keep a record of what you spend, check against your caps, and keep an eye on what you are doing. You will get a better understanding of what's going on with your finances when you see numbers in real time. You don't want to look at your budget once in a blue moon and find yourself 30–40% above your overhead.

There are plenty of ways to keep track of your spending, so figure out which way best works for you. I mentioned a few ways above, but for me, having a file on my computer has helped me the most. It gives me a chance to check my receipts against any bank and credit card statements.

For those on the go, a phone app option sits in the palm of your hand. An advantage of your phone app is having the ability to make snap decisions before a purchase. You find something you want; look at your app to see if you're under budget with your spending. If you're able to afford it, the numbers will tell you.

It's not uncommon, but you might be old-school and carry a nice little pocket pad and pen around. That's right, a good ole' pocket-sized book and pen to keep track of everything. That's where I began my budgeting habits. I know I'm old, but it got the job done.

Let the technique you choose be something you enjoy doing. Enjoying The Process will help create a habit. If you try any method, give it a full cycle—four straight months. As always, during your reevaluation period, decide if your choice is right for you.

The secret is to give yourself time through patience. Nothing is fun, easy, or understood at the beginning of any journey, even for those learning their craft. No one loves practicing when all they want to do is do the thing they are practicing professionally. You have to learn how to do it by actually doing it at a micro level and doing that consistently.

I get it, really, I do. The things we love doing, we put the time into. We even push through the crappy parts of learning our craft because creative people love being creative. This is why I learned guitar so quickly, even though I really hated practicing pick motions, strumming patterns, scale patterns, and speed exercises. Who wants to deal with that crap?

I just wanted to write and play music. But, like all things, you need to put time into a skill until you understand it and it becomes a part of you. When it becomes a part of you, you can make a real assessment of that skill in your life.

2. PAY OFF YOUR DEBT

The evil that men do will live on and on, or so Iron Maiden has said—no, wait, they sang that. The band knew what they were talking about, and though the original lyrics had nothing to do with capital debt, I still think my point stands.

See, what you need to take from this long-winded thought is that, just like in the song, debt will live on and on unless we face it. The debt we create is from our own actions; we're the evil that creates the debt, and we must create good habits to conquer our debt.

Debt is one of those things that will literally pull all your resources, energy, and effort down with it as it gets heavier and heavier to bear. You need to find a way to destroy the weight of your debt by doing two things: pay it down and stop accruing it.

But, Thomas, how do I pay down my debt?

I hear foot pics are really popular now, but honestly, I have hobbit feet, and no one has time for that. So instead, let's look at The Process of paying down your debt and stopping the act of accruing it.

A) PAYING DOWN YOUR DEBT

It takes a considerable amount of consistency to pay down debt. There are a decent number of options out there, but here is one method that helped me. Start with the highest interest-rated card and pay double the minimum. For your other debt, pay the minimum amount (round up to the highest dollar).

Once you pay off the card with the highest interest rate, add what you paid to that card to the next card with the highest interest rate. Continue this until you've paid off all your cards.

These compound payments build momentum and reduce accrued interest costs. As you eliminate each debt, you add more force to the next one. And each card you pay off gives you more financial power to tackle the next highest interest rate card.

But, Thomas, I don't make that kind of money to pay double.

This is why you need to take time to do the research, research, research needed to figure out what would work best for you. Ultimately, there are many options to pay down your debt.

For example, if you have the option to consolidate your debt into one payment by taking out a loan, look into it. Can you borrow money from people? Get a second job that goes toward your debt only?

The goal is to find ways to take care of your debt and make sure it's never at the expense of a relationship or your sanity. The end result should be the same with any action you take: to pay off the debt.

B) STOP ACCRUING DEBT, SORT OF

In general, some debt can help, but not *bad* debt, as it can destroy your net worth in the long run. *Bad* debt forces you to spend the majority of your income, time, and effort trying to pay it down. And if this *bad* debt takes over your life, you could find yourself being forced to pay the debt through legal means: bankruptcy or otherwise.

But, Thomas—

I know, "What is *bad* debt?" *Bad* debt usually has high interest rates, doesn't have cash back options, and, like I said above, it costs you money, time, and effort to chip away at it. *Bad* debt doesn't earn you wealth-generating opportunities or a chance to increase your financial situation. Whereas *good* debt has the potential to increase your net worth over time and influence your generational wealth to fuel your future income.

However, this book isn't about *good* or *bad* debt, so for now, focus on keeping your debt down and under control. In the end, the power to stop accruing debt is in the hands of one person—you. It's on you to accept accountability for what you spend money on, especially when it's more money than you have in the bank.

Yes, I know you needed to put that industry event outfit on a credit card—it was for a major opportunity for your career. But right now, your job responsibility isn't to spend money you don't have. It's to get your Career Business on track by building a strong Financial Foundation Account. This means getting your debt in check, your budget in order, and your finances organized before you launch your Career Business.

A great way to stay away from accrued debt is by maintaining your budget, sticking to what you can afford, and not paying for things you *want* when you *need* to cover your overhead first.

But, Thomas, you mention something about *good* debt.

Oh yes, I did. Like I said above, this book isn't really about *good* and *bad* debt. Good debt comes with investing and organizing your money into your 3 Needs of Purpose. Right now, this section of money management is more about doing just that: managing your money and getting ahead of spending and debt spillage. Other books in this series will cover *good* debt and investing.

3. YOUR CREDIT SCORE

There is a nice residual effect for paying off your debt; it helps to increase your credit score, which will become more important later on for your path.

But, Thomas, how?

The day might come when you want to buy a house or property, one with a hot tub or an investment property for passive income. A good credit score could also lead to credit cards with extra benefits, like travel rewards or lower interest rates, which become valuable tools for managing your Career Business expenses. Trust me, those flyer miles can help with free flights or hotels from time to time.

For those paying attention in the back of the room, a high credit score means you're capable of getting approved for higher credit limits on your credit cards, but also something else: stronger loan options for business opportunities later on in your Career Business and passive income ventures.

> *A fun side note* is that a good credit score helps in life. For reference, a fair score is 580 to 669; a good score is 670 to 739; and a very good score is 740 to 799. If your score is 800 or more, your record is considered excellent.

4. USE CREDIT CARDS INSTEAD OF DEBIT CARDS (OR CASH)

But, Thomas, you just said that I should pay off my debt?

Yes, yes, I did. Using your credit card instead of your debit card (or cash) is not about accruing debt. There are benefits to using a credit card instead of plain old cash or your bank debit card. You should be spending money responsibly within your budget, whether you use a credit card, cash, or a debit card. So why not use a credit card that rewards your spending?

Obviously, you would be using your credit card with the intent of paying off the balance at the beginning of each statement cycle, right? Some credit cards have rewards in the form of money, air miles, or coupons. Some credit cards, depending on your credit score or spending behavior, will give you a zero-interest period. No interest and a reward for spending? That's how you make money—by spending money you would have spent anyway.

One of the most important reasons to use a credit card instead of a debit card is for protection. Imagine your debit card gets compromised, now the money in your actual bank account could be at risk. And if it *is* taken, it could take weeks, months, or years to get that stolen money back, if you get it back at all. No money means no way to pay bills on time, which could mean missing career opportunities while you sort out your finances.

With a credit card, you're not responsible for stolen cards or any accrued expenses that you had nothing to do with. Your actual money is safe in the bank, and you can continue on as if nothing happened. You'll just have to wait for a new credit card to arrive in the mail. This is advice that comes directly from the one and only Frank Abagnale Jr., an FBI consultant.

What I'm saying is that credit cards offer better consumer protection against fraud compared with debit cards. While this is a powerful tool to have on you, you're also building your credit while being responsible for protecting your physical money in the bank.

> *A good rule of thumb* is to contact the credit cards you do have and ask them about the available benefits, rewards, and options. Do your research, research, research, and discover what is available for you.

5. EMERGENCY FUND

Hope for the best; prepare for the worst. That's right, you need to be smarter than the fall when it comes to protecting yourself. This is the benefit of having an emergency fund of at least $1,000 to start. An emergency fund is there to cover you in the event of an unexpected financial blow. By staying on top of what could happen, you're keeping yourself in a position to continue to take calculated risks without being forced backwards.

More importantly, you are protecting yourself from the need to: A) spend outside of your budget; B) take from other accounts designated for fueling your purpose; and C) never allowing your Financial Foundation Account to suffer as a result of your lack of preparation.

You need this emergency money on the side to stay ahead of random occurrences. This becomes even more apparent when you realize you're self-employed now. That's right, a career in the entertainment industry makes you responsible for yourself. And entertainers don't have regular paychecks like a job provides.

With limited startup capital at your disposal at the beginning of your Career Business, every dollar must count toward your mission. And an emergency fund keeps you from spending your startup capital on unexpected expenses outside your control.

> *A good rule of thumb* is to place 60% of any earning income over your safety-net threshold into your emergency fund until it reaches the total amount of $1,000. Once it reaches $1,000, split that 60% surplus into four accounts: security, growth, dream, and the emergency fund.

6. STARTUP CAPITAL (FINANCIAL FOUNDATION ACCOUNT)

In the Foundation Chapter, I went over The Process of figuring out how to get your startup capital together. As a recap, here is the short and sweet version of how to get your startup capital together.

1. Figure out your average monthly overhead by adding up all twelve months' worth of expenses and dividing them by twelve.
2. Multiply that average monthly overhead by eighteen months; this becomes your startup capital total
3. Place your startup capital into a Financial Foundation Account.
4. Live on a tight budget; sacrifice your *wants* to afford your *needs*.
5. Work several jobs to accumulate startup capital for your Financial Foundation Account before starting your Career Business.

> *A fun side note* is that I've always found it fascinating how simple the procedures are. I used to think it was a major process. At times, I made it more complicated in my head than I needed to. My Artist Brain pushed me to believe it was about the *art* for me to be successful. In reality, it was the Business Brain that helped me make a living doing the *art* of it all.

7. TAKE OUT 33% FROM ALL MONEY EARNED

One protective aspect of money management is the 33% Rule. This rule keeps you ahead of the taxman. See, the taxman wants your money, and this rule prepares you for the inevitable deduction from your account.

But, Thomas, why do they want my money if I don't make enough?

You're officially a business when you start your Career Business in the entertainment industry. Because of that, you'll be responsible for paying specific taxes. Even if you weren't an official *business* on paper, working a few jobs in the industry will officially make you a sole proprietorship. This means you're responsible for paying taxes and potentially getting 1099s.

Basically, as you earn money for a service, you'll need to take 33% of earned money and put it aside in a savings account. This is the money that'll be there to protect you if and when you owe taxes. And yes, before you ask, acting, music, writing—all creative skills really—are services.

Owing money happens, and sometimes it doesn't, but you never want to be in a situation where tax season comes and they ask you for three thousand dollars, and you're like, "Where in the hell am I going to get that kind of money?" Or worse, you have money in your Financial Foundation Account, but you have to pay the IRS. This'll leave you with less money to cover your overhead. And remember, a Financial Foundation Account has one job: to cover *your* overhead.

I know a third is a lot of money. But taking that money out now and putting it to the side protects you in the long run. At the end of the day, or rather, more specifically, after your taxes are squared away, you might have extra money remaining. Which means you can place any remaining money back into your Financial Foundation Account. It's like finding free money after the tax season is over. And who doesn't love to find $20 in their pants pockets after doing laundry?

8. ORGANIZE YOUR MONEY

The following information about your 3 Needs of Purpose will be explored in greater detail within another book in this series. This current book in your hands focuses on building a foundation and insight into what's to come. With that said, the next step of your journey is to…

Organize your money into your 3 Needs of Purpose. These three Needs will help you protect yourself, invest in yourself, and reward yourself to fuel your purpose: creating a Career Business within the entertainment industry. And these allocated accounts give you the power to open doors to do just that because they're actionable accounts.

An actionable account is: (A) an account that money is placed into with a purpose; (B) you're getting a return on that purpose; (C) it works to elevate your overall position to take calculated risks; and (D) it strengthens your financial situation by using the 60/40 Split Rule.

> *A good rule of thumb* is that you can activate the 60/40 Split Rule on day one after starting your Career Business. Your Financial Foundation Account is already covering your overhead, so activate the rule: 40% returns to your Financial Foundation Account, and 60% gets distributed evenly among your 3 Needs of Purpose accounts—plus the emergency fund account.

Fueling your purpose affords you the right to make the choices you want to, not because you have to pay bills, but because it fuels your mission forward. Additionally, money management and your 3 Needs of Purpose put you in a position to have control over the outside forces that take away any control.

This is evident when you have to say *yes* to a gig so you can pay your rent. And when you have to say *yes* to gigs outside your brand, mission, or goals because they pay well, you're no longer in control.

The rules of your 3 Needs of Purpose should be a standard part of any person's money management, whether in the entertainment industry or not. There's no point in managing your money if you're not allowing it to do something for you beyond just looking pretty.

Traditionally, people manage their money to do one thing: save it. However, others might manage their money to pay their bills or save just enough to do what they love doing: vacations, cars, new toys. And a small minority of people manage their money to invest in assets.

Each of those things is important separately, but doing all of them at the same time will change favor in your direction. And organizing money into your 3 Needs of Purpose with the 60/40 Split Rule will make it possible to do all of these wonderful things: protect, invest, and reward yourself.

> *A good rule of thumb* is to activate the 60/40 Split Rule after you deduct your 33% for the taxman. The remaining difference gets 40% to your FFA and 60% into your 3 Needs of Purpose and emergency fund accounts.

9. INVEST INTO ASSETS

Do you want to be wealthy? If you answered yes, then assets are for you. Assets generate wealth, while liabilities cost money to maintain. Once your money management has led you to have your finances in order, you'll notice that there's money available. This money is for investing in assets.

That's one of the reasons you have the 3 Needs of Purpose and their associated accounts: Security, Growth, and Dream Accounts. But, with that said, this next part will center on the Growth Account only.

The Growth Account is dedicated to investing money. This allocated cash gives you a chance to invest in one or more of the Assets of Life. Assets help develop passive income streams that lead you one step closer to generating wealth. And invested correctly, assets will create passive income. This in turn creates a system that cycles money back into itself—at which point, you won't be working for money; money will be working for you.

But, Thomas, how would that even work? Money can't work.

Money invested earns you a return, and that return gets filtered through the 60/40 Split Rule, placed back into your Financial Foundation Account and your 3 Needs of Purpose. This process fuels your Career Business while also allowing you to protect yourself, invest back into assets, and reward yourself.

But, Thomas, how would I do that?

Assuming your Financial Foundation Account has money covering your overhead *and* you're below the safety net threshold, do the following:

1. Earn income from working within your field of interest.
2. Remove 33% of your earned income for the taxman.
3. The remaining difference: use the 60/40 Split Rule.
4. Accrue at least $1,000 (or more) in your Growth Account.
5. Invest your Growth Account capital in assets.
6. Create multiple avenues of passive income.
7. Liquidate any earned passive income.
8. Remove 33% of your earned passive income for the taxman.
9. The remaining difference: use the 60/40 Split Rule.
10. Repeat steps 4 through 10.

As you can see, The Process inevitably leads back to fueling your financial system, that is, your Financial Foundation Account, 3 Needs of Purpose, emergency fund account, and any passive income.

And the best part: this system earns you money that'll give you back your time by developing your wealth. Oh, yes, and in this book series, we define wealth as the amount of time one can go without needing to recoup income. Recouping income is when you trade your time for money. And if you're not trading your time for money and have money coming in through passive income, then money is now working for you.

The beautiful part about wealth is that you can only work so many hours a week. But money? Money never sleeps and can work twenty-four hours a day, seven days a week, and 365 days a year. *Drops microphone!*

CHAPTER 6.4
Money Management

6.4 | OVERHEAD

Money management is about knowing your numbers, and knowing them begins with understanding your average monthly overhead. Having an intimate awareness of your overhead will give you control over your money. Without a detailed understanding of your overhead, it just becomes a collection of expenses you can't budget for—budgets keep you in control of your expenses.

But, Thomas, what *is* an overhead?

That's a great question, so here's a general definition: An overhead refers to the ongoing expenses of operating a business and the personal cost of living.

Every person on this planet has expenses, even if those expenses are the bare minimum to survive. Getting a handle on your overhead allows you to justify, organize, and restrict what expenses you can or can't afford. Sure, buying nice things is great, but not everyone *can* afford expensive organic food, but everyone needs to eat. It's about finding ways to meet your needs within your financial reality.

The whole point of understanding your overhead is to take back control over your finances. Once you have control over your numbers, you can start taking action to adjust your lifestyle (that comes later).

Even wealthy people take note of their own overheads. Oh, sure, they have more money coming in and other money invested into assets, but they do this to stay ahead of the game.

But, Thomas, what's the point of knowing your budget intimately?

Here's something to think about: would you go on a cross-country trip without first knowing what that trip would cost? The cost is your trip's overhead. Once you know the cost, you can budget for it and know how much cash you'll need to save to get from point A to point B. That budgeted cash is now your trip's Financial Foundation Account. The budget you created for this trip will show you what and when you can and cannot spend.

But, Thomas, what's a trip have to do with my Career Business?

A trip from New York to California is the same as preparing your Career Business for the entertainment industry. And look, the brain change isn't easy to notice at first, so let's explore a few things.

Creative people look at their careers in the arts differently than their personal lives or opening a business. A career in the arts has expenses as much as a person's life, and opening a business does. And for some weird reason, people look at their creative passion differently than other aspects of their lives. As if wanting a career playing guitar for a living is any different than trying to start a business or working at a company.

Sure, you have specific responsibilities for each, but they all share common requirements: managing your Triangle of Life, securing startup capital to take advantage of opportunities, and covering your overhead.

Ultimately, people who don't budget for their overhead usually end up struggling to stay afloat; while those who understand their overhead usually create options for themselves. The biggest difference is when you make the brain change to do more than *know your budget* and *overhead*—you make changes in your lifestyle to get ahead of your expenses and organize your surplus into assets to generate wealth (as discussed in previous chapters).

But, Thomas, what's this got to do with my overhead?

Everything starts with your overhead. This is where you need to change your brain to make a difference. Approach your passion in the same way you'd approach your lifestyle or business. Be more than your craft; be prepared—Am I the only one who sang the Lion King song just now?

PERSONAL OVERHEAD VS. BUSINESS OVERHEAD

There are two types of overhead: personal and business. Your personal overhead represents the cost of your lifestyle, while your business overhead covers the cost of running your business—in the case of you and this book: your Career Business.

The tricky part is getting these overheads to work together, at least for a short time in the beginning. Ultimately, it's helpful to know where one stops and the other begins. In the beginning, these overheads will feel like one and the same, but the goal is to prepare for the inevitable divide before that happens. You don't want your personal and business expenses blurring into one another once real financial results pour in and tax season comes.

This is why you should keep your personal and business overheads separate on paper from the start. However, at some point in your industry career, there will be a clear divide.

But, Thomas, how will I know what that divide looks like?

Simply put, the divide becomes clear when you start earning money from Career Business opportunities that both afford your business overhead and pay you a salary to cover your lifestyle.

But, Thomas, why would I pay myself a salary if I *am* the business?

The rule is technically that you should *treat your life like a business* and therefore start a legal business. We've already covered S corporations, LLCs, and other business certificates in an earlier chapter, so, with that said, eventually you'll be able to take a salary from your Career Business, which ultimately helps your long-term financial stability.

I'd speak with an accountant or lawyer about these next details, but here's the gist of why it's important to pay yourself a salary: it can help you save on taxes, manage cash flow, and establish a steady income. That steady income will help you manage FICA taxes, deduct from payroll taxes, build social security credits, qualify for unemployment benefits, and more.

Until that day comes, some of your expenses will be both personal and business. After all, you're working from home, and you're still working on solidifying the Financial Foundation Account before you start. But it is important to properly document and allocate them.

Think of these blurred expenses as the following: traveling to meet people, getting to job sites, and going to events. Meeting a friend (to cultivate a relationship with) is part of your job responsibilities. It feels personal, and it is, but it's also one of the many Needs of your Triangle of Life. Essentially, anything you do, including hanging out with people, is both a personal and a business action in the beginning as you're working to develop your Career Business.

At some point, you'll have a personal life outside your business life, and this is when you'll need to allocate money for both. You can't have your business paying for vacations, however your personal life should be able to survive off the salary your business pays you. More so, your business should thrive on the money earned through business opportunities without your personal money paying its overhead.

If you reach this point in your life where your business is earning good income and you're using it to fuel your lifestyle (without a salary), the taxman could come asking questions. So... Don't use your business bank accounts like a piggy bank. Other than not paying your taxes, this is usually how most celebrities end up getting in trouble.

Because, honestly, getting paid to be an actor, musician, or writer doesn't mean you get to keep what you earn. Sure, sometimes it's off the books and you're paid cash in hand, but you're still providing a service from your *Career Business*, which means you can't pocket the full check. As with all payments, you'll have to filter that money through your business accounts to afford your business overhead first and your salary second.

SAFETY NETS

A safety net is a safeguard against financial instability, a tool for awareness, and, of course, money management. Every Financial Foundation Account should have at least one safety net set up to be there as a warning or guide.

But, Thomas, what is a safety net?

It's a specific number that you set against your overhead total. This financial threshold becomes your Financial Foundation Account's safety net. It's there to help indicate what actions to take when the capital inside your FFA is higher than, gets close to, or exceeds its safety net threshold.

For example, if you have $54,000 in your FFA covering eighteen months of your overhead, a good safety net threshold for that amount would be $9,000 to cover a three-month overhead. If you reach or exceed this safety net threshold, you've officially entered the red zone. The red zone will be your bells and whistles going off, telling you to stop and reevaluate.

In reality, your Career Business should already be making money to pay some or all of your bills. But things happen. Life gets in the way, random expenses pop up, and opportunities might not be flying in your direction. And another truth you have to accept: your plan might need adjusting, and that's okay.

At this point, you need to stop what you're doing and recoup your eighteen months of startup capital to start over. Don't worry; at this point, you should have at least some contacts in the industry, among other things connecting to developing your Career Business foundation.

But, Thomas, after all that work, I have to start over?

Yes. You need capital in your FFA covering your overhead so you can make choices that influence your Career Business and missions. If you have to say yes to things to pay your bills, you're not in control of your career. And this can lead to even greater missteps that might take you in a different direction. Capital gives you the power to say *no* to things and *yes* to your missions.

At the end of the day, you need to have capital, whether you're successful or trying to make it. Your startup capital is there to give you a fighting chance to get into the industry and generate opportunities. This safety net threshold tells you when you need to stop, reevaluate, and if you need to start over and get another job, or two, to save up again.

Your safety net threshold also has a benefit to it. You can activate the 60/40 Split Rule as long as your FFA capital is higher than your safety net threshold. The best part—this rule is activated on day one of your venture. That's another reason why I told you to save up eighteen months of startup capital. Eighteen months is a lot higher than your three-month safety net threshold.

A good rule of thumb is to have two safety nets: a six-month (warning) and a three-month (red zone). At six months, stop and reevaluate what you've been doing. If by chance no changes help you earn capital, the three-month safety net is where you'll have to stop and start over again. Rinse and repeat as needed. You won't be the first to start over, and certainly not the last.

REEVALUATE WHAT LED YOU TO THIS POINT

But, Thomas, why would I have to reevaluate and start over?

Your Financial Foundation Account should have eighteen months of startup capital covering your overhead. That money is so you can focus on building your Career Business, opportunities, and developing relationships. I've talked about this in the Foundation chapters, explaining the reason for those eighteen months of startup capital. However, here's a recap to keep you moving forward in this book and series.

Your first-year goals are simple: network, market, and practice.

Those three things will lead you to make a living within your field of interest in 365 days.

But, Thomas, that's less than eighteen months of startup capital.

Those additional six months are there to protect you if something goes wrong. And I promise you, something always does. But that's not a bad thing. This is why we prepare for the inevitable.

And before you ask, "making a living within your industry" doesn't mean that you get to act, do standup, write, or whatever it is *you* would rather be doing for a living. It means that you're covering your bills by working *within* your industry of choice. At the end of the day, it's not about you and the craft, it's about relationships, and not just the first year, but the second, third, fourth, and fifth years in the industry.

> *A fun side note* is that one secret to success is realizing that it's not about being able to do what you love doing at first. You've not earned your place to get cast as a lead in a film, headline a comedy tour, or get a six-figure publishing deal. Success is about getting involved to develop opportunities. Opportunities come when people see you and see you often.

If you're involved in the industry, even on the backend, then you have a chance to network, market, and practice. If you're fooling around trying to get gigs to do what you love doing, then you're not focused on building your Career Business.

Should you say no to acting, comedy gigs, or a chance to do what you love? No, you should say *yes*. If these opportunities *come to you*, then you're doing your *actual* job correctly: building relationships. Relationships lead to the reward of why you're doing all of this in the first place. The reward is that you get to do what you love to do, and the opportunities to do it will absolutely come in time and with effort.

But, Thomas, what does this have to do with starting over?

No money means no options. If you can't afford to say yes to anything I just mentioned above, then those things won't be available for you. No money means that you can't get involved in free opportunities; you can't volunteer your time. And worse still, you can't even say yes to paid opportunities that are for $50 for the day. No money means that you have to start over because you need to save up that startup capital to cover eighteen months.

During that time, reevaluate what you were and were not doing so you can restructure your approach and change things up. When you have that money in your Financial Foundation Account affording your overhead, you can now take action again!

CHAPTER 6.5
Money Management

6.5 | FINAL THOUGHTS

None of this is easy. I repeat: none of this is easy. It's very, very difficult to manage your money. The time it'll take to develop strong financial habits, save up startup capital, organize money into your 3 Needs of Purpose, and develop wealth will be long and drawn-out.

And that long, drawn-out path starts at the bottom of the mountain. A mountain of opportunities you'll have to work hard at to take advantage of. It'll only happen if you have the capital to afford you the freedom to make choices.

When you're at the bottom of Opportunity Mountain, your eyes won't be able to comprehend the long journey ahead of you. Most people will only see the end results: the top of the mountain. Think of it this way: Mount Everest is a quick trip on a map. Then you get there, look up, and it happens: you begin to feel the bitter bite of cold across your masked face. That's when it sets in: the journey is going to be hard. But…

The difference in that moment between success and failure is the willingness to take one step forward. Then, another, and another. And each step is going to be hard, but one step is easier than trying to take the final step at the beginning of your journey. Each step must also be dedicated to the long-term plan of your purpose, mission, and Career Business. This is why you have to ask yourself, "Self, am I ready for this?"

If the answer to that question is yes, then know that you'll have a hard time managing your money, saving it, and investing it. I know, at first, it sounds hard, but those willing to consistently take one step at a time will be rewarded. That reward will lead you to have your startup capital, money to organize into your 3 Needs of Purpose, and develop wealth.

This process will be tedious if you're willing to put in the time and impossible if you're not. However, with each failure and a successful mindset, you'll evolve and grow stronger money management skills.

But, Thomas, all this is just making me not want to try.

Fear not, my fellow entertainer! The good news is that I have faith in you, just as you should have faith in yourself. You, like everyone else with a dream, deserve a chance to be what you want to be, to do what you want to do, and to succeed at making a living in your field of interest. But that success isn't going to come simply by wanting it, feeling you deserve it because you're really good at doing what you love doing, and because you *can* do that specific craft.

Acting, singing, music, writing, producing, directing, drawing—all these things are easy for a person who loves doing it. And you love doing what you do. They're easy because you're willing to suffer through the time it takes to practice your craft to get better, so you *are* better.

I'm with you when it comes to the fun art part. Who wouldn't want to put time into being creative, even if it's for practice? The reward of doing what you love leads to that feeling of accomplishment. Ah, yes, the results of being creative! You love the reward of acting, singing, playing music, writing—doing your passion. Even when you originally really sucked at it, you loved it so much that you'd do whatever you had to do to get better.

What you don't love, what most people don't enjoy, is the bullcrap tasks and responsibilities you have to do to actually become successful. Who wants to waste time saving startup capital, investing, or organizing money?

The Artist Brain believes if they just work a crappy job and do their creative *thing* on the side, that eventually something will happen. Then, and only then, they can finally quit their crappy job and focus on being creative.

I get it. That does sound more fun than running around and meeting people, working several jobs to save up startup capital, writing out business plans—ugh, just listing it out is dreadful and feels dirty—especially when an Artist Brain feels their awesomeness is all they need to get discovered.

But, see, the thing is this: the Artist Brain doesn't want to put the time into anything but their art. It's the old, "I wish I could just focus on being creative and let other people deal with the business stuff" mentality. And I'm telling you this because I care—you *need* to go out there and establish a reputation, relationships, and save up startup capital. That won't happen if you only post on social media and ask people to "come to my event" or "buy my thing," and boom, it sells. It won't happen if you kind of work a job while doing your creativity on the side. It just won't happen.

But... I get it. And oddly enough, so does everyone else. A lot of Artist Brain people do what I just said. They focus on the *dream*, the *art* of it all, and wait around for something to happen. Okay, they don't wait around, but what they do do is perform, perform, and perform. Performance isn't the secret to success. Running the business side of your Career Business is.

Don't believe me? If all those Artist Brains are doing exactly what you're doing and they're not succeeding, shouldn't that tell you something?

Okay, enough dark talk. Let's talk about making it. It's time to shut off your Artist Brain and switch to the Business Brain. Let's talk about my final thoughts on money management, which are:

You'll need money to pay your bills and to afford your overhead, and those things give your Career Business a chance to succeed. Why? Well, being able to afford your overhead allows you to say *yes* to opportunities. Which leads us to the Business Brain path:

1. Create a budget for your overhead
2. Pay off your debt
3. Increase your credit score
4. Use a credit card over your debit card/cash
5. $1,000 emergency fund
6. Save up startup capital
7. Remove 33% from earned money (taxes)
8. Organize money into your 3 Needs of Purpose
9. Invest in assets to generate passive income and wealth
10. Bonus: sacrifice your *wants* to afford your *needs*

Your first level of protection is money management. Whether you magically get discovered out of nowhere or create a Career Business, it's there to protect you. How else will you know what to do once capital starts flowing in, is saved, or you want a specific lifestyle? Money management—that's what'll keep you above water.

> *A fun side note* is that it's not how much you make; it's how much money you save, invest, and organize. There are plenty of *rich* celebrities out there who go broke no matter how much money they earn, simply because they didn't know what to do with it as it came in.

People who complain, make excuses, and try to find a quick way to make it in their industry usually have the same mentality: *We can't figure out a budget, we don't make enough money yet.* This, my friends, is an excuse. It's an excuse because income has nothing to do with your expenses. Your budget is based on your expenses, not what you bring in.

Oh, sure, income can change how you afford your lifestyle and how you organize surplus into your 3 Needs of Purpose, but it doesn't influence how *you* spend your money. A budget is about adding up all your expenses and how you adjust those expenses to fit a lifestyle.

Being consistent with your budget will correct your bad habits and train you to have better money management control. Basically, what I'm saying is that expenses can get expensive if you don't know when to say *no* to your *wants* and learn to afford your *needs* first.

Money management is not easy, but it's still part of The Process.

> *A good rule of thumb* is that less is more. When you spend less, you save more. That's the secret to wealth growth: spending less than you earn.

CHAPTER 7.1
People Management

7.1 | PEOPLE MANAGEMENT

How you manage people will actively affect your goals and the goals of those people. See, the wrong people can influence bad habits as much as the right people can inspire great habits. Which means we have to put time into people, and select how much time we put into the right people.

Ah yes, time. Oh, how it's limited and finite. This isn't a bad thing, per se, but we all have time as a resource. A resource that we can't refill. And more importantly, the moment you're born, that limited resource is being spent. What's more frightening—we don't know how much we have.

But, Thomas, that's… what am I supposed to do with that?

It's supposed to make you reexamine time—your time, life, choices, wants, desires, and the dream of one day making a living within your field of interest. All of it, because it should motivate you to think about The Process and how to get there and what it'll take. That's the magic of being aware.

The time you have is a gift to spend as you wish. When you spend that time and give it to others, it'll take away your limited commodity. Does this mean you shouldn't give time to people if they're not elevating your purpose? No, not at all. All people have value in life. Whether those people give you perspective by being around them or you influence them.

This is why there's wisdom in managing the people in and around your life, and you *will* have to learn to manage people to create longevity. People management is a step toward taking back control over your own value, the value of others, and how we all can influence each other to work, grow, and rise together.

To be fair, this section of chapters isn't about networking or growing your Circle of Influence. In fact, we're probably not even going to touch on what you should do with your Circle of Influence.

My goal is to hopefully give you perspective on your life and those you let into it. These chapters will allow you to understand your worth, how your worth influences others, and how the worth of others influences you.

But, Thomas, are you saying I should use people?

No. Don't use people. Ever. The real purpose of these chapters is to give you direction on determining certain elements about yourself and others. Some of those elements are your morals, missions, and purposes. These elements (which connect deeply to your brand) can help determine what makes a good person great and a great person a powerful part of your life. But hopefully, you'll see how you can do the same for others.

Managing people is a give-and-take action that requires you to look deep into yourself as well as understand the qualities you look for in others. The secret to managing people is to know when to invest time in others and how long to invest that time. The second part of that is knowing your value and worth so you don't waste other people's time.

Ultimately, this approach will determine who you want to surround yourself with and who you want to give your time to. And, of course, not all relationships are meant to last forever. They come and go, and at times, we learn what we can from them. How and what you learn from them—well, the harsh reality of it all is that betrayal is just as much a lesson in life as finding a mentor. The hard truth is that friendships will come and go, but that doesn't mean you should stop making friends.

Take into consideration that it's okay to change up the people you spend time with. Whether those people are amazing or not, you need breaks, adjustments, and change to grow and experience life. Besides, we all know that there's always a chance a good, strong, and cohesive relationship could last a few months or forty years.

But remember, the amount of time you spend with a person isn't indicative of that relationship's true value. You're not responsible for giving people any or all of your time, just as they're not responsible to do the same. True friendships are the ones where time vanishes in our absence, and when you see each other again, it's as if no time has passed.

> *A good rule of thumb* is that the people we hang out with the most become the world we live in. In reality, we take on the qualities and habits of those we surround ourselves with. So, if you really want to be successful in the entertainment industry, hang out with successful entertainers within your field of interest. If you want to be a millionaire, hang out with millionaires.

As you read through this section of chapters, you'll be given tools to take an in-depth look within and acknowledge what qualities are important to you or those around you. Once you figure out what those qualities are, ask yourself if you represent those qualities too.

Now remember, you're not here to make friends with people who can help you. That's using people. You're not here to use people. You're here to make friends with those who will inspire, elevate, and influence you to take action. Their presence alone should motivate you as much as your presence will motivate them. It's about working together.

Using people for their resources is wrong. Period. I repeat, don't do it. I promise you that you won't succeed in your industry if you only have an interest in others because *they* have something that'll help *your* career. It would be the same as if *you* had a passion for a *cause* but diminished that cause by using it as a stepping stone filled with an agenda.

For example, if a person wanted to bring light to mental health, that, by itself, is a great mission. Mixing that into a brand is also wonderful.

But, Thomas, how would that look when played out?

Let's say you're a musician and want to bring light to mental health; the positive way to do this is to use your lyrics or visual themes to represent it. However, the moment you decide to utilize your *mission* or *purpose* to build your platform for something else, say, to get YouTube views or Spotify listens for your music, now you're in questionable territory.

This hidden agenda is visible to others, and when making friends, they can see the truth in you. They'll be able to tell when they're being used for their resources or if you're using a mission for gain.

The same goes for an audience: when they see a *mission* being used to gain notice, it'll absolutely reflect back on your brand in a negative way. That reflection will tarnish how others see you and your brand.

So, whether you use a person or a mission to gain something, it'll only backfire and show your true colors. Don't do it. Don't use people. I know, I'm saying that a lot. The reason is that you shouldn't use people, and I want to make sure you know that before moving forward.

But, Thomas, when I befriend someone to help me, isn't that, well, the same as me using them?

It depends. Are you friends with them because they have a resource or connection that will benefit only you? If you both connect on something specific, like helping people or mental health, then that's a good starting point. In the end, you should always try to meet like-minded people with like-minded goals, trying to accomplish a like-minded mission (that's not the mission to help you and only you).

See, when you look deep within at what's important, you're looking at what qualities and values you deem purposeful.

But, Thomas, what does that mean?

I'm trying to say that *what you do is who you are*. If you believe that people should help one another rather than exploiting them, then you should help others rather than exploiting them. See? You become the truth in what you do, not what you say.

On the other hand, if a person willingly gives you their time, money, and access to the people they know, that's different. There are many reasons for a person to give you their resources. They might believe in you or feel you earned their time because they see similar qualities in you.

Either way, I'd still add that when this happens, be aware of the thin line that connects you to them and their resources. That thin line is going to be the agenda *you* have for that relationship. Yes, they might be giving you their resources, but that doesn't mean you should take advantage of them. Be aware of your behavior and intentions when kindness is helping you.

> ***A good rule of thumb*** is that when a mentor takes you under their wing to teach you the industry, it's best not to use their resources for *your* purpose. Example: If a mentor tries to teach you how to get press for their clients, don't use it as an opportunity to get press for yourself. If you think "*I'll get interviews for myself first, build relationships with the press, and then help their clients*" is a good idea, it's not. You're affecting their business.

CHAPTER 7.2
People Management

7.2 | QUALITIES TO NOTE

Here are three qualities to note in other people and yourself: trusting in people, working as a team, and no person is an island. You want to find people who have these three qualities. In fact, you should want to be that kind of person too. I say this knowing that these three qualities will benefit the proverbial tables of opportunity—either the ones you join or build.

You have to be able to trust the people you associate with, and they need to trust you. And that trust needs to be a two-way street; though, you'll have to figure out what trust truly means to you in the long run. When you decide that, remember, you too have to live by those morals, those values, those qualities.

When it comes to trusting and choosing the right people to have around you, it's the ones that join a table as part of a team, not as a person standing on their shoulders to get ahead. Do you have to create a team to succeed? No. Not at all. But it does mean you need people. And lots of them. These people will be those you help and those who help you.

Speaking of people, when it comes down to the reality of success, no person is an island. We're interconnected, whether you believe it or not. Your success is based on how involved you are within a community. You need to be involved so you can connect with other people. Which means that you need to learn how to depend on others as others need to depend on you.

At the end of the day, isolation is a killer. Being alone and trying to do it all yourself is detrimental. I know how hard it can be to deal with others. To think that your craft and talent will be what gets you to the top. After all, a writer writes *their* books in isolation. A guitarist performs alone on stage left while girls watch *them* fiddle. Actors perform *their* character's lines for a scene. So, I get it. But the truth remains, cutting yourself off from others is harmful to your well-being, success, longevity, and ultimately, your dream career within the entertainment industry.

Allow the following breakdown of each quality to give you some insight on the qualities you should be looking for within others and yourself.

TRUST IN PEOPLE

First, what is trust? Trust is going to be different for you, me—everyone. We all have had different life experiences, from having our trust broken to being surrounded by really great people. Those experiences are why and how we learn to trust and what leads us to distrust.

Before you can trust anyone in the industry, you have to decide what trust means to you. What it really means to you. This'll help guide you with how you behave around people and what's acceptable behavior from them.

The truth is, trust can have different value levels. Your trust can be completely opposite of another's. Don't be surprised if you meet people who are comfortable not being very forthright. The thing is, you can't read minds, so you don't always know. You can't know. But that doesn't mean you can't trust people, nor does it mean you can't get to know someone. And having a baseline for what trust is to you will make The Process easier to identify.

For me, honesty is what builds trust. It's about being truthful with your positions, having accountability, and open communication with your true intentions. To me, this helps everyone be on the same page.

Honesty doesn't mean you have to tell me everything. Just be honest and truthful with what you *do* decide to tell me. If I probe deeper, be honest with your answers or tell me you don't want to go into detail. You have that right, and I want you to speak up.

And when it comes down to it, all I ask is that you're honest with me, even when the results are bad. I'll always be understanding of those who are upfront with their intentions. I'll say that honesty doesn't make one immune to consequences, but it does help maintain a relationship of trust. Of course, a person could be hiding too much information that leads them to be untrustworthy with their shifty, sly, and sneaky behavior.

Alright, now it's your turn to think about what trust is to you. Take your time and think about what matters to you. Make sure your version of trust reflects your morals. Once you determine what kind of trust you want in others, think about how you represent those trusting qualities yourself.

Yes. You set the standard, and those standards reflect who you are in how you behave. Which means, think about how others trust you. Are you trustworthy, honestly trustworthy, to your own standards?

This is the hardest part about growth. This is the moment when you have to look unbiasedly into a deeper critique of yourself. If you only see perfection, you'll never move to change or evolve. You need to trust people, but they need to trust you more. And if you're unable to honestly take a look inside, doors of opportunity will close within your industry. You must be the standard you wish to see in others.

But, Thomas, how can I know if I'm trustworthy?

Ask people if you're trustworthy. Yep. It's that easy. Ask them what qualities they see in you that make you trustworthy. Do they match up with what you believe about yourself or the qualities you wish to see in others?

If yes, great. If not, then it's time to change your habits. It's time for you to do the work and reflect on your own qualities. Yes, you'll have to actually do the work on yourself and make changes. But it's worth it.

But, Thomas, what if I can't trust someone, but they're useful?

Well, remember: Don't use people. However, that question brings me to rules about trust. If you can't trust someone, they must be removed. This is a hard, strong fact that will not only protect you but also allow you to fire quickly and hire slowly. That's right, your life is a business, and it will fail based on the people you waste your time relying on or trusting.

The cold truth is that you have to be able to trust people. If you can't trust them, let them go. But embrace the ones you find who've earned that trust. If they *are* people you recognize as untrustworthy but want them in your life (because they've been there forever—or are family), just keep them at arm's length.

But, Thomas, what should I look for in a trustworthy person?

They buy you pizza. Sorry, that's my requirement. For you, live by this rule: open communication. Trust yourself to do right by others and speak up. You want people who do the same. If you can't trust they'll do right by you, have a conversation.

See, to trust one another, use open communication to make sense of things. Open and honest communication cancels out miscommunication—or *feelings*. "I feel like Chris is avoiding me." You can't know until you ask follow up questions. It'll save everyone from headaches.

But, Thomas, what if open communication upsets them?

It's true, honesty can hurt people's feelings, even when presented in a compassionate, empathetic, and respectful way. You can't know if your approach is respectful beyond being true to your understanding of kindness. For me, I follow the *How I would like to be treated* rule in life. If you don't like being talked down to, don't talk down to people. However, if people insist you're always talking down to them—take a beat and think about it.

At the end of the day, it's not your job to fight, scream, and become frustrated with an individual or a group that you just don't believe or trust anymore. If you can't trust them or communicate openly with them, move on. It's not worth the insanity of their own bubble of inconsistency.

Here's the reality of trust: if you can't trust them without question, it's not worth your time or theirs. Trust means you can depend on each other. Trust is believing and accepting the words that come out of each other's mouths. Trust is the foundation of potential in relationships. Without it, it will collapse on itself.

But, Thomas, why is trust the first element on this list?

Because success can't happen if you don't trust those around you or they don't trust you. Your name must hold the strength of trust, or you'll fade away as people stop thinking of you when opportunities open up.

But, Thomas, how does the trust of others help me in the long run?

Just as you have to trust people you invest time into, that trust must be there when you vouch for them. The time will come when you'll need to help others by introducing them to new people. Equally important is that they'll introduce you to others, knowing they can vouch for you. And in either situation, *trust* suggests you or them will do right by the introduction.

With success, you'll have a chance to build new relationships with older ones. This happens when you meet a new person, Person A, who needs XYZ, and you already know the right person, Person B, who can absolutely help them. Now you can vouch for Person A and B when you make the introduction.

You wouldn't do this if you didn't trust that the introduction would shine positively back on you. However, when you can trust both parties to do right by this new relationship, it'll add value to you and all parties involved in the introduction and future introductions.

When they end up being everything you said they were, you will be able to continue to introduce that person to others. The more people you trust to do right by you and those you introduce them to, the greater influence you'll have with managing people. And this influence you created is considered a Value Set. One that'll carry you into your future, all because the person you introduced was everything you said they were.

Trust: it's a powerful quality to have and to have in others.

WORK AS A TEAM

Yeah, I know, teamwork makes the dream work. That's true—you do need others in your life as much as you're in theirs. However, I'm not saying that you *should* have a team or be in one. What I'm saying is that you and those around you should have a *team mentality*.

A team mentality is much different than having a team do stuff for you or you do stuff for a team. What makes a team mentality powerful is a collection of people all working together toward the same mission goal: to succeed, not for themselves but for something greater.

But, Thomas, the success of my Career Business is my mission goal.

That's not really a mission goal; that's a you thing, and it won't bring you true success. Without a mission, a *real* mission, you'll be working hard to push boulders up a hill by yourself. A real mission goal is more than "I want money," "an Oscar," or "my epic instrumental metal band to win!"

Selfish intent is going to reflect the truth, your truth, that you live by the *me mentality* and not the *we mentality*. You cannot trust a *me mentality* individual except for the fact that you can trust them to choose themselves over others 90% of the time.

The *me mentality* is about taking advantage of others and jumping ship for opportunities so *they* can try to make it to the top. These are people who will leave without any real courtesy warning when other doors open. These are the people who make themselves known during your success but vanish when the ship starts sinking.

Metallica is Metallica because it's four people working toward the same goal: Metallica Inc. This method allows the *brand* to accomplish much more than just music. Metallica Inc. makes movies, owns a record label, and they all individually own businesses too.

But, see, before opening their own businesses, it started with them focusing on a single mission goal for the brand—not the band, but the brand itself. Everything those members did was designed to elevate the Metallica Inc. brand during its uprising. The members established certain rules that they stuck to early on in their careers. One of those rules gave them insight by looking at successful bands, companies, and producers. And those ventures all have something in common: they either stayed together the whole time or got rid of anyone who wasn't part of the *we mentality*.

> *A good rule of thumb* is that you can work with teams. Approach those opportunities with the *we mentality*. And when you do, do right by the people you work with, stand by your word, and communicate openly with them when another opportunity does come up.

I say all of this because if you want success, a mission goal will take your Career Business further. The reason is simple: working to succeed for yourself will always come at the cost of others. Working with others toward a mission goal will connect audiences and like-minded people to your brand.

But, Thomas, what if my mission goal is to be a comedian or writer?

Is that what you're selling your audience? No. It's not what you're selling anyone. If telling jokes or writing a book was all it took, then there would be way more successful people in this industry.

Your mission goal shouldn't be to be a comedian or writer. It should be greater than your dream. No one in the world, other than your mom and dad, will connect to and support your dream. And even that's pushing it. The old, "You should have a plan B and become a doctor" mantra.

What I'm saying is, your mission goal should be something people can connect with. If you're a comedian, the material you do on stage would represent that true mission goal. Maybe that mission goal is to bring light to healthy relationships by exposing the absurdity of unhealthy relationships. Same with writers—write about healthy relationships, and that becomes your brand. And these mission goals can be many, many different things.

But, Thomas, how would my mission goals link with others?

You should always be searching for other people who have similar mission goals as you as much as you do for theirs. And people work harder for the things they believe in. This is why you need people involved who have the *we mentality*. Does that mean you'll always find those people? No. Sometimes the *me mentality* people will sneak in.

When trying to find these people, you want to search for those ever-present red flags of the *me mentality*. The first clue: those who see a mission goal as an opportunity for themselves. Second clue: those who are only concerned with *their* outcome. This means they're more likely to take action if it'll directly influence their mission goals. These are usually people who do not add value to the team or that team's mission unless it showcases their worth and potential.

This goes for people who create teams too. If they have a team and use that team for their own gain, then the mission is there as a ruse. *Me mentality* people try to A) get to the top in the quickest way possible, B) use people and opportunities, and C) have little concern about the bridges they'll burn on the way to success.

The hard truth about all of this is that you can't connect with others in your industry if you only care about yourself and your Career Business. It will always become a chaotic experience when everyone involved *only* cares about themselves. More importantly, you need people; you need like-minded people; and you need others who have a team mentality—the *we mentality*.

NO PERSON IS AN ISLAND

No person is an island—ah, no truer statement had ever been spoken. That hyperbole tells us just enough to pay attention. See, you alone can never and will never truly be self-sufficient. It's impossible.

But, Thomas, isn't my success based on what I do?

Sure. You *are* responsible for making things happen. But no matter what, you're still going to be reliant on others in order to thrive. Beyond the fact that you *need* to connect with others, there are also those who open doors for you, say yes for you, and advocate for you, and that's only a *few* examples. Oh, wait, there's another group of people you need: people who'll buy into your brand enough to pay money for the *thing* you do.

For example, if you were a comedian, you'd need people to enjoy who you are as an actual person before they book you on stage. You need people to manage your career, guide you, and mentor you. And no one will do that because you're awesome. Managers have to like *you* and believe in your brand's mission, and those managers *need* to know the right people to get you booked and paid for performances at festivals.

You, like everyone in the world, need other people in your life and through your Career Business. Honestly, imagine doing an interview all by yourself. Who would ask who the questions? You'd be that wacko talking to yourself in an empty room and asking yourself questions.

But, Thomas, I'm the talent; they need me more than I need them.

Imagine you lived on an island. On that island, you only know how to hunt, but you don't know how to make fire. You know how to swim, but you don't know how to fish. You saw how to build a house on YouTube, but you don't have the tools or real know-how to do it.

If that doesn't hit you the right way, how would you feel in a month, six months, one year... no, three years of living on that island alone? Yeah, that feeling isn't a good feeling. We need people in and around our lives to survive, feel emotions, feel a connection, and stay sane.

I get it though, the Artist Brain thinks: *I need to be seen so people buy into me, since I'm the one who wants to be successful!* That kind of thinking will push you to believe you're the most important person around. It happens;

I've been there. I've lived fully inside the Artist Brain, and Artist Brains love living on that island, searching for the spotlight! Look at me!

The problem with this Artist Brain approach is, until hindsight hits you, you won't know how your selfishness will sabotage your opportunities. Oh sure, you might be nice to people, but I'm talking about the Artist Brain agenda. The things that make it about you and not them.

Thoughts like: your talent is the secret to *your* success. *You* have to blow other performers off the stage with your awesomeness. Or how actors, comedians, or musicians *need* to be the best on stage and have zero care for the other performers. Think like that, and I assure you, that island is going to be lonely at the top.

You need people on your island. In fact, you're on an island that isn't even your island. You're part of a community that is ever-growing. And on that island, everyone is important, each with their own unique ability to do things others cannot. It just doesn't matter who is awesome, amazing, or unique. It matters that everyone tries to work together so they get the best results as a *team*. You should be learning from each other.

You have to think about your life beyond yourself and your needs. Yes, you have needs, and you also have wants; these desires are for *things* that are as far from your grasp as the universe itself, and that's okay. You will work toward them, but it's hard to build a spaceship when you're alone. The thing is, you're not alone, and you shouldn't be alone. No matter what you do in this life, you are a part of something bigger than you.

Focusing on yourself will only lead you down a path of failure. I say this because if you look at successful people, you will discover something interesting: they all have people they rely on and who rely on them.

You know what else they do? They added value to their industry and communities within that industry. In turn, as they worked hard within their industry, their success came from others helping them. And those other people who helped them had help from others along the way.

The ones who have failed in this business are those who are hard to work with, are a problem on set/stage, cause issues with others, people who just don't get along with anyone, and the list goes on. It's not something you can ignore when the proof is the truth. If it didn't work for them, why would it work for you? You're not an island, so don't let your behavior isolate you because no one wants you around.

The truth is that you need other people to connect with. And they'll connect with you through your mission goals. Those goals will guide your behavior and who you get involved with. When you do get involved with those people, you'll leave an impression on them. Mostly because you'll all have something in common with mission goals.

People connect on missions and with people who believe in those missions. And no one is going to connect with you just because you want to be successful, make lots of money, or win awards—none of that is something others will be drawn to or can connect with on a deeper, more emotional level.

But, Thomas, won't awards, money, and my greatness get attention?

Well, it might get people's attention enough to ask you to come and get involved. But the issue here is that it'll be for the wrong reasons. They want your status, your money, the draw from your recent award, and not you as a person. You've become expendable based on your resources alone.

When you realize they're using you, the fun part of working with these people will vanish. Poof. They asked you to join their table to help add attention to *their* project, *their* personal goals, *their* dreams. Your value has now been reduced to your intangible attributes that will absolutely fade with time. You become just a number in the equations of being used and not seen for the value of what you truly bring to the table.

Listen, you're not just one person trying to survive on an island, and you don't have to be either. A person makes that choice to be alone on an island. You? You get to change it up and take action, get involved, and make things happen. Because *you* need to get involved so your Value Sets and brand can be noticed. Which, in the end, is what makes people want to be around you. Or rather, they want you around them. Ah, forming emotional connections with people. Who would have thought?

The island is a lonely place when you're trying to enjoy the love of your passion in an industry that will chew you up and spit you out. What's that old saying? Oh yeah: it's lonely at the top when you don't put the time into forming authentic relationships with others. And this is done by being nice to everyone.

But, Thomas, do I have to be nice to *everyone*?

Yes. It's the first rule of networking: Be nice to everyone, because you never know who someone is or knows. Besides, you want to be nice to people on the way up because you'll meet them all on the way down.

THE TAKEAWAY

These qualities form the foundation of how you'll treat others, what to look for in people, and how to approach every table you join or build. Remember, it's not about *you*; it's about the people you surround yourself with, it's about teams with the *we mentality*, and it's about getting involved with others so you can work, grow, and rise together.

One of the bigger takeaways is that you won't get off any island if you isolate yourself in your greatness. It'll always be harder working alone. You need to work with teams filled with people you can trust and where they can trust you so you can all get off that island. The takeaway is that if you're trapped on that island together, you'll be able to survive the long haul together.

The entertainment industry is an island filled with opportunities, but when you start out, you'll be trapped in the sway of its influence. So, you'll have to work on building your brand, developing relationships, and all the things necessary to create real movement. Because right now, you can't just walk into a room and get what you want simply because you're awesome and feel you deserve it. It takes people, and lots of them, to make things happen. It takes *you* helping others in the industry.

And then, not at first, but eventually, your efforts will lead to you having influence, pull, and the resources to become a maker who can shake things up. Until that day comes, build trust with like-minded people, become a team player, and help others.

CHAPTER 7.3
People Management

7.3 | WHO IS RIGHT FOR YOUR BUS

Who *is* right for your bus? Before we can answer that question, we should define what the bus is. The *bus* represents your life. Everyone in this world is born with a bus. It looks similar for each person too—limited seats, needing gas, people getting on and off, and a limited number of miles.

As you can see, these are all metaphors for what it takes to live. And each person has specific needs and concerns about the finer details of their bus (life), such as windows, style, comfort, power, and the list goes on. I'm sure you're thinking about it right now. Maybe you're concerned about the tires, seating arrangement, and functionality. These are all valid concerns.

Each specific concern has variables you can change based on who you are or who you allow onto your bus. After all, you might have mechanic friends, artists to paint the bus a different color, a group of people to help manage your bus trips, or control the radio. It's amazing how much you can adjust things on *your* bus. And sure, some people have really nice buses because, well, more money, wealth, and resources, and it shows.

However, those things are what make a bus a bus. Which means, with the right amount of money, anyone can make the bus of their dreams. For me, I hope it has AC. I'm not a fan of heat. However, not everyone has loads of money. Which is another reason *you* need to save up startup capital for your Financial Foundation Account (just reminding you).

LIMITED SEATING

Your bus (life) is going to have limited resources. The biggest one being time. Then money, and finally people. Since you have limited resources, your bus has limited space to dedicate to those things. And time is the resource you need to be most aware of. Time vanishes even when you do nothing, when you work for money, and when you put time into people.

The truth is, all kinds of people have come and gone in your life over the years. Some are quick meetings with random strangers; other relationships last over a decade and end with a simple goodbye. These scenarios, and everything in between, are absolutely okay.

The thing is, not everyone can get on your bus, and that's because there's not a lot of room. That limited space means that some people will be left behind, others given priority, and still, you'll need to adjust that limited space from time to time for random people.

But, Thomas, can't I just let people on my bus and figure it out?

If there are a limited number of seats, you'll have to choose wisely. Ask yourself: Who's earned a spot on your bus?

The problem is that you might try to fit everyone you know onto the bus, declaring that no one will be left behind! Now you have a bus filled to the brim with people. Is that better than no people? Maybe, maybe not. But a person can't handle everything on their own. A bus is a lot to handle; after all, the bus itself is *life*.

This brings me to a point where it's time to get real. You might trust yourself more than anyone else in the world. Does that mean you should be driving the bus alone, feeding yourself, spending and allocating the money, fixing the bus, figuring out where you need to go, and entertaining yourself?

No. No, you should not be doing any of it alone. It can become quite overwhelming. And this is why, over time, you have to develop relationships and manage the people on your bus (in your life). And as they enter your bus, get off the bus, and then sometimes get back on the bus, you have to say to yourself, "Who do I *want* on my bus?"

And this is the crazy part: from time to time, you'll be on someone else's bus (involved in their life at their tables). This is where you need to figure out what *you* can add to their bus. Why are you on that bus in the first place? Is it because it'll help you go a few miles before you jump off, or are you trying to sincerely help that bus?

However you approach it, it gets pretty crazy on any bus, trust me. I've been on fun buses, clown buses, musician buses, comedian buses, and actor buses, and each time I had to figure out who was right for my bus or what I could bring to the buses I was right for.

ADD QUALITY TO A BUS

Every situation, every life, every bus needs to be filled with quality people with certain qualities. Those qualities will be different for each bus. You personally will have qualities that are important to you as much as others will have for them.

But, Thomas, what kind of qualities should I look for?

Any qualities you want for your bus. Qualities can be anything from a person's missions, morals, and purposes. You might want specific qualities in a person, like loyalty, kindness, compassion, and a willingness to listen. Whatever it is, you have to figure it out and then seek out people with those qualities. But remember, what you seek out in others should be the standard of what you represent. That's right. Become the change you want to see.

If you're not representing what you wish to receive from others, it'll damage your reputation. A damaged reputation means that no one will want to be around you. If no one wants to be around you, then who'll sit on your bus? In reality, what you do is who you are, even if you don't believe you're doing it.

But, Thomas, if I'm being a good person, who's to say otherwise?

People will see you as they perceive you. If you believe you're doing one thing and others tell you you're doing something else, it's best to listen to what they have to say. It's okay to take their input, especially if it's the majority of what people are saying. Afterwards, consider how to change things up so you can better represent what you feel you want to be seen as.

SETTING THE TONE

Whatever route you take, you'll need to figure out what kind of bus you want. And it's important. Once you figure it out, it'll literally set the tone for your bus. So, once you have it in your head, write it down.

By the way, you might write down that you want people on your bus who are honest, loyal, giving, take action, and have resources that help your mission. Those are standard and basic examples. Remember, you want to set the tone through your missions, morals, and purposes.

The tone of your bus will not be impacted by generic concepts. This is why you need to ask yourself strong questions. Hard questions. The questions that allow you to understand your missions, morals, and purpose. What are you trying to accomplish? How do you want to go about it? Why are your mission and your morals important for you? Knowing the answers will give you a strong, healthy starting point. A starting point that'll allow your principles to set the standard, the tone.

But, Thomas, I don't even know where to start.

Let me use my old progressive doom metal band, Altayon, for this example. You'll see how I take my missions, morals, and purposes to drive (no pun intended) me to the qualities that are important to me.

"The world is filled with misguided evidence to the contrary of right and wrong, and life should inform change through behavior and a series of enlightenments found over the course of being the presented examples, not commanding change of others, but bringing light to the emotional discovery of a united populace as a one world seeking peace in harmony."

It's a simple enough idea, minus the convoluted choice of words. Not all missions are straightforward, and not all poetic messages need to be. For me, the goal with my band's brand (and most of what I do in life) was to tell stories through various mediums (written, visual, audio) and spread a message of change through enlightenment.

If we look through the message, we can discover what kind of people would be right for my bus, or if I'm right for other buses. Because, honestly, I don't have to be driving the bus if I find people fueling similar ideas at the beginning of my Career Business. With that said, I'm going to go through the example a few words at a time.

"The world is filled with misguided evidence to the contrary of right and wrong..."

To me, I'm trying to express that people have been led down a road of what is expected of them through specific morals, behaviors, laws, and ideals that make you a *good* person. Over time, I noticed that what people held dear to them as *doing right by others* isn't always the case. Right and wrong have nuances, but our cultural oppression of human existence has been tampered with through educational systems, government, and those we're directly/indirectly mentored by.

To my point, in the entertainment industry alone, there are people in the industry who *guide* actors to get headshots. Oddly enough, it turns out they're a photographer or *know* a photographer. What's worse than that is when you realize they're not a photographer, nor do they know one.

What happened with that exchange is that they *know* how the industry works, and they only know what they know from what they learned growing up and around others with the same misconceptions.

But, Thomas, why is that worse?

When you realize that they themselves are still doing nothing with their careers and yet their advice is to do XYZ. They were filled with misguided evidence to the contrary of right and wrong for their careers.

Understanding the sentence helps me look at my life in a specific way, but how does this help me find the right people for my bus or find the right bus to be on? It means I should look for people who, at a minimum, see the industry (and life) outside of constructs.

My hope is that I find like-minded people with these views or opinions. Perhaps their belief is that the world needs a change, that what people are being taught isn't helping but destroying. These people would have morals similar to my own. These are the morals that guide them to help others, to learn from one another, and to see past the misguided evidence and identify when something is wrong. Research, research, research.

Okay, next one.

> "...and life should inform change through behavior and a series of enlightenments found over the course of being the presented examples, not commanding change of others..."

I believe deeply that we have no right to ask others to change. What we can do is make better choices for ourselves. Choices that will hopefully inspire others to make a change. It's about influencing change by setting an example. We can't ask others to change if we're not setting the standard.

But, Thomas, how does all of this help your bus?

It helps by filling it up with like-minded people who take action that represents their beliefs. Beliefs where people help one another, guide others, and break the cycles of misinformation. It's about people with similar mindsets who walk the walk and not just talk the talk.

And finally.

> "...but bringing light to the emotional discovery of a united populace as a one world seeking peace in harmony."

This part of my mission is all about doing what we do while getting along with others as best we can. And this is accomplished by compassionately listening to others, by truly hearing what they're saying, seeing them for their truths, and being willing to understand how their mind, body, and soul work.

We should be working to realize that we're a gathering of people who all have diverse points of view and cultures and look for common ground. It's not about changing people but finding ways to unite and accept others. To work toward finding that common ground until we have *peace in harmony.*

A few qualities that meet these standards are people who aren't racist and people who bring others together and not tear them apart. People who try to get along with others and rarely judge them as best they can. I want to be near people who listen to hear, not listen to respond. It's about being around others who want to work, grow, and rise together.

Now it's your turn. Put as much time into this as needed to figure out what your mission is. Break that mission down to see what matters to you. What qualities are important for your bus? After you write it down, examine it. Remember this important rule: you're allowed to change what you come up with.

WHAT DOES ALL THIS MEAN?

At the end of the day, you need to know what's important to you and your mission. Through that mission, you'll discover what qualities are right for your bus. And here's the thing. You might find people for your mission who fit great on your bus. Then one day, they don't fit. People change, grow, regress, and evolve (or devolve); it happens. Which means that you need to know when to pull over and let people out, either because they asked you to (don't fight them on staying) or because you need them to be let out.

> *A fun side note* is that there is an indisputable truth when it comes to your bus. You have the power of choice when it comes to your bus. The power to choose who you want to keep on *your* bus. Additionally, others have the choice to stay on your bus or if they want you on their bus.

When people do get off your bus (for whatever reason), stick to the first rule of networking: be nice to everyone; you never know who someone is or knows. You don't have to keep people in your life who've broken your boundaries or your peace, but you should still be the standard of kindness you want from others.

I'll say this much: you might be driving down the road in your big, beautiful bus and see a person from your past just standing in the rain. The goodness inside of you will want to pull over and check on them. And you should. They might need a ride, or maybe it's for a quick hello. Either way, check on people when they come into view.

This all brings me to the purpose of the chapter: you need to figure out what qualities are most important to you. As you can tell, in my above example, my mission wasn't looking for people who had the best resources to help me achieve *my* mission. It was about their core beliefs; it was about us having things in common; it was about the qualities *we* all brought to the table.

And shared qualities are a powerful truth that bring people together. When people emotionally believe in something, they put effort into it. You should be trying to find people who emotionally believe in your *mission* and whose presence is filled with a desire to help elevate that *mission*. Notice I said *mission* and not *you*. That's right, it's not about you; it's about what you stand for, what others stand for. Success comes from fueling a mission through morals pushed by a purpose.

Let me end with this thought: the people who are right for your bus should appreciate and support the same things that you love (at least in part). And you, yes you, should appreciate and support the same things they love. You know why? Because loving similar things is what brings people together. So, yes, find people who have a similar appreciation for the world beyond what they do creatively. Oh sure, two comedians might connect over comedy, but they'll become friends based on their *approach* to comedy, life, and the business of it all.

That approach is filled with the things they care about, believe in, and not only what led them into comedy, but what they love about comedy. It's all the elements and qualities behind the craft of comedy and not "I tell jokes."

So, figure out what matters to you, what you want to see in others, and how you can become the truth of what you believe in. And I assure you, your bus will fill up with the right people, and if you are true to yourself, you'll be asked to join other buses.

CHAPTER 7.4
People Management

7.4 | ME PERSPECTIVE VS. WE PERSPECTIVE

The *me perspective*: a selfish approach to success that fuels actions for the best results to influence you. Did I jump in too fast? Let's back it up a little. Your success is *not* about you; it's about the people around you. To maintain healthy, strong, collaborative relationships, you need to have a give-and-take approach. This is the *we perspective*, where teams and its players prosper.

But, Thomas, without me, there is no we.

Yeah? Say that to the linemen protecting you. Seriously, I get it. Yes, of course you're part of the equation. Yes, you need to take action. And yes, you're responsible for what you do and don't do. But *you* have to make a choice early on in your Career Business journey on whether it'll be about you, those you work with, or a nice combination of both.

Let's break those down. If it's all about you, *me perspective*, it'll be evident in how you approach each situation. The agenda will be firmly seen within your behavior. Do you make choices for situations where it would solely benefit you? And if it can't benefit you, you want no part of it? Is this an opportunity to advance yourself using the shoulders of others? Yes? Well, that's all *me perspective* thinking.

The opposite of that, you going all in to help those you work with, is just as bad. It's draining, time-consuming, and a path that never ends. In the end, being used to help others is just as painful as using others to help you.

But, Thomas, who should benefit?

Simply put: both parties. Because both parties shouldn't be using each other as stepping stones for success. No one should be anyone's tool. Which brings me to the next point: a nice combination of both.

We perspective: focuses on missions and the people involved in those missions. Every person has missions, morals that drive them, and a purpose fueling their intentions. It's their approach that decides if they're a *me* or *we perspective*.

Not sure who you are? Ask yourself, "How does this help me?" and "How does this elevate the table's mission?" One is about you.

ME PERSPECTIVE

Time to roleplay the *me perspective*. We all love a little roleplaying, and we won't even need a D20 for this.

You're an actor, writer, and filmmaker and decide to write, cast, and make a film. So far, this isn't really that bad. You should always feel comfortable being creative. But your first thought is: *How will this make me money?* Your second thought: *I can use this to get noticed.* And your third thought is that *this film will get me discovered.*

Your toe has now dipped into the *me perspective*. No one will want to work with you if it's about your film, you making money, getting noticed, or even discovered.

But, Thomas, I'm a musician. I don't care about filmmaking.

Alright, imagine you were asked to play in a band, and all you cared about was being the best performer on stage, the one that used the stage time to show off their talent and get noticed. Sure, you like the band, but it's not *your* band. It's just a step to get noticed for your epic instrumental band.

But, Thomas, you said stage performances don't get you noticed.

You're listening. That makes me happy. Alright, you joined a band because you found out they have connections. And joining the band means you can use the right people to your advantage. You might even just be the mascot running around the stage, and when they need a guitarist to stand in, you get upset because they didn't think about you. It's not about you.

This is my favorite one, and I've experienced it: You decide to join a band, and you know they dress up as characters. But that's not *your* thing. So you outright refuse and instead wear your other band's shirt or look like an accountant on stage.

Okay, one more for actors. You're an actor, but *you* only take lead roles. And you hear about a project that's a great opportunity for *your* career. So you ask the writer/producer if you can be an actor in the project. But they tell you they have an actor for the lead. However, they need a production assistant. To which you respond with no. Lead actors get noticed and have lots of lines, and you don't want to be running around like a gofer. Go for this, go for that—get me a cup of coffee.

Caring only if you're the lead to get noticed is about you, the *me perspective*, and not the mission of the project, the team involved, or beyond what you'll gain from working on it.

WE PERSPECTIVE

Role reversal and brain change time! *We perspectives* actively help others and get involved. Especially when missions align and everyone involved is working together with a purpose.

In this roleplay, you're someone who actively seeks out others to help them achieve results in their mission. You actively introduce people to each other who can benefit from one another independently from you. You join missions, doing what you can to elevate it by being available. You get involved because you believe in the mission even if you're not getting to perform (or do what you love doing).

Your mind sees opportunities not for your personal success but for something bigger than you. You're getting involved, and it's not about you; it's about other people. You've learned to get involved beyond your *wants*. To hear that others need a specific person for something—your first reaction is, "I know the right person for them; let me introduce them."

And yes, before you ask, this works for you too. When you have a mission, it should be about the mission, not you being the shining star. I once had a keyboardist play with my second big band. And the band was me on guitar and singing; another guitarist; a bass player; a female co-singer; a drummer; and the keyboardist. The keyboardist asked why they couldn't have their keyboards up front. I asked why he wanted that. He said that he wanted people to see him.

Keep in mind, you can still see him clearly. However, the band did a stage show, a kind of character performance because, you know, we were characters. The keyboardist refused to dress in character and only wore black pants and a band shirt. It wasn't about us; it was about him. And their presence up front would not have added to the mission.

We perspective places the mission before the glory of yourself. That keyboardist didn't care about the show, the band members, or what we were going for. He cared about being noticed. He cared about being seen as an awesome keyboardist. Correction. He might have internally cared about the show in his mind, but his actions spoke louder than his words. To be fair, he also said, "I want the people to see me."

If he had the *we perspective*, he would have dressed in character and thought about how to add to both the show and the mission. Sure, our website was TheGreatestBand.com at the time—but we used it ironically. Originally it was about the greatest "band" of bands in the community. But the name backfired, and we leaned into it. Playing up the ego of it all in an over-the-top, "Of course you're clapping, please, please, keep it coming" way.

The point is: think about how you can elevate missions as a team so you can work, grow, and rise together. It's easier to grow as a group than it is to rise as an individual. Team players are the dream players who take action together.

MANAGE YOURSELF FIRST

You're responsible for your behavior. Your intent. Not how people see you, but when others say your actions don't match your intended beliefs, you have to adjust. It's okay when your actions don't represent what you *feel* you're doing, but listening to others gives you a sense of their perspective. Especially when the majority of people see the opposite of your intent.

Take note of what people tell you about your behavior. This is all part of managing people in your life. Not only are you a person, but for people to want you around, you have to make sure you're behaving as you intended. Now, if you want to be annoying and annoy people, you're fine. Keep it up. I mean, you won't go anywhere. But at least your actions match your intent.

You have to manage yourself first, people second, and adjust based on new information. You're the first line of truth when it comes to how *you* behave. And you have to adjust your behavior when people tell you your behavior feels like the *me mentality* when your intent was the *we mentality*.

But, Thomas, what if I *know* I'm there with the *we mentality*?

Are you doing right by others? Are they doing right by you? Why are you getting involved? Is your choice based on being rewarded? Are you doing it because you believe in the mission?

Of those, which matters most to you? You're an adult, and from time to time, you have to analyze your true intentions. What you do needs to stand for what you believe in. It has to be something more than what you *want*. We all want something: success, money, stability, celebrity, maybe even validation.

And the teams you work with will get those things together, but not if you're doing things with them to get rewarded first. Your *wants* should be rewards for bringing purpose to something greater than yourself. Success comes through the effort of doing right by others, your audience, and your mission. Success is not about pushing through others to get to the top first.

RECOGNIZE THEIR INTENTION

Understanding a person's intention is a major part of managing the people. Whether it's making sure your own intentions match your behavior or you recognize the behavior of others isn't matching up with theirs.

Recognizing the intention within others can save you a lot of time, money, and the cost of your connections within your industry. This is why you need to know what kind of intentions you're searching for in others. What kind of intentions are you trying to avoid? And as always, you have to set the standard for what you're looking for.

Not everyone is going to be upfront with you about their intent. Rarely, if ever, will someone say to you, "I'm helping you to get something out of it." It's good they told you, but it's bad they told you. Don't let them on your bus.

Since they're not going to be that bluntly honest with you, you need to recognize their intent: are they using you or do they believe in the table's mission?

With that said, here are some behavior patterns to look for: how they treat others, how poorly they talk about people who helped them, how often they abandon projects, and how often they keep their word. These are only a few examples. The secret is to watch and research people. A person's truth is their behavior, not their words or a resume. I'd recommend learning to recognize these behaviors in yourself before they become the impression you leave on others.

KNOWING YOUR BOUNDARIES

To break the habit of being used, or if you're using others, you need to set and understand your own personal boundaries. Boundaries can be used as a guideline for how you'll treat others. After all, you should always treat people as you wish to be treated. However, if they tell you their boundaries, *you* have to choose to respect those boundaries or realize you might not be right for this relationship. And that is okay either way.

You don't have to be friends with everyone. You do, however, have to be nice to everyone. Being nice doesn't mean you have to tolerate them by going outside your comfort zone. It means to be nice when walking away from them. Because you deserve to be respected just as much as they do.

There will be times when people disrespect you, and it's okay to let them know. Be verbal in expressing your feelings about how you perceive their behavior. Either the conversation will be productive in healing the relationship or it'll let you know it's over.

And I know that most people don't want to hear that their behavior is not aligning with their belief in that behavior. This is the old argument: what I feel and think is valid no matter how much my actions don't align.

"You keep poking me in the eye."

"Sure, but I respect you."

"Could you stop poking me in the eye?"

"Of course," they said, as they poked them in the eye.

"You don't respect me."

"How dare you tell me what I feel inside. I told you I respect you," they said as they poked them in the eye again.

There isn't enough information to know what's going on inside a person's head, because, well, mind reading and all that. But being poked in the eye after asking them to stop means something is not right. They might feel they respect the person and that poking them in the eye is how they show that respect. We don't know the deeper intent.

What's not happening is the poker is not listening. They need to take a moment and decide if they should change their behavior or not. They both can walk away from the relationship, or they can both accept the people for who they are. I'd suggest ending the relationship.

Boundaries are boundaries and should never be compromised at the expense of your peace and your truth. Like how you might hate watching romance movies, but your best friend loves them. A compromise to watch it so you can hang out with them doesn't attack your peace. Unless it's P.S. I Love You. I'm still crying.

Oh, where was I? Oh yes. You make the compromise because you enjoy being around your best friend. See, boundaries are personal thresholds to what and how you're willing to endure. And understanding them allows you to make choices based on where you're willing to stand firm or adjust.

And of course, you do have to tell people what your boundaries are. Which means boundaries are about communication. And yes, you need to tell them. You can't sit there in silence, ignoring them, and expect them to know your boundaries.

But, Thomas, what if my boundary is not to let them speak with me because our conversations turn into arguments?

Then you need to speak with them at least once about that boundary. And I'll tell you why. If you keep silent while they talk to you, that's not helpful, respectful, or kind, especially if you live or work together. The reason is, they have no idea what's going on. Especially if you confuse them by asking them questions about your career and success when you need to speak but ignore them when they speak with you.

Ultimately, telling them does a lot, and it helps figure out the next step. Oh sure, you might not want to tell them, and that's fine. But that means you need to leave that relationship and situation. However, I'd still tell them it's over. But telling them your boundaries gives you insight into who they are. How they respond to that conversation is quite telling. When you tell them your boundaries, do they go above and beyond to respect them or continue crossing the line?

I'll say this much: the situation can be difficult when you're good friends, partners, lovers, or work directly with each other. It can be even harder to recognize the disrespectful ignorance of a *good* friend when they cross your boundaries. You want to believe that they're your friend first, so why would they cross those boundaries? More so, why would they do it after you confide in them what bothers you about their behavior? It can be even more painful when they use that information against you as a weapon.

> *A fun side note* is that boundaries ensure we're all treated with respect, allowing everyone to work together without compromising our core values or being exploited by agendas. Clear boundaries help understand how to best collaborate together in a transparent, mutually rewarding situation.

GETTING TO THE POINT

Life is short; it really can be. You can have a full seventy years or twenty. It's not worth wasting any time on people that don't believe in the same truths as you. And if your missions align, even slightly, with other people, it's a great feeling to get involved with them.

At the end of the day, it's more than who you're working with and about how you're working with them. Open communication, kindness, and the ability to work towards something greater than yourselves will always be a healthier, stronger, environment to grow in.

Success is wonderful when you achieve it. It's even more powerful when it's with other people who all respect one another. And the greatest strength of all of this is helping others once you start opening doors and especially once you reach the top.

Life is about the *we mentality*, not the *me mentality*. People, teams, groups, and missions bring things to life. So embrace the power of freeing yourself from the ego of need and spotlight, and you'll be rewarded with friends, associates, and people you'd consider family.

CHAPTER 7.5
People Management

7.5 | CUT PEOPLE OUT OF YOUR LIFE

One of the more difficult elements of managing people is knowing when to cut them out of your life. It'll happen, and when it does, you'll have to make the hard decisions to do it. Otherwise, it'll hurt your chance for success, and more importantly, your peace.

You shouldn't keep people in your life who drain your resources of time, money, or the people around you. So, that's why one of your jobs is to pay attention to their behavior. People who:

1. Use others for advancement
2. Push clearly stated boundaries
3. Drain others of their resources
4. Drain others of their energy
5. Suck the joy out of other's life
6. Say sorry and continue doing it

When you notice these or similar behaviors, cut them out of your life. Be nice to them, be compassionate, and be respectful. But, at the end of the day, you're responsible for the people *you* allow into your life and who stay there.

At one point or another, you'll notice that certain people just disrupt your flow, corrupt your habits, and lead you to react in ways that aren't true to who you are. This happens often in younger people, usually due to peer pressure—drink because they drink, smoke because they smoke. People can find themselves doing things outside their morals when hanging around bad influences. If *you* notice their bad influences, cut them out of your life.

You don't need to maintain relationships with people who don't add value to your life—value as in being a good influence, elevating your habits, or inspiring morals. And it's not uncommon for those who don't add value to your life to take advantage of your kindness, willingness to help them, or drain the enthusiasm right from your soul.

It's okay to cut people out of your life. Just as much as it's okay to stand up for yourself and tell people how you feel. In fact, I recommend that you always tell people how you feel. Communication is key to success.

I AM SORRY

But, Thomas, you also said I should cut out people who say sorry.

Oh, yes. Now, don't get me wrong, occasionally, people are actually sorry when they say it. And those who say sorry and take accountability can stay. That's the healthy kind of sorry. The unhealthy version of saying sorry comes from people who are *always* sorry.

As an example, you're working with someone, and it's a small thing too, but you ask them to please set up an email signature. They agree to do it, understand how to do it, and promise to have it done by the end of the week. The week comes to an end and no signature. This is where their truth begins to show behind their behavior. They again say that they're sorry and will take care of it by the end of *this* week. Another week passes and there's still no email signature. Rinse and repeat until you just can't trust them. Or, cut them out.

What's the value of being sorry if you continue to repeat the thing you're sorry about? A sincere sorry, at the minimum, is for an accident. At the most, a sorry is for a mistake. But what truly makes it a sincere apology is how they learn from it and adjust their behavior.

It's a pattern of insincerity when it becomes a repeated experience. Sure, they might believe that they're sincerely apologizing, but unchanged behavior is going to disrupt you, those around you, and your peace.

What I'm saying is you can only tolerate certain things for so long before they become destructive. Thus, know your limitations, know your boundaries, and become aware of people who use you. No one is ever truly worth your peace.

And, as always, you must be aware of your own behavior. This gives you the power to change, adjust, and correct yourself when your behavior is outside what you intended. Besides, you set the standard of what you expect from others. You have to change your behavior when it becomes the same as those you'd cut out of your life for.

> *A good rule of thumb* is that when others do not see their negative behavior or their intentions as clearly as their actions have spoken, it is absolutely okay to cut them out of your life. People Management 101 is knowing when to teach, promote, or get rid of a person. Stop your bus and let them out.

THE POWER OF RESPONSIBILITY

It's a liberating feeling to have the strength to cut people out of your life. It truly is. But it's also a responsibility to yourself to cut out the right people and not to abuse the rule.

This rule can feel so freeing at times that you might start cutting everyone out. They do one thing and boom, gone. As much as I agree with "reclaiming my time," you never want to do it at the cost of ending up alone.

You need people to challenge you, push back on your ideas, and keep you thinking, guessing, and growing. You need that around you. You need to be able to listen and make choices based on disagreements. And most of all, you don't want to live in an echo chamber.

However, don't let people take advantage of you. And that's the rub. That's where your responsibility comes in. You are in control of your own choices and behavior, what you're willing to tolerate, and what is a hard no. And that power, that responsibility, isn't easy.

Cutting the wrong person out could end up scaring people away from you. Worried that you're hard to work with, or that they can't be themselves around you. And the right cuts, getting rid of the people who drain, could elevate the tables you build or join. The wrong person could end up talking poorly to a future possibility. The right person could be someone no one likes.

But, Thomas, who do I cut out?

You can cut out the people who show a pattern of negative behavior. Not those one-and-done people. Not the, well, they did it twice in a year people. Not even they lied to me six times in ten years, people. It's a pattern of consistency. A pattern so common that their nickname becomes what they're known for. Mr. Used Me For My Connections over here.

However, if they *only* call when you're working on something to be part of it, that's a consistent pattern. When someone *only* decides to call so they can ask you for career advice, that's a consistent pattern. When people never help you, but you're always helping them, that's a consistent pattern.

Simply pay attention to how people behave consistently, match it to your boundaries, and make a choice based on evidence. Life is short, and I'll be the first to say it. So don't go wasting it away on people who are draining you of the limited time you have. Choose wisely, honorably, and be respectful when you do end up chopping them from the block!

CHAPTER 7.6
People Management

7.6 | FINAL THOUGHTS

People management is more than how you manage people; it's also about how you take responsibility for yourself. It's a two-way street that takes effort, self-awareness, and a willingness to change your behavior.

Self-awareness is important for the success of your Career Business and the relationships you develop. The thing is, other people don't need to manage their relationships or even think about their own behavior. You, on the other hand, do. You're in control of the world you live in. Remember, people can break the rules; you can't. You're the one that wants to be successful.

But, Thomas, don't they want to be successful too?

Oh sure, however, you're not responsible for how they behave. It's not your job to watch over how they treat people, or to course correct them. You're responsible for your own behavior and who you choose to give your time to. You're in control of those around you. And I don't mean you *control* others; I mean you're in control of who you keep around you.

It's all about how you choose to reflect on yourself and those around you, open communication, and organizing your Circle of Influence. You have to be transparent enough to understand another person's thoughts and perspectives so you can have a clear position on their ideas, missions, morals, and purposes.

Their answers will give you insight into how much time you should give or if you should keep them in your circles. Simply by how they behave or don't behave. If their behavior doesn't match their missions, morals, and purposes, it'll be quite revealing of their truth.

To best manage people in your life, you must become the standard for what you wish to see in others. Your goal should be to inspire others through your behavior, not just your words. Your behavior should reflect the value of your words, not just how you feel you intended it.

To truly reflect your words through your actions, take some time to work on your missions, morals, and purposes. The more you understand this on a fundamental level, the better you can represent them through your actions. And knowing them inside and out also allows you to seek out like-minded people with similar beliefs.

In the end, it'll always come down to you. You can't expect people to behave a certain way or listen to you as you try to communicate yourself. It gets harder to gain the trust of those people when you're not abiding by your own principles as you invite people onto your bus. Before you can set the tone for what you want to see in others, you have to set the tone for how you take action around them.

And from time to time, you'll want to invite people on your bus, and when it's not working out, kick them off. That's because kicking people off your bus is just as important as knowing what kind of people you want on it.

Then there are the buses that other people own. Think about how you will add to their buses. Are you the standard for the same kind of person you'd want on your bus? Become the person you'd hire.

The summed-up version of this section is as follows:

1. Do right by others as you wish them to do to you
2. Know and communicate your boundaries
3. Cut people out before they crash your bus
4. Have common missions, morals, and purposes
5. Your missions, morals, and purposes will guide you
6. People are not the value of what they can do for you
7. Who a person is, is more important than their craft/skill
8. Actions speak louder than words

And to hit the idea home about missions, realize this much: missions are the foundation of your character. Strong, selfless missions will draw the right people to you. And when you represent those beliefs through action, it'll shine a light out into the world of who you are.

The power of missions can change the world. Missions invented the automobile, shipped us over oceans, flew us across the country, and sent us to the moon. None of those things were initially developed for money. Each inventor had a mission that pushed them forward, and people joined them on that mission. Think bigger than your desires, and surround yourself with people who have visions bigger than their own glory.

CHAPTER 8.1
Acknowledgments

8.1 | ACKNOWLEDGEMENTS

These acknowledgments go out to the people who've molded me into who I am today. Individuals who pushed and encouraged me to improve, think deeper, and helped me take responsibility for my actions to earn my success. For that, I wish to begin my list with the worst of them all.

And before you think this'll be a negative list, I'll clarify. These are the people *you* should get up and thank for being in your life. These people indirectly gave me my missions, my morals, and my purposes. They drove me to inform others of misconceptions, the darker truth of success, and the reality of the entertainment industry.

Because of these people, I chose to teach, guide, and elevate others. I chose to protect people with truth, knowledge, and the tools to help them rise above those who see them as competition or the next step in their career.

Life isn't going to be easy, especially in the entertainment industry, and absolutely if you never learn that your knowledge is limited—for when all you know is all you know, it'll destroy your chances for success.

And that right there is how people can get lost on their journey to success. With that said, I'd like to thank *the people*...

Who told me no.
Who believed I should have a Plan B.
Who I knew not to trust before the truth was revealed.
Who were gatekeepers and took advantage of the uninformed.
Who gave up on me when the ship was going down.
Who used me for my resources to elevate their careers.
Who praised me to my face but talked poorly behind my back.
Who used the word loyalty for gain.
Who lied, cheated, and stole.
Who "faked it until they make it."
Who chose to abandon their child for their career.
Who cheered for you only while wishing you to fail.
Who reluctantly said yes.
Who were askholes.
Who promised one thing and did another.
Who has to always be right.
Who needed to be front and center on stage.
Who doesn't feel good until all the heavy lifting and work is done.
Who didn't keep their word… or do cocaine (hard drugs).
Who made it all about themselves when joining teams and tables.

And I assure you that the list goes on. Especially if you add all the people who made you angry, lied to you, or took advantage of you. Who gave you hope knowing what their true intentions were all along.

But enough about those above people. It's time to thank the people who truly matter—the people who made it worthwhile, changed my life, and reminded me of my peace. I'd like to thank *the people*…

Who gave me their time when I was young, dumb, and didn't listen.
Who told me to believe in myself.
Who took me under their wing and told the whys and hows of it all.
Who loved me.
Who guided me with compassion.
Who lifted me up when I fell.
Who were there when I lost all my opportunities to cancer.

Who were there when I failed and had to start over.
Who went out of their way to see a show.
Who bought one of my products.
Who supported a cause I believed in.
Who gave their all and more to make The Rose Theater happen.
Who held me when my chronic depression took over.
Who sat and ate pizza with me.
Who said yes and let me work my way up from the bottom.
Who let me stay with them when I had nothing.
Who were there when my parents died.
Who told me they loved me and meant it.
Who understood that my anxiety makes it hard to leave the house.
Who let me work on their film and TV sets.
Who gave me a chance to prove myself.
Who didn't give up on me even when I gave up on myself.
Who celebrated and helped one another beyond their selfishness.
Who came out and celebrated my one-year cancer-free event.

And again, this list could go on and on. Everyone has a list like this. For you, for me, for those you know and don't know—these lists and their variables exist. It's good to know your own list and the people who belong on it. For when you realize that both lists will shape you into the person you were meant to be, it'll pull you up and out of the maybe mindset and into the possible one.

At the end of the day, the good, the bad, and the ugly will always be part of your life as you follow the north star of your heart. Remember, in the end, none of it matters if you can't enjoy laughter and a good slice of pizza with friends.

Author Friends

Dawn Aurora Hunt
www.CucinaAurora.com

Dr. Sheena Howard
www.SheenacHoward.com

Ellen Karis
www.EllenKaris.com

Eloise Bahr
www.EloiseBahr.com

Emma Bennet
www.Emma-Bennet.co.uk

J. Carson Rose
www.TheGreyWoods.com

Jim Avelli
www.JimAvelli.com

JM Celi
www.JMCeli.com

Jody J. Sperling
www.JodyJSperling.com

Leni Flowers
amzn.to/429sCNz

Lilla Glass
www.LillaGlass.com

Lori Hayes
www.LoriHayesAuthor.com

Mark London Williams
amzn.to/3DSq2SP

Nicole Pierman
www.NicolePierman.com

Thomas J. Bellezza
www.MakeARightLeftHere.com
www.BBRProductions.com
www.Altayon.com

Thomas R Clark
www.ThomasRClark.com

WORK, GROW, AND RISE TOGETHER

www.ingramcontent.com/pod-product-compliance
Lightning Source LLC
Chambersburg PA
CBHW050523100526
44581CB00002B/90